Lecture Notes in Computer Science   8552

Commenced Publication in 1973
Founding and Former Series Editors:
Gerhard Goos, Juris Hartmanis, and Jan van Leeuwen

More information about this series at http://www.springer.com/series/7408

Ugo Dal Lago · Ricardo Peña (Eds.)

Foundational and Practical Aspects of Resource Analysis

Third International Workshop, FOPARA 2013
Bertinoro, Italy, August 29–31, 2013
Revised Selected Papers

 Springer

Editors
Ugo Dal Lago
Università di Bologna
Bologna
Italy

Ricardo Peña
Universidad Complutense de Madrid
Madrid
Spain

ISSN 0302-9743   ISSN 1611-3349   (electronic)
ISBN 978-3-319-12465-0   ISBN 978-3-319-12466-7   (eBook)
DOI 10.1007/978-3-319-12466-7

Library of Congress Control Number: 2014953270

LNCS Sublibrary: SL2 – Programming and Software Engineering

Springer Cham Heidelberg New York Dordrecht London

Printed on acid-free paper

Springer is part of Springer Science+Business Media (www.springer.com)

Preface

The Third International Workshop on Foundational and Practical Aspects of Resource Analysis (FOPARA 2013) was held in Bertinoro, Italy, during August 29–31, 2013. It was hosted by the Bertinoro International Conference Center. In this edition, FOPARA was co-located with the 13th International Workshop on Termination (WST 2013). Given the thematic proximity of the events, the Program Chairs decided to have not only a co-location, but also interleaved sessions, so as to stimulate exchange of ideas between the two communities.

The FOPARA workshop serves as a forum for presenting original research results that are relevant to the analysis of resource consumption by computer programs. The workshop aims at bringing together researchers who work on foundational issues with researchers who focus more on practical results. Therefore, both theoretical and practical contributions were encouraged. Papers that combined theory and practice were also welcome. The scientific program of this edition included three invited talks, all of them joint with WST 2013:

- Gilles Barthe, from IMDEA Software, on "Computer-Aided Cryptographic Proofs";
- Amir Ben-Amram, from The Academic College of Tel-Aviv Yaffo, on "Ranking Functions for Linear-Constraint Loops";
- Byron Cook, from Microsoft Research, who gave a talk entitled "Beyond Termination."

Of the 10 contributed talks, seven were on traditional approaches to complexity analysis, while three were on topics that were hardly treated in previous editions of the workshop, including differential privacy and probabilistic analysis of programs. During the workshop lively, inspiring discussions emerged between the more practical and the more theoretical researchers. The interaction with researchers attending WST 2013 was strong.

The FOPARA workshop is held every two years. The first two workshops of this series were organized by the Radboud University Nijmegen at Eindhoven (The Netherlands) in November 2009 and by the Universidad Complutense de Madrid at Madrid (Spain) in May 2011. After the workshop, nine of the presented works were submitted for formal publication. Also, an open call for more contributions was issued and three more works were included in the formal peer-reviewing process. The Program Committee then selected nine papers for publication which are the ones included in this volume. Each submission was reviewed by at least three Program Committee members.

We thank all the speakers, the authors, the Program Committee, and the rest of the participants for contributing to the success of FOPARA 2013. We also acknowledge the generous funding and support of the Department of Computer Science and Engineering of the University of Bologna.

August 2014

Ugo Dal Lago
Ricardo Peña

Organization

Program Committee

Roberto M. Amadio	Université Paris Diderot, France
Ugo Dal Lago	University of Bologna, Italy
Marco Gaboardi	University of Dundee, UK
Miguel Gomez-Zamalloa	Universidad Complutense de Madrid, Spain
Steffen Jost	University of St Andrews, UK
Hans-Wolfgang Loidl	Heriot-Watt University, UK
Damiano Mazza	CNRS, UMR 7030, LIPN, Université Paris 13, Sorbonne Paris Cité, France
Georg Moser	University of Innsbruck, Austria
Ricardo Peña	Universidad Complutense de Madrid, Spain
Ulrich Schöpp	Ludwig-Maximilians-Universität München, Germany
Marko Van Eekelen	Radboud University Nijmegen, The Netherlands
Pedro Vasconcelos	University of Porto, Portugal

Additional Reviewers

Alonso, Diego Esteban
Avanzini, Martin
Correas, Jesus
Eguchi, Naohi
Gimenez, Stéphane
Hoffmann, Jan

Hsu, Justin
Kersten, Rody
Montenegro, Manuel
Perrinel, Matthieu
van Gastel, Bernard

Contents

Certified Complexity (CerCo). 1
   Roberto M. Amadio, Nicolas Ayache, Francois Bobot, Jaap P. Boender,
   Brian Campbell, Ilias Garnier, Antoine Madet, James McKinna,
   Dominic P. Mulligan, Mauro Piccolo, Randy Pollack,
   Yann Régis-Gianas, Claudio Sacerdoti Coen,
   Ian Stark, and Paolo Tranquilli

On the Modular Integration of Abstract Semantics for WCET Analysis 19
   Mihail Asăvoae and Irina Măriuca Asăvoae

Can a Light Typing Discipline Be Compatible with an Efficient
Implementation of Finite Fields Inversion?. 38
   Daniele Canavese, Emanuele Cesena, Rachid Ouchary, Marco Pedicini,
   and Luca Roversi

Probabilistic Analysis of Programs: A Weak Limit Approach 58
   Alessandra Di Pierro and Herbert Wiklicky

Predicative Lexicographic Path Orders: An Application of Term Rewriting
to the Region of Primitive Recursive Functions. 77
   Naohi Eguchi

A Hoare Logic for Energy Consumption Analysis. 93
   Rody Kersten, Paolo Parisen Toldin, Bernard van Gastel,
   and Marko van Eekelen

Reasoning About Resources in the Embedded Systems Language Hume 110
   Hans-Wolfgang Loidl and Gudmund Grov

On Paths-Based Criteria for Polynomial Time Complexity in Proof-Nets 127
   Matthieu Perrinel

Collected Size Semantics for Strict Functional Programs over General
Polymorphic Lists 143
   Olha Shkaravska, Marko van Eekelen, and Alejandro Tamalet

Author Index 161

Certified Complexity (CerCo)

Roberto M. Amadio[4], Nicolas Ayache[3,4], Francois Bobot[3,4], Jaap P. Boender[1],
Brian Campbell[2], Ilias Garnier[2], Antoine Madet[4], James McKinna[2],
Dominic P. Mulligan[1(✉)], Mauro Piccolo[1], Randy Pollack[2],
Yann Régis-Gianas[3,4], Claudio Sacerdoti Coen[1], Ian Stark[2],
and Paolo Tranquilli[1]

[1] Dipartimento di Informatica - Scienza e Ingegneria,
Universitá di Bologna, Bologna, Italy
dominic.p.mulligan@gmail.com
[2] LFCS, School of Informatics, University of Edinburgh, Edinburgh, UK
[3] INRIA (Team πr^2), Paris-Rocquencourt, France
[4] Universitè Paris Diderot, Paris, France

Abstract. We provide an overview of the FET-Open Project CerCo
('Certified Complexity'). Our main achievement is the development of
a technique for analysing non-functional properties of programs (time,
space) at the source level with little or no loss of accuracy and a small
trusted code base. The core component is a C compiler, verified in Matita,
that produces an instrumented copy of the source code in addition to gen-
erating object code. This instrumentation exposes, and tracks precisely,
the actual (non-asymptotic) computational cost of the input program
at the source level. Untrusted invariant generators and trusted theorem
provers may then be used to compute and certify the parametric execution time of the code.

1 Introduction

Programs can be specified with both functional constraints (what the program
must do) and non-functional constraints (what time, space or other resources
the program may use). In the current state of the art, functional properties are
verified by combining user annotations—preconditions, invariants, and so on—
with a multitude of automated analyses—invariant generators, type systems,
abstract interpretation, theorem proving, and so on—on the program's high-
level source code. By contrast, many non-functional properties are verified using
analyses on low-level object code, but these analyses may then need information
about the high-level functional behaviour of the program that must then be
reconstructed. This analysis on low-level object code has several problems:

- It can be hard to deduce the high-level structure of the program after compiler
optimisations. The object code produced by an optimising compiler may have
radically different control flow to the original source code program.

The project CerCo acknowledges the financial support of the Future and Emerg-
ing Technologies (FET) programme within the Seventh Framework Programme for
Research of the European Commission, under FET-Open grant number: 243881.

© Springer International Publishing Switzerland 2014
U. Dal Lago and R. Peña (Eds.): FOPARA 2013, LNCS 8552, pp. 1–18, 2014.
DOI: 10.1007/978-3-319-12466-7_1

– Techniques that operate on object code are not useful early in the development process of a program, yet problems with a program's design or implementation are cheaper to resolve earlier in the process, rather than later.
– Parametric cost analysis is very hard: how can we reflect a cost that depends on the execution state, for example the value of a register or a carry bit, to a cost that the user can understand looking at the source code?
– Performing functional analyses on object code makes it hard for the programmer to provide information about the program and its expected execution, leading to a loss of precision in the resulting analyses.

Vision and approach. We want to reconcile functional and non-functional analyses: to share information and perform both at the same time on high-level source code. What has previously prevented this approach is the lack of a uniform and precise cost model for high-level code as each statement occurrence is compiled differently, optimisations may change control flow, and the cost of an object code instruction may depend on the runtime state of hardware components like pipelines and caches, all of which are not visible in the source code.

We envision a new generation of compilers that track program structure through compilation and optimisation and exploit this information to define a precise, non-uniform cost model for source code that accounts for runtime state. With such a cost model we can reduce non-functional verification to the functional case and exploit the state of the art in automated high-level verification [18]. The techniques currently used by the Worst Case Execution Time (WCET) community, who perform analyses on object code, are still available but can be coupled with additional source-level analyses. Where our approach produces overly complex cost models, safe approximations can be used to trade complexity with precision. Finally, source code analysis can be used early in the development process, when components have been specified but not implemented, as modularity means that it is enough to specify the non-functional behaviour of missing components.

Contributions. We have developed *the labelling approach* [5], a technique to implement compilers that induce cost models on source programs by very lightweight tracking of code changes through compilation. We have studied how to formally prove the correctness of compilers implementing this technique, and have implemented such a compiler from C to object binaries for the 8051 microcontroller for predicting execution time and stack space usage, verifying it in an interactive theorem prover. As we are targeting an embedded microcontroller we do not consider dynamic memory allocation.

To demonstrate source-level verification of costs we have implemented a Frama-C plugin [10] that invokes the compiler on a source program and uses it to generate invariants on the high-level source that correctly model low-level costs. The plugin certifies that the program respects these costs by calling automated theorem provers, a new and innovative technique in the field of cost analysis. Finally, we have conducted several case studies, including showing that the plugin can automatically compute and certify the exact reaction time of Lustre [7] data flow programs compiled into C.

2   Project Context and Approach

Formal methods for verifying functional properties of programs have now reached a level of maturity and automation that their adoption is slowly increasing in production environments. For safety critical code, it is becoming commonplace to combine rigorous software engineering methodologies and testing with static analyses, taking the strengths of each and mitigating their weaknesses. Of particular interest are open frameworks for the combination of different formal methods, where the programs can be progressively specified and enriched with new safety guarantees: every method contributes knowledge (e.g. new invariants) that becomes an assumption for later analysis.

The outlook for verifying non-functional properties of programs (time spent, memory used, energy consumed) is bleaker. Most industries verify that real time systems meet their deadlines by simply performing many runs of the system and timing their execution, computing the maximum time and adding an empirical safety margin, claiming the result to be a bound for the WCET of the program. Formal methods and software to statically analyse the WCET of programs exist, but they often produce bounds that are too pessimistic to be useful. Recent advancements in hardware architecture have been focused on the improvement of the average case performance, not the predictability of the worst case. Execution time is becoming increasingly dependent on execution history and the internal state of hardware components like pipelines and caches. Multi-core processors and non-uniform memory models are drastically reducing the possibility of performing static analysis in isolation, because programs are less and less time composable. Clock-precise hardware models are necessary for static analysis, and obtaining them is becoming harder due to the increased sophistication of hardware design.

Despite these problems, the need for reliable real time systems and programs is increasing, and there is pressure from the research community for the introduction of hardware with more predictable behaviour, which would be more suitable for static analysis. One example, being investigated by the Proartis project [8], is to decouple execution time from execution history by introducing randomisation.

In CerCo [2] we do not address this problem, optimistically assuming that improvements in low-level timing analysis or architecture will make verification feasible in the longer term. Instead, the main objective of our work is to bring together the static analysis of functional and non-functional properties, which in the current state of the art are independent activities with limited exchange of information: while the functional properties are verified on the source code, the analysis of non-functional properties is performed on object code to exploit clock-precise hardware models.

2.1   Current Object-Code Methods

Analysis currently takes place on object code for two main reasons. First, there cannot be a uniform, precise cost model for source code instructions (or even basic blocks). During compilation, high level instructions are broken up and reassembled in context-specific ways so that identifying a fragment of object code and a single high level instruction is infeasible. Even the control flow of the object and source code can be very different as a result of optimisations, for example aggressive loop optimisations may completely transform source level loops. Despite the lack of a uniform, compilation- and program-independent cost model on the source language, the literature on the analysis of non-asymptotic execution time on high level languages assuming such a model is growing and gaining momentum. However, unless we provide a replacement for such cost models, this literature's future practical impact looks to be minimal. Some hope has been provided by the EmBounded project [11], which compositionally compiles high-level code to a byte code that is executed by an interpreter with guarantees on the maximal execution time spent for each byte code instruction. This provides a uniform model at the expense of the model's precision (each cost is a pessimistic upper bound) and the performance of the executed code (because the byte code is interpreted compositionally instead of performing a fully non-compositional compilation).

The second reason to perform the analysis on the object code is that bounding the worst case execution time of small code fragments in isolation (e.g. loop bodies) and then adding up the bounds yields very poor estimates as no knowledge of the hardware state prior to executing the fragment can be assumed. By analysing longer runs the bound obtained becomes more precise because the lack of information about the initial state has a relatively small impact.

To calculate the cost of an execution, value and control flow analyses are required to bound the number of times each basic block is executed. Currently, state of the art WCET analysis tools, such as AbsInt's aiT toolset [1], perform these analyses on object code, where the logic of the program is harder to reconstruct and most information available at the source code level has been lost; see [17] for a survey. Imprecision in the analysis can lead to useless bounds. To augment precision, the tools ask the user to provide constraints on the object code control flow, usually in the form of bounds on the number of iterations of loops or linear inequalities on them. This requires the user to manually link the source and object code, translating his assumptions on the source code (which may be wrong) to object code constraints. The task is error prone and hard, especially in the presence of complex compiler optimisations.

Traditional techniques for WCET that work on object code are also affected by another problem: they cannot be applied before the generation of the object code. Functional properties can be analysed in early development stages, while analysis of non-functional properties may come too late to avoid expensive changes to the program architecture.

2.2   CerCo's Approach

In CerCo we propose a radically new approach to the problem: we reject the idea of a uniform cost model and we propose that the compiler, which knows how the code is translated, must return the cost model for basic blocks of high level instructions. It must do so by keeping track of the control flow modifications to reverse them and by interfacing with processor timing analysis.

By embracing compilation, instead of avoiding it like EmBounded did, a CerCo compiler can both produce efficient code and return costs that are as precise as the processor timing analysis can be. Moreover, our costs can be parametric: the cost of a block can depend on actual program data, on a summary of the execution history, or on an approximated representation of the hardware state. For example, loop optimisations may assign a cost to a loop body that is a function of the number of iterations performed. As another example, the cost of a block may be a function of the vector of stalled pipeline states, which can be exposed in the source code and updated at each basic block exit. It is parametricity that allows one to analyse small code fragments without losing precision. In the analysis of the code fragment we do not have to ignore the initial hardware state, rather, we may assume that we know exactly which state (or mode, as the WCET literature calls it) we are in.

The CerCo approach has the potential to dramatically improve the state of the art. By performing control and data flow analyses on the source code, the error prone translation of invariants is completely avoided. Instead, this work is done at the source level using tools of the user's choice. Any available technique for the verification of functional properties can be immediately reused and multiple techniques can collaborate together to infer and certify cost invariants for the program. There are no limitations on the types of loops or data structures involved. Parametric cost analysis becomes the default one, with non-parametric bounds used as a last resort when the user decides to trade the complexity of the analysis with its precision. A priori, no technique previously used in traditional WCET is lost: processor timing analyses can be used by the compiler on the object code, and the rest can be applied at the source code level. Our approach can also work in the early stages of development by axiomatically attaching costs to unimplemented components.

Software used to verify properties of programs must be as bug free as possible. The trusted code base for verification consists of the code that needs to be trusted to believe that the property holds. The trusted code base of state-of-the-art WCET tools is very large: one needs to trust the control flow analyser, the linear programming libraries used, and also the formal models of the hardware under analysis, for example. In CerCo we are moving the control flow analysis to the source code and we are introducing a non-standard compiler too. To reduce the trusted code base, we implemented a prototype and a static analyser in an interactive theorem prover, which was used to certify that the costs added to the source code are indeed those incurred by the hardware. Formal models of the hardware and of the high level source languages were also implemented in the interactive theorem prover. Control flow analysis on the source code has been obtained using invariant generators, tools to produce proof obligations from generated invariants and automatic theorem provers to verify the obligations. If these tools are able to generate proof traces that can be independently checked, the only remaining component that enters the trusted code base is an off-the-shelf invariant generator which, in turn, can be proved correct using an interactive theorem prover. Therefore we achieve the double objective of allowing the use of more off-the-shelf components (e.g. provers and invariant generators) whilst reducing the trusted code base at the same time.

3   The Typical CerCo Workflow

We illustrate the workflow we envisage (on the right of Fig. 1) on an example program (on the left of Fig. 1). The user writes the program and feeds it to the CerCo compiler, which outputs an instrumented version of the same program that updates global variables that record the elapsed execution time and the stack space usage. The red lines in Fig. 2 introducing variables, functions and function calls starting with __cost and __stack are the instrumentation introduced by the compiler. For example, the two calls at the start of count say that 4 bytes of stack are required, and that it takes 111 cycles to reach the next cost annotation (in the loop body). The compiler measures these on the labelled object code that it generates.

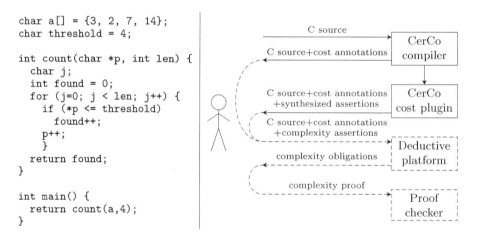

```
char a[] = {3, 2, 7, 14};
char threshold = 4;

int count(char *p, int len) {
  char j;
  int found = 0;
  for (j=0; j < len; j++) {
    if (*p <= threshold)
      found++;
    p++;
  }
  return found;
}

int main() {
  return count(a,4);
}
```

Fig. 1. On the left: C code to count the number of elements in an array that are less than or equal to a given threshold. On the right: CerCo's interaction diagram. Components provided by CerCo are drawn with a solid border.

The annotated program can then be enriched with complexity assertions in the style of Hoare logic, that are passed to a deductive platform (in our case Frama-C). We provide as a Frama-C cost plugin a simple automatic synthesiser for complexity assertions which can be overridden by the user to increase or decrease accuracy. These are the blue comments starting with /*@ in Fig. 2, written in Frama-C's specification language, ACSL. From the assertions, a general purpose deductive platform produces proof obligations which in turn can be closed by automatic or interactive provers, ending in a proof certificate.

Twelve proof obligations are generated from Fig. 2 (to prove that the loop invariant holds after one execution if it holds before, to prove that the whole program execution takes at most 1358 cycles, and so on). Note that the synthesised time bound for count, $178 + 214 * (1 + \text{len})$ cycles, is parametric in the length of the array. The CVC3 prover closes all obligations within half a minute on routine commodity hardware. A simpler non-parametric version can be solved in a few seconds.

4   Main Scientific and Technical Results

First we describe the basic labelling approach and our compiler implementations that use it. This is suitable for basic architectures with simple cost models. Then we will discuss the dependent labelling extension which is suitable for more advanced processor architectures and compiler optimisations. At the end of this section we will demonstrate automated high level reasoning about the source level costs provided by the compilers.

4.1   The (basic) Labelling Approach

The labelling approach is the foundational insight that underlies all the developments in CerCo. It allows the evolution of basic blocks to be tracked throughout the compilation process in order to propagate the cost model from the object code to the source code without losing precision in the process.

Problem statement. Given a source program P, we want to obtain an instrumented source program P', written in the same programming language, and the object code O such that: (1) P' is obtained by inserting into P some additional instructions to update global cost information like the amount of time spent during execution or the maximal stack space required; (2) P and P' must have the same functional behaviour, i.e. they must produce that same output and intermediate observables; (3) P and O must have the same functional behaviour; (4) after execution and in interesting points during execution, the cost information computed by P' must be an upper bound of the one spent by O to perform the corresponding operations (*soundness* property); (5) the difference between the costs computed by P' and the execution costs of O must be bounded by a program-dependent constant (*precision* property).

The labelling software components. We solve the problem in four stages [5], implemented by four software components that are used in sequence.

The first component labels the source program P by injecting label emission statements in appropriate positions to mark the beginning of basic blocks.

```
int __cost = 33, __stack = 5, __stack_max = 5;
void __cost_incr(int incr) { __cost += incr; }
void __stack_incr(int incr) {
  __stack += incr;
  __stack_max = __stack_max < __stack ? __stack : __stack_max;
}

char a[4] = {3, 2, 7, 14};  char threshold = 4;

/*@ behavior stack_cost:
      ensures __stack_max <= __max(\old(__stack_max), 4+\old(__stack));
      ensures __stack == \old(__stack);
    behavior time_cost:
      ensures __cost <= \old(__cost)+(178+214*__max(1+\at(len,Pre), 0));
*/
int count(char *p, int len) {
  char j;  int found = 0;
  __stack_incr(4);  __cost_incr(111);
  __l: /* internal */
  /*@ for time_cost: loop invariant
        __cost <= \at(__cost,__l)+
                214*(__max(\at((len-j)+1,__l), 0)-__max(1+(len-j), 0));
      for stack_cost: loop invariant
        __stack_max == \at(__stack_max,__l);
      for stack_cost: loop invariant
        __stack == \at(__stack,__l);
      loop variant len-j;
  */
  for (j = 0; j < len; j++) {
    __cost_incr(78);
    if (*p <= threshold) { __cost_incr(136); found ++; }
    else { __cost_incr(114); }
    p ++;
  }
  __cost_incr(67);  __stack_incr(-4);
  return found;
}

/*@ behavior stack_cost:
      ensures __stack_max <= __max(\old(__stack_max), 6+\old(__stack));
      ensures __stack == \old(__stack);
    behavior time_cost:
      ensures __cost <= \old(__cost)+1358;
*/
int main(void) {
  int t;
  __stack_incr(2);  __cost_incr(110);
  t = count(a,4);
  __stack_incr(-2);
  return t;
}
```

Fig. 2. The instrumented version of the program in Fig. 1, with instrumentation added by the CerCo compiler in red and cost invariants) added by the CerCo Frama-C plugin in blue. The __cost, __stack and __stack_max variables hold the elapsed time in clock cycles and the current and maximum stack usage. Their initial values hold the clock cycles spent in initialising the global data before calling main and the space required by global data (and thus unavailable for the stack).

These are the positions where the cost instrumentation will appear in the final output. The syntax and semantics of the source programming language is augmented with label emission statements. The statement "EMIT ℓ" behaves like a NOP instruction that does not affect the program state or control flow, but its execution is observable. For the example in Sect. 3 this is just the original C code with "EMIT" instructions added at every point a __cost_incr call appears in the final code.

The second component is a labelling preserving compiler. It can be obtained from an existing compiler by adding label emission statements to every intermediate language and by propagating label emission statements during compilation. The compiler is correct if it preserves both the functional behaviour of the program and the traces of observables, including the labels 'emitted'.

The third component analyses the labelled object code to compute the scope of each of its label emission statements, i.e. the instructions that may be executed after the statement and before a new label emission is encountered, and then computes the maximum cost of each. Note that we only have enough information at this point to compute the cost of loop-free portions of code. We will consider how to ensure that every loop is broken by a cost label shortly.

The fourth and final component replaces the labels in the labelled version of the source code produced at the start with the costs computed for each label's scope. This yields the instrumented source code. For the example, this is the code in Fig. 2, except for the specifications in comments, which we consider in Sect. 4.5.

Correctness. Requirements 1 and 2 hold because of the non-invasive labelling procedure. Requirement 3 can be satisfied by implementing compilation correctly. It is obvious that the value of the global cost variable of the instrumented source code is always equal to the sum of the costs of the labels emitted by the corresponding labelled code. Moreover, because the compiler preserves all traces, the sum of the costs of the labels emitted in the source and target labelled code are the same. Therefore, to satisfy the soundness requirement, we need to ensure that the time taken to execute the object code is equal to the sum of the costs of the labels emitted by the object code. We collect all the necessary conditions for this to happen in the definition of a *sound* labelling: (a) all loops must be broken by a cost emission statement; (b) all program instructions must be in the scope of some cost emission statement. This ensures that every label's scope is a tree of instructions, with the cost being the most expensive path. To satisfy also the precision requirement, we must make the scopes flat sequences of instructions. We require a *precise* labelling where every label is emitted at most once and both branches of each conditional jump start with a label emission statement.

The correctness and precision of the labelling approach only rely on the correctness and precision of the object code labelling. The simplest way to achieve that is to impose correctness and precision requirements on the source code labelling produced at the start, and to demand that the compiler preserves these properties too. The latter requirement imposes serious limitations on the compilation strategy and optimisations: the compiler may not duplicate any code that contains label emission statements, like loop bodies. Therefore various loop optimisations like peeling or unrolling are prevented. Moreover, precision of the object code labelling is not sufficient *per se* to obtain global precision: we implicitly assumed that a precise constant cost can be assigned to every instruction. This is not possible in the presence of stateful hardware whose state influences the cost of operations, like pipelines and caches. In Sect. 4.4 we will see an extension of the basic labelling approach which tackles these problems.

In CerCo we have developed several cost preserving compilers based on the labelling approach. Excluding an initial certified compiler for a 'while' language, all remaining compilers target realistic source languages—a pure higher order functional language and a large subset of C with pointers, gotos and all data structures—and real world target processors—MIPS and the Intel 8051 processor family. Moreover, they achieve a level of optimisation that ranges from moderate (comparable to GCC level 1) to intermediate (including loop peeling and unrolling, hoisting and late constant propagation). We describe the C compilers in detail in the following section.

Two compilation chains were implemented for a purely functional higher-order language [3]. The two main changes required to deal with functional languages are: (1) because global variables and updates are not available, the instrumentation phase produces monadic code to 'update' the global costs; (2) the requirements for a sound and precise labelling of the source code must be changed when the compilation is based on CPS translations. In particular, we need to introduce labels emitted before a statement is executed and also labels emitted after a statement is executed. The latter capture code that is inserted by the CPS translation and that would escape all label scopes.

4.2   The CerCo C Compilers

We implemented two C compilers, one implemented directly in OCaml and the other implemented in Matita, an interactive theorem prover [4]. The first acted as a prototype for the second, but also supported MIPS and acted as a testbed for more advanced features such as the dependent labelling approach in Sect. 4.4.

The second C compiler is the *Trusted CerCo Compiler*, whose cost predictions are formally verified. The executable code is OCaml code extracted from the Matita implementation. The Trusted CerCo Compiler only targets the C language and the 8051/8052 family, and does not yet implement any advanced optimisations. Its user interface, however, is the same as the other version for interoperability purposes. In particular, the Frama-C CerCo plugin descibed in Sect. 4.5 can work without recompilation with both of our C compilers.

The 8051 microprocessor is a very simple one, with constant-cost instructions. It was chosen to separate the issue of exact propagation of the cost model from the orthogonal problem of low-level timing analysis of object code that may require approximation or dependent costs.

The (trusted) CerCo compiler implements the following optimisations: cast simplification, constant propagation in expressions, liveness analysis driven spilling of registers, dead code elimination, branch displacement, and tunnelling.

The two latter optimisations are performed by our optimising assembler [14]. The back-end of the compiler works on three address instructions, preferred to static single assignment code for the simplicity of the formal certification.

The CerCo compiler is loosely based on the CompCert compiler [13], a recently developed certified compiler from C to the PowerPC, ARM and x86 microprocessors. In contrast to CompCert, both the CerCo code and its certification are fully open source. Some data structures and language definitions for the front-end are directly taken from CompCert, while the back-end is a redesign of a compiler from Pascal to MIPS used by François Pottier for a course at the École Polytechnique. The main differences in the CerCo compiler are:

– All the intermediate languages include label emitting instructions to implement the labelling approach, and the compiler preserves execution traces.
– Instead of targeting an assembly language with additional macro-instructions which are expanded before assembly, we directly produce object code in order to perform the timing analysis, using an integrated optimising assembler.
– In order to avoid the additional work of implementing a linker and a loader, we do not support separate compilation and external calls. Adding them is orthogonal to the labelling approach and should not introduce extra problems.
– We target an 8-bit processor, in contrast to CompCert's 32-bit targets. This requires many changes and more compiler code, but it is not fundamentally more complex. The proof of correctness, however, becomes much harder.
– We target a microprocessor that has a non-uniform memory model, which is still often the case for microprocessors used in embedded systems and that is becoming common again in multi-core processors. Therefore the compiler has to keep track of data and it must move data between memory regions in the proper way. Moreover the size of pointers to different regions is not uniform.

4.3   Formal Certification of the CerCo Compiler

We have formally certified in Matita that the cost models induced on the source code by the Trusted CerCo Compiler correctly and precisely predict the object code behaviour. There are two cost models, one for execution time and one for stack space consumption. We show the correctness of the prediction only for those programs that do not exhaust the available stack space, a property that— thanks to the stack cost model—we can statically analyse on the source code in sharp contrast to other certified compilers. Other projects have already certified the preservation of functional semantics in similar compilers, so we have not attempted to directly repeat that work and assume functional correctness for most passes. In order to complete the proof for non-functional properties, we have introduced a new, structured, form of execution trace, with the related notions for forward similarity and the intensional consequences of forward similarity. We have also introduced a unified representation for back-end intermediate languages that was exploited to provide a uniform proof of forward similarity.

The details on the proof techniques employed and the proof sketch can be found in the CerCo deliverables and papers [9]. In this section we will only hint at the correctness statement, which turned out to be more complex than expected.

The correctness statement. Real time programs are often reactive programs that loop forever responding to events (inputs) by performing some computation followed by some action (output) and continuing as before. For these programs the overall execution time does not make sense. The same is true for reactive programs that spend an unpredictable amount of time in I/O. Instead, what is interesting is the reaction time — the time spent between I/O events. Moreover, we are interested in predicting and ruling out crashes due to running out of space on certain inputs. Therefore we need a statement that talks about sub-runs of a program. A natural candidate is that the time predicted on the source code and spent on the object code by two corresponding sub-runs are the same. To make this statement formal we must identify the corresponding sub-runs and how to single out those that are meaningful. We introduce the notion of a *measurable* sub-run of a run which does not exhaust the available stack before or during the sub-run, the number of function calls and returns in the sub-run is the same, the sub-run does not perform any I/O, and the sub-run starts with a label emission statement and ends with a return or another label emission statement. The stack usage is bounded using the stack usage model that is computed by the compiler.

The statement that we formally proved is: for each C run with a measurable sub-run, there exists an object code run with a sub-run, with the same execution trace for both the prefix of the run and the sub-run itself, and where the time spent by the object code in the sub-run is the same as the time predicted on the source code using the time cost model generated by the compiler.

We briefly discuss the constraints for measurability. Not exhausting the stack space is necessary for a run to be meaningful, because the source semantics has no notion of running out of memory. Balancing function calls and returns is a requirement for precision: the labelling approach allows the scope of a label to extend after function calls to minimize the number of labels. (The scope excludes the called function's execution.) If the number of calls/returns is unbalanced, it means that there is a call we have not returned to that could be followed by additional instructions whose cost has already been taken in account. The last condition on the start and end points of a run is also required to make the bound precise. With these restrictions and the 8051's simple timing model we obtain *exact* predictions. If we relax these conditions then we obtain a corollary with an upper bound on the cost. Finally, I/O operations can be performed in the prefix of the run, but not in the measurable sub-run. Therefore we prove that we can predict reaction times, but not I/O times, as desired.

4.4   Dependent Labelling

The core idea of the basic labelling approach is to establish a tight connection between basic blocks executed in the source and target languages. Once the connection is established, any cost model computed on the object code can be transferred to the source code, without affecting the code of the compiler or its proof. In particular, we can also transport cost models that associate to each label a *function* from the hardware state to a natural number. However, a problem arises during the instrumentation phase that replaces label emission statements with increments of global cost variables. They are incremented by the result of applying the label's cost function to the hardware state at the time of execution of the block. However, the hardware state comprises both the functional state that affects the computation (the value of the registers and memory) and the non-functional state that does not (the pipeline and cache contents, for example). We can find corresponding information for the former in the source code state, but constructing the correspondence may be hard and lifting the cost model to work on the source code state is likely to produce cost expressions that are too complex to understand and reason about. Fortunately, in modern architectures the cost of executing single instructions is either independent of the functional state or the jitter—the difference between the worst and best case execution times—is small enough to be bounded without losing too much precision. Therefore we only consider dependencies on the 'non-functional' parts of the state.

The non-functional state is not directly related to the high level state and does not influence the functional properties. What can be done is to expose key aspects of the non-functional state in the source code. We present here the basic intuition in a simplified form: the technical details that allow us to handle the general case are more complex and can be found in [16]. We add to the source code an additional global variable that represents the non-functional state and another one that remembers the last few labels emitted. The state variable must be updated at every label emission statement, using an update function which is computed during the processor timing analysis. This update function assigns to each label a function from the recently emitted labels and old state to the new state. It is computed by composing the semantics of every instruction in a basic block restricted to the non-functional part of the state.

Not all the details of the non-functional state needs to be exposed, and the technique works better when the part of state that is required can be summarised in a simple data structure. For example, to handle simple but realistic pipelines it is sufficient to remember a short integer that encodes the position of bubbles (stuck instructions) in the pipeline. In any case, it is not necessary for the user to understand the meaning of the state to reason over the properties of the program. Moreover, the user, or the invariant generator tools that analyse the instrumented source code produced by the compiler, can decide to trade precision of the analysis for simplicity by approximating the cost by safe bounds that do not depend on the processor state. Interestingly, the functional analysis of the code could determine which blocks are executed more frequently in order to use more aggressive approximations for those that are executed least.

Dependent labelling can also be applied to allow the compiler to duplicate blocks that contain labels (e.g. in loop optimisations) [16]. The effect is to assign a different cost to the different occurrences of a duplicated label. For example, loop peeling turns a loop into the concatenation of a copy of the loop body for the first iteration and the conditional execution of the loop for successive iterations. Further optimisations will compile the two copies of the loop differently, with the first body usually taking more time.

By introducing a variable that keeps track of the iteration number, we can associate to the label a cost that is a function of the iteration number. The same technique works for loop unrolling without modification: the function will assign one cost to the even iterations and another cost to the odd ones. The optimisation code that duplicates the loop bodies must also modify the code to correctly propagate the update of the iteration numbers. The technical details are more complicated and can be found in the CerCo reports and publications. The implementation, however, is quite simple (and forms part of our OCaml version of the compiler) and the changes to a loop optimising compiler are minimal.

4.5   Techniques to Exploit the Induced Cost Model

We now turn our attention to synthesising high-level costs, such as the reaction time of a real-time program. We consider as our starting point source level costs provided by basic labelling, in other words annotations on the source code which are constants that provide a sound and sufficiently precise upper bound on the cost of executing the blocks after compilation to object code.

The principle that we have followed in designing the cost synthesis tools is that the synthesised bounds should be expressed and proved within a general purpose tool built to reason on the source code. In particular, we rely on the Frama-C tool to reason on C code and on the Coq proof-assistant to reason on higher-order functional programs. This principle entails that the inferred synthetic bounds are indeed correct as long as the general purpose tool is, and that there is no limitation on the class of programs that can be handled, for example by resorting to interactive proof.

Of course, automation is desirable whenever possible. Within this framework, automation means writing programs that give hints to the general purpose tool. These hints may take the form, say, of loop invariants/variants, of predicates describing the structure of the heap, or of types in a light logic. If these hints are correct and sufficiently precise the general purpose tool will produce a proof automatically, otherwise, user interaction is required.

The Cost plugin and its application to the Lustre compiler. Frama-C [10] is a set of analysers for C programs with a specification language, ACSL. New analyses can be added dynamically via plugins. For instance, the Jessie plugin [12] allows deductive verification of C programs with respect to their specification in ACSL, with various provers as back-end tools. We developed the CerCo Cost plugin for the Frama-C platform as a proof of concept of an automatic environment exploiting the cost annotations produced by the CerCo compiler. It consists of an OCaml program which essentially uses the CerCo compiler to produce a related C program with cost annotations, and applies some heuristics to produce a tentative bound on the cost of executing the C functions of the program as a function of the value of their parameters. The user can then call the Jessie plugin to discharge the related proof obligations. In the following we elaborate on the soundness of the framework and the experiments we performed with the Cost tool on C programs, including some produced by a Lustre compiler.

Soundness. The soundness of the whole framework depends on the cost annotations added by the CerCo compiler, the verification conditions (VCs) generated by Jessie, and the external provers discharging the VCs. Jessie can be used to verify the synthesised bounds because our plugin generates them in ACSL format. Thus, even if the added synthetic costs are incorrect (relatively to the cost annotations), the process as a whole is still correct: indeed, Jessie will not validate incorrect costs and no conclusion can be made about the WCET of the program in this case. In other terms, the soundness does not depend on the cost plugin, which can in principle produce any synthetic cost. However, in order to be able to actually prove a WCET bound for a C function, we need to add correct annotations in a way that Jessie and subsequent automatic provers have enough information to deduce their validity. In practice this is not straightforward even for very simple programs composed of branching and assignments (no loops and no recursion) because a fine analysis of the VCs associated with branching may lead to a complexity blow up.

Experience with Lustre. Lustre [7] is a data-flow language for programming synchronous systems, with a compiler which targets C. We designed a wrapper for supporting Lustre files. The C function produced by the compiler is relatively simple loop-free code which implements the step function of the synchronous system and computing the WCET of the function amounts to obtaining a bound on the reaction time of the system. We tested the Cost plugin and the Lustre wrapper on the C programs generated by the Lustre compiler. For programs consisting of a few hundred lines of code, the cost plugin computes a WCET and Alt-Ergo is able to discharge all VCs automatically.

Handling C programs with simple loops. The cost annotations added by the CerCo compiler take the form of C instructions that update a fresh global variable called the cost variable by a constant. Synthesizing a WCET bound of a C function thus consists of statically resolving an upper bound of the difference between the value of the cost variable before and after the execution of the function, i.e. finding the instructions that update the cost variable and establish the number of times they are passed through during the flow of execution. To perform the analysis the plugin assumes that there are no recursive functions in the program, and that every loop is annotated with a variant. In the case of 'for' loops the variants are automatically inferred where a loop counter can be syntactically detected.

The plugin computes a call-graph and proceeds to calculate bounds for each function from the leaves up to the main function. The computation of the cost of each function is performed by traversing its control flow graph, where the cost of a node is the maximum of the costs of the successors. In the case of a loop with a body that has a constant cost for every step of the loop, the cost is the product of the cost of the body and of the variant taken at the start of the loop. In the case of a loop with a body whose cost depends on the values of some free variables, a fresh logic function f is introduced to represent the cost of the loop in the logic assertions. This logic function takes the variant as a first parameter. The other parameters of f are the free variables of the body of the loop. An axiom is added to account for the fact that the cost is accumulated at each step of the loop. The cost of the function is added as post-condition of the function.

The user can also specify more precise variants and annotate functions with their own cost specifications. The plugin will use these instead of computing its own, allowing greater precision and the ability to analyse programs which the variant generator does not support.

In addition to the loop-free Lustre code, this method was successfully applied to a small range of cryptographic code. See [5] for more details. The example in Sect. 3 was also produced using the plug-in. The variant was calculated automatically by noticing that j is a loop counter with maximum value len. The most expensive path through the loop body ($78 + 136 = 214$) is then multiplied by the number of iterations to give the cost of the loop.

C programs with pointers. Using first-order logic and SMT solvers to specify and verify programs involving pointer-based data structures such as linked-lists or graphs shows some limitations. Separation logic, a program logic with a new notion of conjunction to express spatial heap separation, is an elegant alternative. Bobot has recently introduced automatically generated separation predicates to simulate separation logic reasoning in the Jessie plugin where the specification language, the verification condition generator, and the theorem provers were not designed with separation logic in mind [6]. CerCo's plugin can exploit these predicates to automatically reason about the cost of execution of simple heap manipulation programs such as an in-place list reversal.

5   Conclusions and Future Work

All CerCo software and deliverables may be found on the project homepage [9].

The results obtained so far are encouraging and provide evidence that it is possible to perform static time and space analysis at the source level without losing accuracy, reducing the trusted code base and reconciling the study of functional and non-functional properties of programs. The techniques introduced seem to be scalable, cover both imperative and functional languages and are compatible with every compiler optimisation considered by us so far.

To prove that compilers can keep track of optimisations and induce a precise cost model on the source code, we targeted a simple architecture that admits a cost model that is execution history independent. The most important future work is dealing with hardware architectures characterised by history-dependent stateful components, like caches and pipelines. The main issue is to assign a parametric, dependent cost to basic blocks that can be later transferred by the labelling approach to the source code and represented in a meaningful way to the user. The dependent labelling approach that we have studied seems a promising tool to achieve this goal, but more work is required to provide good source level approximations of the relevant processor state.

Other examples of future work are to improve the cost invariant generator algorithms and the coverage of compiler optimisations, to combining the labelling approach with the type and effect discipline of [15] to handle languages with implicit memory management, and to experiment with our tools in the early phases of development. Larger case studies are also necessary to evaluate the CerCo's prototype on realistic, industrial-scale programs.

References

1. AbsInt: aiT WCET analysis tools. http://www.absint.com/ait/
2. Amadio, R., Asperti, A., Ayache, N., Campbell, B., Mulligan, D.P., Pollack, R., Régis-Gianas, Y., Coen, C.S., Stark, I.: Certified complexity. Procedia Comput. Sci. **7**, 175–177 (2011). Proceedings of the 2nd European Future Technologies Conference and Exhibition 2011 (FET 11)
3. Amadio, R.M., Régis-Gianas, Y.: Certifying and reasoning on cost annotations of functional programs. In: Peña, R., van Eekelen, M., Shkaravska, O. (eds.) FOPARA 2011. LNCS, vol. 7177, pp. 72–89. Springer, Heidelberg (2012). Extended version to appear in Higher Order and Symbolic Computation
4. Asperti, A., Ricciotti, W., Sacerdoti Coen, C., Tassi, E.: The matita interactive theorem prover. In: Bjørner, N., Sofronie-Stokkermans, V. (eds.) CADE 2011. LNCS, vol. 6803, pp. 64–69. Springer, Heidelberg (2011)
5. Ayache, N., Amadio, R.M., Régis-Gianas, Y.: Certifying and reasoning on cost annotations in C programs. In: Stoelinga, M., Pinger, R. (eds.) FMICS 2012. LNCS, vol. 7437, pp. 32–46. Springer, Heidelberg (2012). http://dx.doi.org/10.1007/978-3-642-32469-7_3
6. Bobot, F., Filliâtre, J.-C.: Separation predicates: a taste of separation logic in first-order logic. In: Aoki, T., Taguchi, K. (eds.) ICFEM 2012. LNCS, vol. 7635, pp. 167–181. Springer, Heidelberg (2012). http://dx.doi.org/10.1007/978-3-642-34281-3_14
7. Caspi, P., Pilaud, D., Halbwachs, N., Plaice, J.: Lustre: a declarative language for programming synchronous systems. In: POPL, pp. 178–188. ACM Press (1987)
8. Cazorla, F., Quiñones, E., Vardanega, T., Cucu, L., Triquet, B., Bernat, G., Berger, E., Abella, J., Wartel, F., Houston, M., Santinelli, L., Kosmidis, L., Lo, C., Maxim, D.: Proartis: probabilistically analysable real-time systems. Trans. Embed. Comput. Syst. (2012)
9. The Certified Complexity (CerCo) project web site. http://cerco.cs.unibo.it
10. Correnson, L., Cuoq, P., Kirchner, F., Prevosto, V., Puccetti, A., Signoles, J., Yakobowski, B.: Frama-C user manual. CEA-LIST, Software Safety Laboratory, Saclay, F-91191. http://frama-c.com/
11. Hammond, K., Dyckhoff, R., Ferdinand, C., Heckmann, R., Hofmann, M., Jost, S., Loidl, H.W., Michaelson, G., Pointon, R.F., Scaife, N., Sérot, J., Wallace, A.: The EmBounded project (project start paper). Trends Funct. Program. TFP **6**, 195–210 (2005)
12. Jessie Frama-C plugin. http://krakatoa.lri.fr/
13. Leroy, X.: Formal verification of a realistic compiler. Commun. ACM **52**(7), 107–115 (2009)

14. Mulligan, D.P., Sacerdoti Coen, C.: On the correctness of an optimising assembler for the intel MCS-51 microprocessor. In: Hawblitzel, C., Miller, D. (eds.) CPP 2012. LNCS, vol. 7679, pp. 43–59. Springer, Heidelberg (2012)
15. Talpin, J.P., Jouvelot, P.: The type and effect discipline. Inf. Comput. **111**(2), 245–296 (1994)
16. Tranquilli, P.: Indexed labels for loop iteration dependent costs. In: QAPL. EPTCS, vol. 117, pp. 19–23 (2013)
17. Wilhelm, R., Engblom, J., Ermedahl, A., Holsti, N., Thesing, S., Whalley, D.B., Bernat, G., Ferdinand, C., Heckmann, R., Mitra, T., Mueller, F., Puaut, I., Puschner, P.P., Staschulat, J., Stenström, P.: The worst-case execution-time problem-overview of methods and survey of tools. ACM Trans. Embedded Comput. Syst. **7**(3), 1–53 (2008)
18. Wögerer, W.: A survey of static program analysis techniques. Technical report, Technische Universität Wien (2005)

On the Modular Integration of Abstract Semantics for WCET Analysis

Mihail Asăvoae$^{(\boxtimes)}$ and Irina Măriuca Asăvoae

VERIMAG/UJF, Gières, France
{mihail.asavoae,irina.asavoae}@imag.fr

Abstract. We propose here a modular resource analysis which is constructed around a rewrite-based formal specification of an embedded system. Designing and analyzing embedded systems considers both hardware and software behavioral aspects which we capture using the modular notion of system configuration. Hence, we use a configuration-based design methodology and we instantiate parts of the configuration to accommodate data and control-flow abstractions. These instantiations require no modifications of the original formal specification. We implement in this manner a particular resource analysis, namely worst case execution time (WCET), and evaluate it with respect to a reusability metric.

1 Introduction

Interaction between an embedded system and the external environment could be stated as a set of constraints, usually produced by resource analyses. For example, a proper scheduling requires an analysis of the time resource, the constraints being generally set in terms of upper/lower bounds. A schedulability analysis requires some of the constraints to be in terms of safe and tight worst case execution time (WCET) bounds. However, to achieve accurate WCET bounds, one has to formalize low-level aspects, e.g., assembly languages and hardware architecture.

The standard workflow for WCET analysis [27] exploits the modularity of the systems (i.e. programs running on specified architectures) by separate analyses for the control-flow and the processor behavior. The control-flow analysis derives flow facts without architectural considerations. The processor behavior analysis computes invariants w.r.t. how instructions behave in the presence of the architecture elements. A successful approach for WCET analysis proposes a mix of integer linear programming (ILP) for path analysis of the control-flow graph (CFG) [19,20] and abstract interpretation (AI) [9] for various architecture elements or their combination [15,18,25,26]. This method (ILP + AI) achieved success through tools as aiT [1] which is used in substantial industrial projects, e.g., Airbus certification. Because of the industry's quality requirements, aiT is sharpen to produce precise bounds for WCET. However, to the best of our knowledge, the modularity in aiT is resumed to the two aspects mentioned above.

© Springer International Publishing Switzerland 2014
U. Dal Lago and R. Peña (Eds.): FOPARA 2013, LNCS 8552, pp. 19–37, 2014.
DOI: 10.1007/978-3-319-12466-7_2

We approach the resource (in particular WCET) analysis workflow from a slightly different perspective, originated from the observation that *a programming language semantics has all the necessary information to define, for any program written in this language, the set of all possible concrete executions.* This view together with the fact that any abstraction is based on (sets of) concrete executions, lead to the idea of a workflow for semantics-based resource analysis. Its core is the *formal executable language semantics* (i.e., basically, a compact representation of the set of concrete executions). The formal aspect of the semantics distills the correct programs from the incorrect ones up to the semantics specification, while the executability aspect allows to thoroughly test such programs and gain confidence in the semantics. These two aspects attest that the language semantics specification forms a *trusted core* which sets a foundation for the integration of abstractions for resource analysis.

We introduce in [3], and use here, the trusted core of a formal executable definition of the MIPS assembly language supported by the Simplescalar toolset [6]. Furthermore, we extend, in [2], the language core with a parametric modeling of instruction caches. In this way, we set the grounds for a standard WCET analysis workflow where the *language semantics* is used in the *control flow analysis* and the *architecture specification* is used in the *processor behavior analysis*. While our approach has been investigated only w.r.t. sequential processors, these settings allow a similar modular integration of other hardware components, e.g., pipeline specification or multicore processors with FPU, as well as of other resource analyses, e.g., power consumption or memory usage. However, we consider fixed the analysis method, i.e., abstract interpretation.

In this paper we present a methodology for the modular integration of abstractions for resource analysis over a trusted core - the concrete semantics specification of a system. We instantiate this methodology on analyses for WCET [28] (e.g., control flow analyses such as constant propagation [8] and interval analysis [22], and processor behavior analyses, namely, may and must for data and instruction caches [25]). Our contribution focusses more on the engineering aspects of integrating two formal methods: the concrete semantics of systems (which are formally specified and tested to form a trusted core) and the abstract semantics for resource analyses (the resource exemplified here is the execution time). The integration of these two formal methods is mutually building strength to both of them. Namely, making the abstraction to draw its abstract operators directly from the concrete ones available in the trusted core builds confidence that the analysis is applied to a model which is faithful to the system of origin. In turns, the system specified by a trusted core, besides being tested w.r.t. the accuracy of the semantics specification, is now also guaranteed to work correctly w.r.t. more subtle properties, e.g., tight and safe resource bounds.

Our tactics to integrate abstractions over the concrete semantics specification starts by identifying a set of semantic entities used to "cut" slices through the concrete execution. Then, the abstraction-specific semantic entities are combined with the concrete slices, in a modular fashion. A more intuitive view of the tactics used for abstractions is given in Fig. 1. The system specification, in Fig. 1

(left), is described structurally by a configuration *Config*, and semantically by a set of rewrite rules of the form $X \Rightarrow X'$. The underlying modularity of the specification, in Fig. 1 (middle), is captured with the possibly overlapping sub-configurations (i.e., C_1 and C_2) of *Config*. A sub-configuration identifies a part of the system with it afferent functionality (e.g., since X, X' are subterms of C_1, the rule $X \Rightarrow X'$ implements the functionality of C_1). An operator "?" (also called guard) specifies how these parts communicate between them. i.e., $?(X' \cap Y)$ means that $Y \Rightarrow Y'$ (in C_2) is applied after $X \Rightarrow X'$ (in C_1). If we see the specification as a program, then "?" is an `assert (cond)` statement which allows the execution to proceed if `cond` is true. The abstraction integration, in Fig. 1 (right), is done in two steps. First, an abstract configuration, CA, encapsulates the necessary information from the existing sub-configurations (e.g., the parts of C_1 and C_2 used by X, X' and respectively Z, Z') and isolates, in this way, the important rules (e.g., the rules using the $\#$ operator). Second, the abstraction specify how to control the system at the points of interest. For example, the two conditions in **Abstraction** enable the following execution steps (represented with the dashed lines): rule $Z \Rightarrow Z'$, the guard/assert statement $?(\#Z' \cap \#X)$ and rule $X \Rightarrow X'$. The second guard $?(\#X' \cap \#Y)$ fails and this execution stops. **Abstraction** has the mechanism (i.e., rewrite rules) to perform such executions, to collect and to process their results.

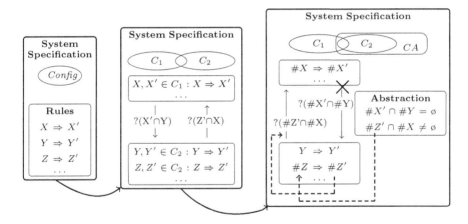

Fig. 1. Workflow for modular resource analysis: in the initial specification (left), we identify the components and the inter-component communication (middle), in order to apply abstractions over an existing (part of the) infrastructure (right).

The formal and executable features of the semantics are provided by a specialized framework, called $\mathbb{K}$ [24] which emerged from the rewriting logic [21]. In the graph theory κ represents the connectivity of a graph. Likewise, $\mathbb{K}$ aims to connect different semantics paradigms such as (modular) small/big step, continuation, or reduction semantics distilled into a cell-based notation á la Chemical

Abstract Machine. $\mathbb{K}$ integrates the main features of all these semantics into the algebraic environment of rewriting logic which sets solid foundations, i.e., the trusted core, for automated verification. Our modular resource analysis is prototyped in $\mathbb{K}$-Maude [10], the implementation of $\mathbb{K}$ on top of the rewriting logic tool Maude [7]. The experimental results are presented with respect to a reusability metric which measures the implementation from the following perspective: keeping the formal semantics, how much of the concrete system is used, while the abstractions are applied. Hence, with this metric we asses how much of the effort spent in specifying the concrete system is actually used by abstraction. We select and conduct experiments on a subset of the Mälardalen benchmarks [13].

Related Work. There are several works concerning formal development of WCET analysis workflows. We mention here the general resource-driven methodology advocated by the Hume project [14], the theorem proving-based framework, via Coq [5], which aims towards the WCET-certifiable compilation and the use of symbolic execution to prove the bounds, while tightening them [4].

The Hume project uses a domain-specific, multi-level (low- to higher-order) language called Hume [14]. Hume combines concurrent finite-state automata (called boxes) as the specification mechanism with the executability support of the functional programming (i.e., through pattern-matching and rich typing information). Both Hume and our approach share similar principles w.r.t. modularity. To a Hume box it corresponds a $\mathbb{K}$ module which is a rewriting-logic theory (through its compilation into a Maude module). To a Hume wiring (connection between boxes) it corresponds communication tokens between $\mathbb{K}$ modules. One key difference is how the abstractions are handled: Hume embeds the abstractions in the workflow, while our methodology advocates for a more flexible scheme, lifting the definition of abstractions at the application level.

The work in [5] uses the infrastructure of the CompCert [17] verified C compiler to formally prove a specific control-flow analysis - the loop bound estimation. As in our methodology for modular integration of abstractions, the Coq formalization of a loop bound analysis is also integrated into an existing workflow (i.e., of CompCert). The working language is the CompCert RTL intermediate representation which is augmented with loop scoping in order to extract control-flow information from loops. While we share a similar low-level language representation, our methodology does not explicitly extend the existing concrete configuration, but it slices it using the wrapping. Another difference is that the Coq formalization of the loop-bound abstraction is fully proved within the workflow, while our approach relies on offline proving of the abstractions.

The WCET analysis workflow is wrapped into a counterexample guided abstraction refinement cycle, in [4]. The point is to consider a WCET bound and to further tighten/prove it using a symbolic execution engine. Both our methodology and [4] follow the same ILP + AI method, w.r.t. the infrastructure for WCET analysis. The key difference is in the workflow, the symbolic execution approach is formal w.r.t. the results of the WCET analysis, while our methodology also proves that the computation for the WCET bound is correct (i.e., up to the specification). The combined ILP + AI approach for WCET analysis was straightforwardly encoded in [2]. In this paper we propose a general methodology to integrate abstract executions and show how our previous encoding of ILP + AI is just an instance of this methodology. Moreover, we present the implementation and experiments w.r.t. the quality of integration.

While the general approach to evaluate abstractions is through experimentation, several techniques address this problem from the more systematic perspective - that of a metric definition. The flow is simple: define a standard (i.e., a set of characteristics) and project each abstraction on this standard. For [12], the abstraction-refinement procedures are compared w.r.t. a standard counterexample. In other words, the metric evaluates the capabilities (i.e., accuracy, performance) of an abstraction. Along the same lines, the standard (i.e., a collection of metrics) defined in [23] captures predictability aspects of cache memories w.r.t. the impact on the WCET analysis. Our metric does not measure the accuracy of an abstraction, as in [12,23]. We propose as standard, the structure of the concrete semantics, hence an abstraction is measured from a more structural point of view. It is more closely related to the metrics in software engineering [11] which evaluate integration of design patterns (in fact our integration of abstraction could be assimilated with a design pattern).

Paper Outline. This paper is organized as follows: Sect. 2 covers some background notions of $\mathbb{K}$ and overviews some aspects of the abstract interpretation and its application to WCET analysis. Sections 3 and 4 overview the general system design and, respectively, its instance for the timing analysis. Section 5 covers some implementation and experimental details with the current prototype while Sect. 6 contains the conclusions.

2   Preliminaries

The $\mathbb{K}$ framework: We introduce $\mathbb{K}$ and illustrate some key concepts in our approach by using a simple specification of an embedded application running on a very basic architecture.

Example 1. Without restricting the generality, we consider a toy system given by: (1) a RISC assembly language as the programming language of choice which consists of representatives of the arithmetic-logic instructions - add, the branch and jump instructions - beq, and the memory-access instructions - lw and sw; (2) the architecture which features a minimal direct-mapped data cache (with one data assigned per cache line) and a main memory module.   □

Next, we introduce the development platform - the $\mathbb{K}$ framework - which is a specialization of rewriting logic for the specification and analysis of programming languages. A $\mathbb{K}$ specification consists of *configurations*, *rules*, and *computations*. A *configuration* defines all the semantic entities necessary for representing the system (or program) states. Namely, the $\mathbb{K}$ configuration is a nested set of $\mathbb{K}$-cells where the $\mathbb{K}$-cell is essentially a generic type formed by a *label* giving the identity of the cell, and the sort of the cell's contents, defined as $\langle\ ContentSort\ \rangle_{\mathsf{label}}$.

Example 2. Our toy RISC assembly language configuration, $Cfg_{toyRISC}$, is:

$$Cfg_{toyRISC} \equiv \langle K \rangle_{\mathsf{k}} \; \langle Reg \rangle_{\mathsf{pc}} \; \langle Reg \mapsto Val \rangle_{\mathsf{regs}}$$

where k, pc, and regs are $\mathbb{K}$-cells, and Reg and Val are sorts for registers and respectively stored values. The cell called k is specially designated in $\mathbb{K}$ to contain the list of computational tasks (of sort K), according to the continuation-based semantics. Hence, the cell k is supposed to be the functional engine of the $\mathbb{K}$-specification. The cell pc holds the program counter register while the cell regs maintains the integer register file - a map from registers to values. In a similar fashion, the configurations for the data cache memory - Cfg_{ToyDC} - and the main memory - Cfg_{toyMM} - are as follows:

$$Cfg_{ToyDC} \equiv \langle K \rangle_{\mathsf{k}} \; \langle CAddr \mapsto Val \rangle_{\mathsf{dc}}$$

where dc is the content mapping cache addresses $CAddr$ to data Val and

$$Cfg_{toyMM} \equiv \langle K \rangle_{\mathsf{k}} \; \langle MAddr \mapsto Instr \rangle_{\mathsf{cmem}} \langle MAddr \mapsto Val \rangle_{\mathsf{dmem}}$$

where the $\mathbb{K}$-cells cmem and dmem are the code and respectively data memory mapping addresses $MAddr$ to instructions $Instr$ and, respectively, to data Val. $\square$

The *rules* in $\mathbb{K}$ describe patterns of system execution which produce changes in the states of the system (i.e., in the instantiations of the configuration). For example, the rules over subterms of $Cfg_{toyRISC}$ give semantics to the language constructs (i.e., the instructions add, beq, lw and sw of our toy RISC language) while the rules over Cfg_{ToyDC} or Cfg_{toyMM} give semantics to the architecture (e.g., cache hit/miss on read/write requests and main memory read/write operations). The rules are classified as: *computational rules*, which may be interpreted as transitions in a program execution, and *structural rules* that modify a term to enable the application of a computational rule. Unless labeled with the keyword [structural], a $\mathbb{K}$-rule is computational.

Example 3. The semantics of the load instruction - lw Rd, Off(Rs); updates a destination register Rd with the value at the memory address calculated based on a source register value Rs and an offset Off. The following $\mathbb{K}$ rules encode the semantics of lw - rule R_LW and of register update - rule R_RU:

$$\frac{\langle \quad\quad \mathtt{lw}\; Rd, Off(V_1); \quad\quad \rangle_{\mathsf{k}}}{\mathtt{updReg}(\boxed{\mathtt{getd}(V_1 + \mathit{Off})}, Rd)} \quad\quad [\text{R\_LW, structural}]$$

$$\frac{\langle \mathtt{updReg}(V, R) \rangle_{\mathsf{k}} \; \langle \cdots \; R \mapsto \underset{V}{\underline{\quad \_ \quad}} \; \cdots \rangle_{\mathsf{regs}}}{\cdot} \quad [\text{R\_RU}]$$

A $\mathbb{K}$ rule uses a specialized bi-dimensional notation to specify the *rewriting context* and the location of the rewriting. For example, in the rule R_LW, the lw instruction appearing inside cell k is transformed into a register update, via a getd data request from the main memory. Note that in rule R_LW the context is given by the cell k. Moreover, the boxing of the term $\mathtt{getd}(V_1 + Off)$

shows that over this term we apply the reduction semantics. Namely, when a term T is boxed at the top of k cell in the context C, i.e., $\langle C\boxed{T}\ \cdots\rangle_k$, then $\mathbb{K}$ applies the reduction semantics style, by pushing T - called redex - outside the box, at the top of the continuation, i.e., $\langle T \curvearrowright C\square\ \cdots\rangle_k$. Hence, the reduction-based feature of $\mathbb{K}$ pushes $\mathtt{getd}(V_1 + Off)$ at the top of the k cell, i.e., $\langle \mathtt{getd}(V_1 + Off) \curvearrowright \mathtt{updReg}(\square, Rd)\ \cdots\rangle_k$. After the reduction of $\mathtt{getd}(V_1 + Off)$ to its normal form, an integer in this case, the result is pushed back into the box, i.e., $\langle \mathtt{updReg}(\boxed{V}, Rd)\ \cdots\rangle_k$, then the box is dissolved leaving $\mathtt{updReg}(V, Rd)$ at the top of k.

The rule R_RU can be applied after the rule R_LW, which places the $\mathtt{updReg}$ operation on top of cell k. The result is twofold: in k, the new computation is the empty task, represented by "." notation standing for the *void element*, and *somewhere* in the regs cell *any* previous value associated to R is replaced by V. Note that the $\mathbb{K}$ notation for *somewhere* is given by the ellipses "$\cdots$" appearing near the walls of cell regs (i.e., the ellipses stand for *other elements in the respective cell*, the "." included). Also, note that *any* value (contained in the register R) is denoted by the wildcard "_" (i.e., $R \mapsto$ _). $\qquad\square$

A *computation* in $\mathbb{K}$ is a sequence of rewrite rules applications.

Example 4. Let us consider yet another rule for our toy specification which captures a data request from a given memory address $Addr$:

$$\frac{\langle \mathtt{getd}(Addr)\ \cdots\rangle_k\ \langle\cdots\ Addr \mapsto V\ \cdots\rangle_{dmem}}{\mathtt{retd}(V)}\quad [\text{R\_MD}]$$

Note that this rule, R_MD, is working on the configuration Cfg_{toyMM}, according to the cells used by this rule. Note also that while R_RU has to be part of $Cfg_{toyRISC}$, for R_LW we have no restrictions but we prefer to place it in $Cfg_{toyRISC}$ as well. We then observe that the sequence of rule applications R_LW, R_MD, R_RU, intercalated with the reduction mechanism (denoted as $\sqcap$ for pushing the redex out of the box, and $\sqcup$ for pushing it inside the box), is a $\mathbb{K}$-computation. Namely, the evolution of the continuation - the contents of the k cell - for the substitution $Rd/5, Off/1, V_1/3, Addr/4$ and $V/7$, is:

$$\langle \mathtt{lw}\ 5, 1(3);\rangle_k \overset{\text{R\_LW}}{\to} \langle \mathtt{updReg}(\boxed{\mathtt{getd}(3+1)}, 5)\rangle_k \overset{\sqcap}{\to} \langle \mathtt{getd}(\boxed{3+1}) \curvearrowright \mathtt{updReg}(\square, 5)\rangle_k$$

$$\overset{\sqcap}{\to} \langle (3+1 \curvearrowright \mathtt{getd}(\square)) \curvearrowright \mathtt{updReg}(\square, 5)\rangle_k \overset{\text{R+}}{\to} \langle 4 \curvearrowright \mathtt{getd}(\square) \curvearrowright \mathtt{updReg}(\square, 5)\rangle_k$$

$$\overset{\sqcup}{\to} \langle \mathtt{getd}(4) \curvearrowright \mathtt{updReg}(\square, 5)\rangle_k\ \langle\cdots\ 4 \mapsto 7\ \cdots\rangle_{dmem} \overset{\text{R\_MD}}{\to} \langle \mathtt{retd}(7) \curvearrowright \mathtt{updReg}(\square, 5)\rangle_k$$

$$\overset{\text{R\_RD}}{\to} \langle 7 \curvearrowright \mathtt{updReg}(\square, 5)\rangle_k \overset{\sqcup}{\to} \langle \mathtt{updReg}(7, 5)\rangle_k\ \langle\cdots\ 5 \mapsto 2\ \cdots\rangle_{regs} \overset{\text{R\_RU}}{\to} \langle\cdot\rangle_k\ \langle\cdots\ 5 \mapsto 7\ \cdots\rangle_{regs},$$

where the rule R_RD simply rewrites $\mathtt{retd}(V)$ into V if V is an integer (i.e., a basic value in Val). Hence, this computation starts from the module corresponding to $Cfg_{toyRISC}$, via R_LW, and goes to Cfg_{toyMM} to execute R_MD, and it ends in $Cfg_{toyRISC}$ with R_MD. $\square$

In the settings of *Example 1*, the rule R_MD specifies part of the main memory behavior. This rule emphasizes two key features of our approach. First, the configuration Cfg_{toyMM} of the main memory has also a code memory cell (i.e., cmem in *Example 2*) which is not used in the rule R_MD. The reason is the *configuration abstraction* mechanism of $\mathbb{K}$, which allows compact representations of the rewrite rules (and hides a rule completion mechanism). The intuition is to use only the relevant semantic entities when writing a particular rule. Second, the `getd` request is placed on top of cell k after applying the rule R_LW, as seen in *Example* 3, and it enables the application of the rule R_MD. At its turn, R_MD places `retd` at the top of communication to signal the enabling of R_RU. Hence, we specify an inter-component communication via `getd` and `retd`.

Abstract Interpretation: Since it was introduced in [9], abstract interpretation established itself as one of the major program reasoning techniques, along with model checking and deductive verification. For a given programming language, abstract interpretation is used to systematically design abstract semantics which target the analysis of specific properties. We introduce the settings of abstract semantics for WCET analysis, as in [28].

A program analysis relies on the following two elements: an abstract domain and an abstract semantics. The abstract domain is defined by a complete semi-lattice, a pair of monotonic (with respect to partial orderings, both in concrete and abstract) functions - called representation and concretization. The representation function maps/represents concrete to abstract states while the concretization function maps abstract states to sets of concrete states. The following translation holds: a concrete state is represented by an abstract state which is concretized to a set of states containing the particular concrete state. A third function, called abstraction, is defined in terms of the representation function and, together with the concretization function, forms a Galois connection. An essential part is the abstract semantics which re-implements the transfer functions of the concrete semantics, under certain requirements. The abstract semantics is used to solve the program analysis problem, by employing a fixpoint computation.

In the context of our approach for modular integration of abstractions, and according to [28], we consider abstract interpretation-based analyses both at the level of the program (i.e., value analyses), and architecture (i.e., cache analyses).

3   A General System Design

Let us consider a complex computational system, specified in $\mathbb{K}$, that has the configuration C_{global} which comprises *all* semantic entities that are necessary to capture the system behavior. We take the C_{global} configuration and split it into a number of (not necessarily disjoint) sub-configurations: $C_1, C_2, \ldots, C_n$. Informally, each sub-configuration handles a well-defined component of the system. The configuration splitting induces a first stage of modularization of the semantics. As such, we distinguish two types of modules *functional* and *structural*, according to the presence or, respectively, the absence of the k cell in the sub-configuration associated with the module. Given that cell k handles the sequencing of the computations, the (functional) modules containing this cell are to be responsible of producing slices of computations.

Example 5. For our simple specification, introduced in *Example* 1, the C_{global} is:

$$\langle K \rangle_k \langle Reg \rangle_{pc} \langle Reg \mapsto Val \rangle_{regs} \langle CAddr \mapsto Val \rangle_{dc} \langle MAddr \mapsto Val \rangle_{cmem} \langle MAddr \mapsto Val \rangle_{dmem}$$

while the modularization consists of the sub-configurations $Cfg_{toyRISC}$, Cfg_{ToyDC}, and Cfg_{toyMM}, each inducing a functional module. Moreover, the specification is equipped with a structural module, which contains the arithmetic (i.e., the rules for the add, lw, and sw instructions) and logic operations (i.e., for the beq instruction) on 32-bits. □

Apart from its computational purpose, the cell k also facilitates the inter-modular communication through tokens (e.g., getd is the token for data request from the main memory as seen in *Example* 4). Structurally, a token is part of the module interface and semantically, it is a computational task which acts like a guarded message passing between modules. Therefore, any execution in this system is an interleaving of inner-module computations and guarded messages that are exchanged between the modules. We assume that any token is sent and received by one module, however this model is amenable to extensions to accommodate concurrent exchanges of tokens.

The configuration abstraction of $\mathbb{K}$ completes the partially defined rules with the cells which were omitted. The mechanism of rule completion identifies first the nesting structure of the configuration, then it inserts the missing cells in the correct place, defining like this the notion of *rule context*. As such, it heavily relies on the shape defined by the configuration. Our idea is to integrate abstractions by changing the configuration shape, through $\mathbb{K}$ cell wrapping, creating in this way new rule contexts.

Example 6. The rule R_MD (i.e., in *Example* 4) is completed according to Cfg_{toyMM} as:

$$\langle \underbrace{\text{getd}(Addr)}_{\text{retd}(V)} \cdots \rangle_k \langle \cdots Addr \mapsto V \cdots \rangle_{dmem} \langle C \rangle_{cmem} \qquad [\text{R\_MD\_completed}]$$

where the code memory content C, in cmem cell, is unchanged. However, if the cells k and dmem are wrapped in a new cell then the rule completion does not add cmem. Hence, getd acts like a guarded message, the guard being here the structure of Cfg_{toyMM}. Moreover, we can use also other types of guarded messages by giving the message rule as a conditional rule where the guard is the predicate in the condition. Note that the conditional rules are denoted in $\mathbb{K}$ by the keyword "when", i.e., "$l \Rightarrow r$ when p" where l and r are the left-and, respectively, the right-part of the rewrite while p is the predicate denoting the condition which has to be met in order for the rewrite to be triggered. For example, such a guarded message is retd and the conditional rule associated to it is denoted as: $\frac{\text{"retd}(V)}{V}$ when $\text{isInt}(V) =_{Bool} true$ [R_RD]". □

We present the abstraction integration methodology as a meta-algorithm, in Fig. 2, then we instantiate it for the WCET analysis workflow. The integration considers a set of modules M_i, each being represented by sub-configurations

Input:

M_i - $\mathbb{K}$ modules with corresponding sub-configurations C_i, with $i = 1..n$;
$T = \{t_{i,j} \mid i, j = 1..n, i \neq j\}$ - tokens between the modules M_i and M_j;
$\langle\langle \cdot \rangle_k \langle S_0 \rangle_{\text{states}} \langle RE \rangle_{\text{slicePattern}} \ Rest \rangle_{\text{abst}} \langle \cdot \rangle_{\text{concr}}$ - the abstract configuration inside cell abst where S_0 is the initial abstract state, RE the slicing pattern given as, e.g., a regular expression over T, and $Rest$ being other abstraction-specific information, and an empty concrete configuration inside the concr cell.

Output:

$\langle\langle S \rangle_{\text{states}} \langle RE \rangle_{\text{slicePattern}} \ Rest \rangle_{\text{abst}}$ - the final state S of the abstraction, identified by the absence of the abstract computation cell k inside cell abst.

INIT
$$\frac{\langle\langle \underbrace{t_{i,j} \curvearrowright t_{k,l}}_{\text{wait}(t_{k,l})} \cdots \rangle_k \langle S \rangle_{\text{states}} \cdots \rangle_{\text{abst}} \quad \langle \underline{\qquad\cdot\qquad} \rangle_{\text{concr}}}{\langle t_{i,j} \rangle_k \langle \flat(S) \rangle_{\text{state}}}$$

STOP
$$\frac{\langle\langle \underbrace{\qquad\text{wait}(t_{k,l})\qquad}_{\text{process}_{k,l}(c \sqcup S) \curvearrowright t_{k,l}} \cdots \rangle_k \langle S \rangle_{\text{states}} \cdots \rangle_{\text{abst}} \quad \langle\langle t_{k,l} \cdots \rangle_k \langle \sharp(c) \rangle_{\text{state}} \rangle_{\text{concr}}}{\cdot}$$

RESUME
$$\frac{\langle\langle \underbrace{\text{processed}_{k,l}(S')}\ \cdots \rangle_k \quad \langle S \rangle_{\text{states}} \cdots \rangle_{\text{abst}} \quad \langle \cdot \rangle_{\text{concr}}}{\cdot} \qquad \text{when} \quad S' < S$$

$$\frac{\langle\langle \underbrace{\text{processed}_{k,l}(S')}\ \cdots \rangle_k \langle \underset{S'}{\underline{S}} \rangle_{\text{states}} \cdots \rangle_{\text{abst}}}{\cdot} \qquad \text{when} \quad S' \not< S$$

REPEAT
$$\frac{\langle\langle \ \cdot\ \rangle_k \langle RE \rangle_{\text{slicePattern}} \cdots \rangle_{\text{abst}}}{RE}$$

Fig. 2. The meta-algorithm for modular integration of abstractions.

wrapped into the abstract configuration. M_is use the token sets $t_{j,k}$ to communicate, via the cell k. The structural modules are not part of the set of M_is, but their rules can be applied wherever necessary (e.g., the rule for integer addition R+ used in the computation from *Example* 4).

This meta-algorithm identifies the following stages: INIT, STOP, RESUME, and REPEAT and it uses $\langle RE \rangle_{\text{slicePattern}}$ as the regular pattern of slicing the concrete executions. The pattern RE is repeatedly pushed in the abstract continuation via the rule REPEAT. As such, the flow of the rules in the meta-algorithm is (REPEAT.(INIT.STOP.RESUME)*)*. Namely, the sequence INIT.STOP.RESUME is repeatedly executed until the abstraction reaches the fixpoint (the first rule of RESUME) or the slicing pattern RE is consumed. If, however, RE is consumed without reaching the fixpoint, i.e., the abstract k cell is empty, then the rule REPEAT is applied so (INIT.STOP.RESUME) is triggered again.

The connection INIT.STOP is made at the top of the abstract k cell via "wait($t_{k,l}$)" which means that the abstract computation is waiting for the concrete computation triggered by INIT to reach the stage where the token $t_{k,l}$ is computed in concrete. We recall that these tokens are functioning as execution guards which, based on the evaluation of the concrete state (the contents of cell state), let the concrete execution pass to another module. However, $\flat(S)$, the concretization of the abstract state S, produces a wrapping around the concrete state - $\sharp(c)$ - which does not allow the triggering of the concrete rule via the context abstraction mechanism. Hence, the concrete execution is cut at $t_{k,l}$ and the rule STOP is triggered. Also, we assume that "process$_{k,l}$"- which processes the assimilation of the newly discovered concrete state c into the abstract state S - reaches the normal form "processed$_{k,l}$". This assumption ensures the connection STOP.RESUME. Finally, the eventual repetition of the sequence, i.e., the connection RESUME.INIT, is produced by the second rule in RESUME which consumes the "processed$_{k,l}(S')$" top of the continuation and clears the way for a new application of the INIT rule. Note that we make use of a mechanism of unfolding the regular expression RE into computation tasks $t \curvearrowright t'$ but we do not insist over this aspect here.

Example 7. Let us assume that we integrate a *value analysis* over the specification described in *Example 1*. This analysis returns the sign of the values referred by load/store instructions, where the sign lattice is $\{?, +, -, 0, 0+, -0, -0+\}$. The meta-algorithm takes the modules M_1 - $Cfg_{toyRISC}$, M_2 - Cfg_{ToyDC}, M_3 - a part of Cfg_{toyMM} (i.e., only k and data memory dmem cells because the analysis focuses on data). As observed in *Example 6*, the token $t_{1,3}$ is getd, used as a memory request for a cache miss on lw, while $t_{3,1}$ is retd. Note that $t_{1,2}$ also contains tokens used for the store instruction sw but, for brevity, we decide not include them here.

When we integrate the value analysis, we wrap in the concr cell only a part of M_3, i.e., the cells k and dmem. In this way, we isolate the necessary behavior to capture the accesses to the data memory. In other words, the wrapping in concr slices the main memory specification. The abstraction-specific semantic entities are wrapped in the abst cell in the *Rest* part which, for this value analysis, contains a representation of the control-flow graph (CFG). Note that CFG is extracted using a similar integration of an abstraction for CFG extraction into the meta-algorithm.

Now, if the slicing pattern RE unfolds into $\langle\langle \mathtt{getd}(A) \curvearrowright \mathtt{retd}(V) \curvearrowright \mathrm{CFG}\rangle_k \cdots\rangle_{\mathsf{abst}}$ then the INIT rule with the abstract state $\langle\cdots \langle\cdots 4 \mapsto ? \cdots\rangle_{\mathsf{states}} \cdots\rangle_{\mathsf{abst}}$ pushes into the concrete cell $\langle\langle\mathtt{getd}(4)\rangle_k \langle\cdots 4 \mapsto \sharp(7) \cdots\rangle_{\mathsf{dmem}}\rangle_{\mathsf{concr}}$. The concrete computation stops with $\mathtt{retd}(\sharp(7))$ at the top of the k cell, since rule R_RD cannot be triggered due to the fact that the rule condition $\mathtt{isInt}(\sharp(7))$ is not *true*. Then, the rule STOP is enabled, $\sharp(7)$ goes into the abstract continuation as $\langle\cdots \langle\mathtt{process}(\sharp(7) \sqcup (4 \mapsto ?)) \cdots\rangle_k \cdots\rangle_{\mathsf{abst}}$. Next, $\mathtt{process}(\sharp(7) \sqcup (4 \mapsto ?))$ reaches the normal form "$\mathtt{processed}(4 \mapsto +))$" and the second rule in RESUME is triggered. Note that the slicing pattern RE depends on the CFG, so the rule REPEAT will trigger the fixpoint computation for the entire program abstracted into the CFG containing only loads and stores. Finally, we remark that we show here only the part of RE for loads and we omit the part for stores. □

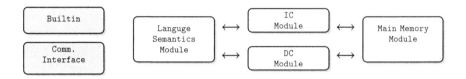

Fig. 3. The modular organization of our WCET analysis workflow with structural (i.e., support operations and communication interface) and functional modules (i.e., language semantics, cache and main memories).

4   Modular Timing Analysis

The System: Our proposed system consists of the formal executable semantics of the MIPS IV assembly language (which plays the role of the processor), parametric specifications of instruction and data caches, of the main memory, as well as specialized support modules. The parametrization refers to both the cache structure (e.g., size, associativity) and functionality (e.g., replacement policies, writing policies).

The overall system, shown in Fig. 3, consists of several $\mathbb{K}$ modules. Next we elaborate the structural modules Builtin and Interface as well as the functional modules Language Semantics, IC and Main Memory. For each of these modules, we discuss the corresponding concrete configurations, which from our methodology perspective described in Fig. 2, are wrapped into the concr cell. The complete configuration, containing both concr and abst, is described in Sect. 4.2 - for the data analyses and Sect. 4.3 - for the ILP + AI method.

Language Semantics - We encode the MIPS IV assembly language as supported by the Simplescalar toolset. Its complete configuration Cfg_{Lang} is given as an extension of $Cfg_{toyRISC}$ from Example 2:

$$Cfg_{Lang} \equiv Cfg_{toyRISC} \langle Reg \rangle_{\mathsf{lo}} \langle Reg \rangle_{\mathsf{hi}} \langle Reg \rangle_{\mathsf{ra}} \langle Val \rangle_{\mathsf{fcc}} \langle Val \rangle_{\mathsf{break}} \langle FReg \mapsto Val \rangle_{\mathsf{fregs}}$$

The concrete language configuration has the cells k, pc and regs from $Cfg_{toyRISC}$, the floating-point register file, fregs, and also two flags, break and fcc (for abrupt termination of execution and respectively a floating point parameter). It also features several specialized registers for the multiplication/division results, lo and hi, and the return address of a function call, ra. Each $\mathbb{K}$ cell displays sorting information.

Main Memory - We emulate the organization of an assembly file into code and data sections, represented in the cmem cell and respectively dmem cell in *Example 2*. The concrete main memory configuration, Cfg_{toyMM}, plays an important role in both control and data abstractions because it stores the input program.

IC Memory - The instruction cache configuration, Cfg_{IC}, captures both structural and functional aspects of a cache memory:

$$Cfg_{IC} \equiv Cfg_{toyIC} \langle Addr \mapsto Val \rangle_{\mathsf{ages}} \langle Addr \rangle_{\mathsf{repl}} \langle Prm \mapsto Val \rangle_{\mathsf{prm}} \langle Val \rangle_{\mathsf{ilen}} \langle Addr \rangle_{\mathsf{faddr}} \langle Type \mapsto Val \rangle_{\mathsf{profl}}$$

The k cell and instruction content ic cell are inherited from the Cfg_{ToyIC} configuration. The ages cell contains, for each cache line, the associated age information of its content. The repl cell has the address of the cache block as the next eviction candidate (computed based on the age information). The profl and prm cells store the hit/miss counts and the cache parameters (e.g., size, associativity), while the ilen and faddr are the instruction length and the address of the first instruction in the program, respectively. The data cache configuration of the DC Module (not presented) is an extension of Cfg_{IC} with new cells to capture parametric modeling for writing policies (i.e., FIFO or LRU).

Builtin - It is a structural module containing definitions for semantic operations on 16- and 32-bit signed and unsigned integers, and single and double precision for floats.

Interface - This structural module contains the communication tokens, $t_{i,j}$s, between two arbitrary modules M_i and M_j, as described in Fig. 2.

This system is designed to simulate the execution of a program on an underlying architecture. We call this the *concrete specification* of the system. The execution of one instruction consists of a sequence of code and data requests to the memory system described by several $\mathbb{K}$ modules (IC Module, DC Module, and Main Memory in Fig. 3).

The modularity of our design allows us to define abstractions directly over the existing modules while these are kept unmodified. The abstract configuration has two components: (a) a definition-based set of $\mathbb{K}$ cells, derived from the concrete definition of the system and (b) an abstraction-specific set of $\mathbb{K}$ cells, to represent abstract datatypes and other necessary auxiliary constructs. We elaborate next on how we encode four abstractions: constant propagation and the interval analysis in Sect. 4.2, and the ILP+AI combined method in Sect. 4.3.

The Data Abstractions: The constant propagation and the interval analysis are widely used static analyses for WCET analysis, according to [28]. In this section we discuss how these two analyses are integrated within our methodology.

A constant propagation analysis produces, at each program point, the set of variables (i.e., register values) having constant values. According to the general scheme for an abstract interpretation based analysis, from Sect. 2.2, we need to define the abstract domain and abstract versions of the language operations. The unknown value of a variable is abstractly represented by a special symbolic value. Also, the abstract operations extend the concrete ones (in Builtin Module) with the unknown value case.

To encode the constant propagation we retain, from the concrete system, the language registers and the code memory, wrapped in the concr cell. The abstraction-specific component, abst, is empty. Therefore, the configuration for the constant propagation, restricted to the integer domain, is the following:

$$\langle\langle Reg \mapsto Val\rangle_{\mathsf{regs}}\langle Val\rangle_{\mathsf{break}}\langle Val\rangle_{\mathsf{lo}}\langle Val\rangle_{\mathsf{hi}}\langle Addr \mapsto Val\rangle_{\mathsf{cmem}}\rangle_{\mathsf{concr}}$$

The interval analysis from [22] relies on an abstract representation of a language value as an interval. Our assembly language uses several types of values: integers and floats, and the interval-based values applies to all of them. Next, we refer to the interval analysis encoding on the integer domain. We follow the same design steps as before: we start with the abstract domain and define new sort information to represent the interval bounds. This integration is seamless with respect to the semantics rules in language semantics module, however a new `Builtin` is required. Once the abstract domain and the `Builtin` module are defined, we proceed to integrate the interval analysis in the same spirit. Since this analysis generalizes the constant propagation, the following relation exists between Cfg_{CP} and Cfg_{IA} (defined below). The abst cell content of Cfg_{CP} remains the same (modulo interval-related sorting) and we add an abstraction-specific cell, called mdop. The configuration for the interval analysis is defined as: $Cfg_{IA} \equiv \langle Cfg_{CP} \langle Val \rangle_{\mathsf{mdop}} \rangle_{\mathsf{abst}}$. The cell mdop is necessary because the multiplication and division operations require two special registers hi and lo to store the result (for the multiplication) or the quotient and the remainder (for the division). After such arithmetic operation, the interval analysis suffers due to rounding errors for lower and upper bounds of the interval result. For example, when multiplying two intervals, we temporarily store the result in mdop before we transfer it into the hi and lo from concr.

The ILP+AI Approach: A successful approach for WCET analysis proposes (1) an integer linear programming (ILP) solution, for path analysis, and (2) uses abstract interpretation (AI) for the processor behavior analysis. In (1) the program becomes an ILP problem with structural (i.e., automatically extracted) and functional constraints (i.e., via analyses or manual annotations). In (2) the program blocks are classified w.r.t. their cache behavior two main types of behavior parameters - may/must hit/miss.

The ILP representation captures the flow information of a program, as ILP constraints. Therefore, the core component of this abstraction is the program counter, pc, wrapped in concr. The configuration of the ILP constraints extraction is in Fig. 4.

$$Cfg_{ILP} \equiv \langle\langle\langle Addr \rangle_{\mathsf{gaddr}} \langle Val \rangle_{\mathsf{ctridx}} \langle PC \mapsto K \rangle_{\mathsf{sconstr}} \rangle_{\mathsf{ilp}} \rangle_{\mathsf{abst}} \langle\langle Val \rangle_{\mathsf{pc}} \langle Addr \mapsto Val \rangle_{\mathsf{cmem}} \rangle_{\mathsf{concr}}$$
$$Cfg_{CA} \equiv \langle\langle K \rangle_{\mathsf{atype}} \langle PC \mapsto K \rangle_{\mathsf{collect}} \langle K \rangle_{\mathsf{jres}} \rangle_{\mathsf{abst}}$$
$$\langle\langle\langle Addr \mapsto Val \rangle_{\mathsf{ic}} \langle Addr \mapsto Val \rangle_{\mathsf{ages}} \rangle_{\mathsf{aic}} \langle Addr \mapsto Val \rangle_{\mathsf{prm}} \langle Addr \rangle_{\mathsf{faddr}} \langle Val \rangle_{\mathsf{ilen}} \rangle_{\mathsf{concr}}$$

Fig. 4. Cfg_{ILP} - the $\mathbb{K}$ configuration for the ILP structural constraints extraction, and Cfg_{CA} - the $\mathbb{K}$ configuration for the AI-based cache analysis.

The abstraction-specific part of Cfg_{ILP} uses the sconstr cell to collect the ILP constraints and, for each program point, keeps the constraint index in the ctridx cell and the target address (for a branch/jump instruction), in the gaddr cell.

Example 8. In Fig. 5 we present the $\mathbb{K}$ rule to extract, for a branch instruction, the ILP constraints. The branch instruction *Ins* is at a program point *PC* and has the fall-through address *N* and the target address *J*. The flow information which

$$\langle\langle\cdots \quad \frac{\langle \text{wait}(PC) \quad \cdots\rangle_k \langle \begin{array}{c} J \\ \hline \cdot \end{array} \rangle_{\text{gaddr}} \langle \begin{array}{c} I \\ \hline I+2 \end{array} \rangle_{\text{ctridx}}}{J \frown N}$$

$$\langle \cdots \quad PC \mapsto \frac{(InsPC, OutsPC)}{(InsPC, \{I, I+1\} \cup OutsPC)}$$

$$N \mapsto \frac{(InsN, OutsN)}{(\{I+1\} \cup InsN, OutsN)} \quad J \mapsto \frac{(InsJ, OutsJ)}{(\{I\} \cup InsJ, OutsJ)} \quad \cdots\rangle_{\text{sconstr}}$$

$$\cdots\rangle_{\text{ilp}}\rangle_{\text{abst}}$$

$$\frac{\langle\langle Ins \quad \cdots\rangle_k \langle N\rangle_{\text{pc}} C\rangle_{\text{concr}}}{\cdot} \quad \text{when} \quad \text{isBranchInstr}(Ins) =_{Bool} true$$

Fig. 5. Rule for structural ILP constraints generation from a branch instruction.

corresponds to the test instruction could be expressed as: the execution count of the condition is equal with the sum of execution counts of the two branches. This rewrite rule represents the case STOP in Fig. 2. If the current instruction is a test - as reflected by the condition "when isBranchInstr(Ins)"- then the computation in concr is stopped (i.e., it rewrites to "·") and the "processing" computation in abst starts. In the cell k of abst, the token "wait(PC)" identifies the program point where the concrete execution stopped. The token is transformed into a sequence of abstract computational tasks, for the instructions at addresses J and N. The gaddr cell is emptied, because the corresponding input constraint for the jump address J is generated at this step. This rewrite rule generates two new constraint indexes, I and $I+1$, hence the next available index is $I+2$ (deposited in the cell ctridx). The constraints are collected in sconstr, where each program point is represented by its input $InsPC/N/J$ and output $OutsPC/N/J$ sets. The exit flow for the test at PC is reflected in an updated $OutPC$ (with the two new indexes), while the entry flow for the two branches are in $InsN/J$. When the algorithm terminates, each program point has a set of constraints with the property that the sum of input constraints is equal to the sum of output constraints.   □

The AI-based analysis for the instruction cache behavior computes sets of abstract cache states to classify each program instruction w.r.t. its cache activity. Hence, an instruction could be always-hit (after a must analysis) or always-miss (after a may analysis). The core of this abstraction is the pair of cache content, in ic and its corresponding age information, in ages. The associated join operations are based on intersection (for must analysis) and reunion (for may analysis) of abstract states. These abstractions are presented in details in [25]. In our methodology, the configuration Cfg_{CA} for the instruction cache analysis is given in Fig. 4. The set of abstraction-specific cells include the analysis type (may or must) in atype, the result of the corresponding join operation, in jres, and the abstraction results in collect. Also, the two data abstractions and the cache behavior abstraction could include, in their abstraction-specific part of the configuration, a special cell cfg for a previously extracted control flow graph.

name	#lines	ILP extraction	AI may instr. cache	AI must instr. cache
icrc1	42	70.5%(647)	23%(22422)	22.1%(23287)
duffcopy	104	70.8%(1519)	23.4%(44064)	19.5%(53368)
expint	185	70.5%(2761)	23.4%(91158)	17.96%(120064)
adpcm decode	312	71.08%(4403)	23.81%(109560)	12.91%(201942)
adpcm encode	327	71.08%(4645)	23.79%(119052)	12.83%(220679)

Fig. 6. Results for some Mälardalen programs for ILP structural constraints extraction, AI may-analysis for instruction cache, and must-analysis for instruction cache.

5   Implementation

We implement in $\mathbb{K}$-Maude [10] our general framework for resource-related analysis in the context of the WCET analysis. For illustration purposes, we opt to experiment with the ILP + AI method rather than the data abstractions, because of the more complex configurations, i.e., $Config_{ILP}$ and $Config_{CA}$.

The ILP monitors the execution between the language semantics and the main memory; a single token (an instruction fetch request) is necessary to stop the concrete execution. The AI part involves the cache memory module and, thus, it is more complex due to the parametrization based on the cache structure and functionality (i.e., cache size, associativity, or replacement policy) and due to the parametrization on the analysis type (i.e., may and must). Regarding the configuration size, the concrete system has 22 $\mathbb{K}$-cells, the ILP constraints extraction needs 9 $\mathbb{K}$-cells (with 4 abstraction-specific ones) and the cache analyses needs 21 $\mathbb{K}$ cells (with 12 abstraction-specific cells).

Moreover, we measure a reusability degree of the concrete specification, when various types of abstractions are integrated. The computation, after an abstraction integration, presents three kinds of rules: two kinds are coming from the concrete and the abstract specification and a third kind, generated by $\mathbb{K}$-Maude. When we measure the percentage of the abstract execution steps with respect to the total number of execution steps, we ignore the tool generated ones.

We select several of the Mälardalen benchmarks [13] and run on a 2.4 GHz Intel Core i5 MacBook Pro. We conduct the experiments on the following programs: the cycle redundancy check computation *icrc1*, the Duff device *duffcopy*, the exponential integral function computation *expint*, and the adaptive pulse code modulation algorithm of *encode* and *decode*. The size of each program is listed in the column #**lines** in Fig. 6.

The table in Fig. 6 shows the integration of the ILP constraints generation and the results on the AI-based instruction cache analyses (i.e., may and must). For each analysis, we present in its designated column the percentage of concrete rewrite rules in the execution and, in the bracket, the number of rewrites of this particular execution.

We observe a higher reusability percentage in the case of the ILP analysis than for the AI for cache analyses. The reason is that the ILP wrapped concrete configuration, Cfg_{ILP}, is simpler than the cache analyses configuration, Cfg_{CA}

(we recall that only the pc register and the code memory are necessary to detect the program flow). Running both may and must analyses under an implicit CFG produces results as low as 12 % reusability, for the *adpcm encode* benchmark program (on must analysis) and not higher than 24 % for the *adpcm decode* program (on may analysis). These results emphasize that, in the worst case scenario, when the join function is executed at every program point, there is still some percentage of the concrete specification that can be reused. Actually, this scenario proposes a lower bound for the reusability factor w.r.t. the system specification. However, running these analyses with an explicit CFG reduces drastically the number of join points and the reusability factor is as high as 85 % for the *adpcm encode* and *adpcm decode* programs.

6 Conclusions

In this paper we proposed a framework for modular resource analysis which relied on a trusted core formed by a modular formal executable semantics of the analyzed system. The work was motivated by the time resource and was constructed around analyses applied in WCET computation. The modularity aspect is both functional and structural. Namely, the functional modularity is at the level of the analysis and stemmed from a systematic integration of abstractions over the trusted core. In its turn, the structural modularity resides in the formal specification of the assembly language and the underlying architecture. We showed how to integrate into the resource analysis workflow the following WCET analyses: the constant propagation, the interval analysis, and the combined ILP+AI approach. We described the implementation and its testing w.r.t. an integration factor which we set to the reusability degree of the concrete specification in the abstract one. Our future work includes (1) a specification of pipeline behavior and analysis (requiring parameterized $\mathbb{K}$ modules - currently in development as described in [16]) and (2) further investigations on integrating other resource analyses into our proposed framework.

Acknowledgments. We thank very much to the anonymous reviewers for their comments and suggestions which helped us to focus and improve our work in this paper.

References

1. AbsInt Angewandte Informatik: aiT Worst-Case Execution Time Analyzers
2. Asăvoae, M., Asăvoae, I.M., Lucanu, D.: On abstractions for timing analysis in the $\mathbb{K}$ framework. In: Peña, R., van Eekelen, M., Shkaravska, O. (eds.) FOPARA 2011. LNCS, vol. 7177, pp. 90–107. Springer, Heidelberg (2012)
3. Asavoae, M., Lucanu, D., Roşu, G.: Towards semantics-based WCET analysis. In: WCET (2011) (to appear)
4. Biere, A., Knoop, J., Kovács, L., Zwirchmayr, J.: The auspicious couple: Symbolic execution and WCET analysis. In: WCET, pp. 53–63 (2013)

5. Blazy, S., Maroneze, A., Pichardie, D.: Formal verification of loop bound estimation for WCET analysis. In: Cohen, E., Rybalchenko, A. (eds.) VSTTE 2013. LNCS, vol. 8164, pp. 281–303. Springer, Heidelberg (2014)
6. Burger, D., Austin, T.M.: The SimpleScalar tool set, version 2.0. SIGARCH Comput. Archit. News **25**, 13–25 (1997)
7. Clavel, M., Durán, F., Eker, S., Lincoln, P., Martí-Oliet, N., Meseguer, J., Talcott, C. (eds.): All About Maude - A High-Performance Logical Framework. LNCS, vol. 4350. Springer, Heidelberg (2007)
8. Cousot, P., Cousot, R.: Systematic design of program analysis frameworks. In: POPL, pp. 269–282 (1979)
9. Cousot, P., Cousot, R.: Abstract interpretation: a unified lattice model for static analysis of programs by construction or approximation of fixpoints. In: POPL, pp. 238–252. ACM Press (1977)
10. Şerbănuţă, T.F., Roşu, G.: K-Maude: a rewriting based tool for semantics of programming languages. In: Ölveczky, P.C. (ed.) WRLA 2010. LNCS, vol. 6381, pp. 104–122. Springer, Heidelberg (2010)
11. Cutumisu, M., Onuczko, C., Szafron, D., Schaeffer, J., McNaughton, M., Roy, T., Siegel, J., Carbonaro, M.: Evaluating pattern catalogs: the computer games experience. In: ICSE, pp. 132–141 (2006)
12. Dams, D.: Comparing abstraction refinement algorithms. ENTCS **89**(3), 405–416 (2003)
13. Gustafsson, J., Betts, A., Ermedahl, A., Lisper, B.: The Mälardalen WCET benchmarks: Past, present and future. In: WCET, pp. 136–146 (2010)
14. Hammond, K., Ferdinand, C., Heckmann, R., Dyckhoff, R., Hofmann, M., Jost, S., Loidl, H.W., Michaelson, G., Pointon, R.F., Scaife, N., Sérot, J., Wallace, A.: Towards formally verifiable WCET analysis for a functional programming language. In: WCET (2006)
15. Healy, C.A., Whalley, D.B., Harmon, M.G.: Integrating the timing analysis of pipelining and instruction caching. In: RTSS, pp. 288–297 (1995)
16. Hills, M., Roşu, G.: Towards a module system for K. In: Corradini, A., Montanari, U. (eds.) WADT 2008. LNCS, vol. 5486, pp. 187–205. Springer, Heidelberg (2009)
17. Leroy, X.: Formal verification of a realistic compiler. CACM **52**(7), 107–115 (2009)
18. Li, X., Mitra, T., Roychoudhury, A.: Accurate timing analysis by modeling caches, speculation and their interaction. In: DAC, pp. 466–471 (2003)
19. Li, Y.T.S., Malik, S.: Performance analysis of embedded software using implicit path enumeration. In: DAC, pp. 456–461 (1995)
20. Li, Y.T.S., Malik, S., Wolfe, A.: Efficient microarchitecture modeling and path analysis for real-time software. In: IEEE RTSS, pp. 298–307 (1995)
21. Meseguer, J.: Twenty years of rewriting logic. J. Log. Algebr. Program. **81**(7–8), 721–781 (2012)
22. Moore, R.E., Kearfott, R.B., Cloud, M.J.: Introduction to Interval Analysis. SIAM, Philadelphia (2009)
23. Reineke, J., Grund, D., Berg, C., Wilhelm, R.: Timing predictability of cache replacement policies. Real-Time Syst. **37**(2), 99–122 (2007)
24. Roşu, G., Şerbănuţă, T.F.: An overview of the K semantic framework. J. Logic Algebraic Program. **79**(6), 397–434 (2010)
25. Theiling, H., Ferdinand, C., Wilhelm, R.: Fast and precise WCET prediction by separated cache and path analyses. Real-Time Syst. **18**(2/3), 157–179 (2000)
26. Wilhelm, R.: Why AI + ILP is good for WCET, but MC is Not, Nor ILP alone. In: Steffen, B., Levi, G. (eds.) VMCAI 2004. LNCS, vol. 2937, pp. 309–322. Springer, Heidelberg (2004)

27. Wilhelm, R., Engblom, J., Ermedahl, A., Holsti, N., Thesing, S., Whalley, D., Bernat, G., Ferdinand, C., Heckmann, R., Mitra, T., Mueller, F., Puaut, I., Puschner, P., Staschulat, J., Stenström, P.: The worst-case execution-time problem–overview of methods and survey of tools. TECS **7**(3), 1–53 (2008)
28. Wilhelm, R., Wachter, B.: Abstract interpretation with applications to timing validation. In: Gupta, A., Malik, S. (eds.) CAV 2008. LNCS, vol. 5123, pp. 22–36. Springer, Heidelberg (2008)

Can a Light Typing Discipline Be Compatible with an Efficient Implementation of Finite Fields Inversion?

Daniele Canavese[1]([⊠]), Emanuele Cesena[2], Rachid Ouchary[1],
Marco Pedicini[3], and Luca Roversi[4]

[1] Dipartimento di Automatica e Informatica, Politecnico di Torino, Torino, Italy
{daniele.canavese,rachid.ouchary}@polito.it
[2] Theneeds Inc., San Francisco, CA, USA
ec@theneeds.com
[3] Dipartimento di Matematica e Fisica, Università degli Studi Roma Tre, Roma, Italy
pedicini@mat.uniroma3.it
[4] Dipartimento di Informatica, Università degli Studi di Torino, Torino, Italy
roversi@di.unito.it

Abstract. We focus on the fragment TFA of λ-calculus. It contains terms which normalize in polynomial time only. Inside TFA we translated BEA, a well known, imperative and fast algorithm which calculates the multiplicative inverse of binary finite fields. The translation suggests how to categorize the operations of BEA in sets which drive the design of a variant that we called DCEA. On several common architectures we show that these two algorithms have comparable performances, while on UltraSPARC and ARM architectures the variant we synthesized from a purely functional source can go considerably faster than BEA.

1 Introduction

In [1] we started to develop a project for contributing the long term goal of supplying toolboxes able to automatically produce high-performance solutions from natural specifications in the area of cryptography[1]. We proposed to contribute by following a growing mainstream which sees functional programming patterns and languages as relevant when getting good optimized and parallelizable implementations [2].

Since we already knew that cryptographic algorithms are in the feasible range of complexity bounds (i.e., FPTIME) we chose to program the main components of such algorithms into a fragment of λ-calculus for which a polynomial time execution certification exists. The fragment is called TFA (i.e., typeable functional assembly), a variant of DLAL [3]. When a λ-term has a type in TFA and represents a function from (a representation of) binary words to binary

---

[1] See, for example, the European Project "Computer Aided Cryptography Engineering (CACE) at http://www.cace-project.eu.

© Springer International Publishing Switzerland 2014
U. Dal Lago and R. Peña (Eds.): FOPARA 2013, LNCS 8552, pp. 38–57, 2014.
DOI: 10.1007/978-3-319-12466-7_3

words, we know we can compute the result in a time which is polynomial in the dimension of the word.

The components of cryptographic algorithms we give in [1] are addition, modular reduction, squaring and multiplication over binary finite fields. After that experience, we were able to develop the multiplicative inversion by encoding the binary euclidean algorithm (BEA), as given in Fig. 1, which is an efficient implementation [4].

INPUT: $a \in \mathbb{F}_{2^m}, a \neq 0$.
OUTPUT: $a^{-1} \mod f$.
    1. $u \leftarrow a, v \leftarrow f, g_1 \leftarrow 1, g_2 \leftarrow 0$.
    2. While z divides u do:
        (a) $u \leftarrow u/z$.
        (b) If z divides g_1 then $g_1 \leftarrow g_1/z$ else $g_1 \leftarrow (g_1 + f)/z$.
    3. If $u = 1$ then return(g_1).
    4. If $deg(u) < deg(v)$ then $u \leftrightarrow v, g_1 \leftrightarrow g_2$.
    5. $u \leftarrow u + v, g_1 \leftarrow g_1 + g_2$.
    6. Goto Step 2.

Fig. 1. Binary field inversion as in **Algorithm 2.2** at page 1048 in [4].

We present for the first time the main design ideas about how implementing BEA as a term wInv (a mnemonic for "inversion on binary words") of TFA (see Sect. 3).

Although the existence of wInv as a term of TFA might be a result by itself, this work is mainly a report on how we can see wInv as a proof that supports the meaningfulness of our initial project. We recall we aim at supplying functional programming patterns that help getting implementations of cryptographic libraries whose efficiency, in the best case, should not require *hand-made tuning* which, for example, must take into account the length of the word in the given running architecture.

The design of wInv must obey the rigid type discipline of TFA which enforces the bound on the normalization time. In general, writing a term in TFA requires to constantly trying to approximate at the best a linear term, i.e., a term that can by typed with linear types. When not possible, because the term could not compute what it is needed, one carefully relaxes the structure of the term to allow a non-linear use of variables.

This very constraining programming strategy can have a payoff.

When writing wInv we were forced to group the operations we found in BEA in four categories which we call *forward*, *backward*, *bidirectional* and *undirected*. The *forward* operations can be naturally completed by traversing a binary word from its least significant bit (lsb) to its most significant bit (msb). For example, testing $u = 1$, as shown in Fig. 1, is implemented as a visit of the representation of u from right to left. The *backward* operations proceed in the opposite direction, such as the test that finds which between u and v has the highest degree.

In the *undirected* category we place operations like the bitwise and carry-free sum of two polynomials in a binary finite field such as $g_1 + g_2$. The *bidirectional* operations include the simultaneous shifting to the right of (the representations of) u and g_1 or $g_1 + f$. We can complete the first half of the operations moving from the lsbto the msbof the two polynomials, and the second half by moving in the opposite direction. This is due to the typing discipline of TFA which requires a careful representation of a state which we must bitwise update as the computation on the main data proceeds.

To us the most interesting fact is that the categorization that the functional setting forces us to adopt is meaningful in the imperative side because it suggests the algorithm DCEA (see Sect. 4), a slight variation of BEA which is obtained by applying source code rearrangements, like decomposition of shifts u and g_1 or $g_1 + f$ in two phases.

Section 5 details the payoff. It shows that DCEA stays very close to the execution time of BEA on Intel architectures, while it can be considerably faster on the two RISC architectures UltraSPARC and ARM. We conjecture that the outcome is a direct consequence of how the optimizer of the C language compiler can take advantage of a code which seems to be compiled in a more uniform sets of assembly code blocks. The reason to support this idea is that compiling DCEA and BEA without any optimization results in an object code of DCEA which is far bigger and slower than BEA's one.

2   Typeable Functional Assembly

We now introduce the strictly necessary notions about TFA from [1]. TFA is the type assignment for λ-terms in Fig. 2. It is DLAL [3] whose set of formulas is quotiented by a specific recursive equation we will subsequently recall from [1].

$$\frac{}{\emptyset \mid \mathbf{x}{:}A \vdash \mathbf{x}{:}A} \; a \qquad \frac{\Delta \mid \Gamma \vdash \mathtt{M}{:}A}{\Delta,\Delta' \mid \Gamma,\Gamma' \vdash \mathtt{M}{:}A} \; w \qquad \frac{\Delta, \mathbf{x}{:}A, \mathbf{y}{:}A \mid \Gamma \vdash \mathtt{M}{:}B}{\Delta, \mathbf{z}{:}A \mid \Gamma \vdash \mathtt{M}\{{}^z/_{\mathbf{x}}\,{}^z/_{\mathbf{y}}\}{:}B} \; c$$

$$\frac{\Delta \mid \Gamma, \mathbf{x}{:}A \vdash \mathtt{M}{:}B}{\Delta \mid \Gamma \vdash (\backslash\mathbf{x}.\mathtt{M}){:}A \multimap B} \; \multimap\mathrm{I} \qquad \frac{\Delta \mid \Gamma \vdash \mathtt{M}{:}A \multimap B \quad \Delta' \mid \Gamma' \vdash \mathtt{N}{:}A}{\Delta,\Delta' \mid \Gamma,\Gamma' \vdash (\mathtt{MN}){:}B} \; \multimap\mathrm{E}$$

$$\frac{\Delta, \mathbf{x}{:}A \mid \Gamma \vdash \mathtt{M}{:}B}{\Delta \mid \Gamma \vdash (\backslash\mathbf{x}.\mathtt{M}){:}!A \multimap B} \; \Rightarrow\mathrm{I} \qquad \frac{\Delta \mid \Gamma \vdash \mathtt{M}{:}!A \multimap B \quad \emptyset \mid \Delta' \vdash \mathtt{N}{:}A \quad |\Delta'| \leq 1}{\Delta,\Delta' \mid \Gamma \vdash (\mathtt{MN}){:}B} \; \Rightarrow\mathrm{E}$$

$$\frac{\emptyset \mid \Delta, \Gamma \vdash \mathtt{M}{:}A}{\Delta \mid \S\Gamma \vdash \mathtt{M}{:}\S A} \; \S\mathrm{I} \qquad \frac{\Delta \mid \Gamma \vdash \mathtt{N}{:}\S A \quad \Delta' \mid \mathbf{x}{:}\S A, \Gamma' \vdash \mathtt{M}{:}B}{\Delta,\Delta' \mid \Gamma,\Gamma' \vdash \mathtt{M}\{{}^N/_{\mathbf{x}}\}{:}B} \; \S\mathrm{E}$$

$$\frac{\Delta \mid \Gamma \vdash \mathtt{M}{:}A \quad \alpha \notin \mathrm{fv}(\Delta,\Gamma)}{\Delta \mid \Gamma \vdash \mathtt{M}{:}\forall\alpha.A} \; \forall\mathrm{I} \qquad \frac{\Delta \mid \Gamma \vdash \mathtt{M}{:}\forall\alpha.A}{\Delta \mid \Gamma \vdash \mathtt{M}{:}A[{}^B/_{\alpha}]} \; \forall\mathrm{E}$$

Fig. 2. Type assignment system in TFA.

Every judgment $\Delta \mid \Gamma \vdash \mathtt{M} : A$ comes with two different kinds of contexts. The formula A is assigned as a type to the λ-term $\mathtt{M}$ with hypothesis from the *polynomial context* Δ and the *linear context* Γ.

In TFA we define every single ground data type.

Let $\mathcal{G}$ be a countable set of *variables*. We use lowercase Greek letters to range over $\mathcal{G}$. Any *type* A belongs to the quotient $\mathcal{F}/\approx$ of the following language $\mathcal{F}$ of *formulas*:

$$F ::= \mathcal{G} \mid F \multimap F \mid !F \multimap F \mid \forall \mathcal{G}.F \mid \S F$$

We define the quotient on $\mathcal{F}$ when introducing the *Sequences of booleans* below. *Uppercase Latin letters* A, B, C, D will range over $\mathcal{F}/\approx$. The *modal* formula $!A$ can occur in negative positions only. The notation $A[^B/_\alpha]$ is the capture-free substitution of B for every free occurrence of α in A.

The λ-term $\mathtt{M}$ belongs to Λ, the λ-calculus given by:

$$\mathtt{M} ::= \mathcal{V} \mid (\backslash\mathtt{x}.\mathtt{M}) \mid (\mathtt{M}\,\mathtt{M}) \tag{1}$$

where $\mathcal{V}$ is the set of variables we range over by *any lowercase Latin teletype letter*. *Uppercase teletype Latin letters* $\mathtt{M}, \mathtt{N}, \mathtt{P}, \mathtt{Q}, \mathtt{R}$ will range over terms of Λ. We shall write $\backslash\mathtt{x}.\mathtt{M}$ in place of $(\backslash\mathtt{x}.\mathtt{M})$ in absence of ambiguity. Application $((\mathtt{M_1M_2})...\mathtt{M_n})$ is left associative and we shall tend to shorten it as $\mathtt{M_1M_2}...\mathtt{M_n}$. The set of free variables of $\mathtt{M}$ is $\mathrm{fv}(\mathtt{M})$. The standard β-reduction $\rightarrow^*$ on λ-terms is the reflexive, transitive, and contextual closure of:

$$(\backslash\mathtt{x}.\mathtt{M})\,\mathtt{N} \rightarrow \mathtt{M}\{^\mathtt{N}/_\mathtt{x}\}$$

Both polynomial and linear contexts are maps $\{\mathtt{x_1} : A_1, \ldots, \mathtt{x_n} : A_n\}$ from the domain of variables $\mathcal{V}$ to the co-domain of formulas $\mathcal{F}$. The difference between the two kinds of context is that variables in the polynomial context may occur an arbitrary number of times in the *subject* $\mathtt{M}$ of $\Delta \mid \Gamma \vdash \mathtt{M} : A$. Every variable in the linear context must occur at most once in $\mathtt{M}$. Every pair $\mathtt{x} : A$ of any kind of context is a *type assignment for a variable*. The notation $\S\Gamma$ is a shorthand for $\{\mathtt{x_1} : \S A_1, \ldots, \mathtt{x_n} : \S A_n\}$, if Γ is $\{\mathtt{x_1} : A_1, \ldots, \mathtt{x_n} : A_n\}$.

Finite types are functions that project one argument out of the many they have:

$$\mathbb{B}_n \equiv \forall \alpha.\mathbb{B}_n[\alpha] \text{ with } \mathbb{B}_n[\alpha] \equiv \overbrace{\alpha \multimap \cdots \multimap \alpha}^{n+1} \multimap \alpha.$$

Finite types with $n = 2$ are *lifted booleans* we denote by $\mathbb{B}_2$. Their canonical representatives are:

$$1 \equiv \backslash\mathtt{x}.\backslash\mathtt{y}.\backslash\mathtt{z}.\mathtt{x} : \mathbb{B}_2 \qquad 0 \equiv \backslash\mathtt{x}.\backslash\mathtt{y}.\backslash\mathtt{z}.\mathtt{y} : \mathbb{B}_2 \qquad \mathtt{B} \equiv \backslash\mathtt{x}.\backslash\mathtt{y}.\backslash\mathtt{z}.\mathtt{z} : \mathbb{B}_2$$

We need $\mathtt{B}$ in order to simplify the definition of the functions we want to program.

The type *Tuples* is:

$$(A_1 \otimes \ldots \otimes A_n) \equiv \forall \alpha.(A_1 \otimes \ldots \otimes A_n)[\alpha] \multimap \alpha \text{ with } (A_1 \otimes \ldots \otimes A_n)[\alpha] \equiv A_1 \multimap \cdots \multimap A_n \multimap \alpha$$

We can extend Definition (1) with tuples: $M ::= \ldots \mid <M, \ldots, M> \mid \backslash\langle \mathcal{V}, \ldots, \mathcal{V}\rangle.M$. Obvious derivable rules that type the new constructors exist in TFA which preserve β-reduction extended with $(\backslash\langle x_1, \ldots, x_n\rangle.M)<N_1, \ldots, N_n> \to M\{{}^{N_1}/x_1, \ldots, {}^{N_n}/x_n\}$.

The *Sequences of booleans*, or simply Sequences, is the following recursive type:

$$\mathbb{S} \approx \forall\alpha.\mathbb{S}[\alpha] \text{ with } \mathbb{S}[\alpha] \equiv (\mathbb{B}_2 \multimap \alpha) \multimap ((\mathbb{B}_2 \otimes \mathbb{S}) \multimap \alpha) \multimap \alpha \tag{2}$$

The recursive definition of $\approx$ in (2) determines the equivalence relation $\mathcal{F}/\approx$ on formulas. We take $\mathcal{F}$ up to such a relation, i.e., if M has type $\mathbb{S}$, then we can equivalently use any of the "unfolded forms" of $\mathbb{S}$ as type of M. The canonical values of type $\mathbb{S}$ are:

$$[\varepsilon] \equiv \backslash t.\backslash c.t\ B : \mathbb{S}$$
$$[b_{n-1} \ldots b_0] \equiv \backslash t.\backslash c.c\ \langle b_{n-1}, [b_{n-2} \ldots b_0]\rangle : \mathbb{S} \tag{3}$$

In accordance with (2), the Sequence $[b_{n-1} \ldots b_0]$ that occurs in (3) is a function that takes two constructors as inputs and yields a Sequence. Only the second constructor is used in (3) to build a Sequence out of a pair whose first element is b_{n-1}, and whose second element is — recursively! — another Sequence $[b_{n-2} \ldots b_0]$. It is well known that adding recursive equations among the formulas of DLAL is harmless as far as polynomial time soundness is concerned [3,5].

2.1   Basic Types and Combinators

This subsection introduces the essential set of elements which allows to justify at an intuitive level why the term wInv of Sect. 3 belongs to TFA.

Church numerals. Their type is $\mathbb{U} \equiv \forall\alpha.\mathbb{U}[\alpha]$ where $\mathbb{U}[\alpha] \equiv !(\alpha \multimap \alpha) \multimap \S(\alpha \multimap \alpha)$ with canonical representatives:

$u\varepsilon \equiv \backslash f.\backslash x.x : \mathbb{U} \qquad \overline{n} \equiv \backslash f.\backslash x.f\ (\cdots (f\ x)\ldots) : \mathbb{U}$ with n occurrences of f

Lists. Their type is $\mathbb{L}(A) \equiv \forall\alpha.\mathbb{L}(A)[\alpha]$ where $\mathbb{L}(A)[\alpha] \equiv !(A \multimap \alpha \multimap \alpha) \multimap \S(\alpha \multimap \alpha)$ with canonical representatives:

$$\{\varepsilon\} \equiv \backslash f.\backslash x.x : \mathbb{L}(A)$$
$$\{M_{n-1} \ldots M_0\} \equiv \backslash f.\backslash x.f\ M_{n-1}(\cdots (f\ M_0\ x)\ldots) : \mathbb{L}(A) \text{ with } n \text{ occurrences of } f$$

Church words $\{b_{n-1} \ldots b_0\}$, with all b_is booleans, are the typical instance of lists with type $\mathbb{L}_2 \equiv \mathbb{L}(\mathbb{B}_2)$ we need. In every Church word $\{b_{n-1} \ldots b_0\}$, or simply *word*, the *least significant bit* (lsb) is b_0, while the *most significant bit* (msb) is b_{n-1}. The same convention holds for every Sequence $[b_{n-1} \ldots b_0]$.

The combinator Xor. It has type $\mathbb{B}_2 \multimap \mathbb{B}_2 \multimap \mathbb{B}_2$. It extends the standard *exclusive or*:

Xor 0 0 $\to^*$ 0	Xor 1 1 $\to^*$ 0	
Xor 0 1 $\to^*$ 1	Xor 1 0 $\to^*$ 1	
Xor B b $\to^*$ b	Xor b B $\to^*$ b	(where b : $\mathbb{B}_2$)

Whenever one argument is B then it gives back the other argument. This is an application oriented choice [1].

The combinator wRev. It has type $\mathbb{L}_2 \multimap \mathbb{L}_2$ and *reverses the bits* of a word:

$$\text{wRev}\,\{b_{n-1}\ldots b_0\} \to^* \{b_0 \ldots b_{n-1}\}$$

Meta-combinator MapThread[·]. Let $F : \mathbb{B}_2 \multimap \mathbb{B}_2 \multimap A$ be a closed term. Then, MapThread[F] $: \mathbb{L}_2 \multimap \mathbb{L}_2 \multimap \mathbb{L}(A)$ applies F to the elements of the input list. If $((F\,a_i)\,b_i) \to^* c_i$, for every $0 \le i \le n-1$:

$$\text{MapThread[F]}\,\{a_{n-1}\ldots a_0\}\,\{b_{n-1}\ldots b_0\} \to^* \{c_{n-1}\ldots c_0\}$$

In particular, MapThread[\a.\b.<a, b>] $: \mathbb{L}_2 \multimap \mathbb{L}_2 \multimap \mathbb{L}(\mathbb{B}_2^2)$ is such that:

$$\text{MapThread[\a.\b.<a,b>]}\,\{a_{n-1}\ldots a_0\}\,\{b_{n-1}\ldots b_0\} \to^* \{<a_{n-1}, b_{n-1}> \ldots <a_0, b_0>\}\,.$$

The meta-combinator wHeadTail[Last, Body]. It has two parameters Last and Body. It builds on the core mechanism of the predecessor for Church numerals [5,6] inside the typing systems like TFA. For any types A, α, let $X \equiv (A \multimap \alpha \multimap \alpha) \otimes A \otimes \alpha$. By definition, wHeadTail[Last, Body] is as follows:

$$\text{wHeadTail[Last, Body]} \equiv \text{\w f x.L (w (wHTStep[Body] f) (wHTBase x))} : \mathbb{L}(A) \multimap \mathbb{L}(A)$$
$$\text{wHTStep[Body]} \equiv \text{\f e.\<ft, et, t>.Body[f, e, ft, et, t]}$$
$$\text{wHTBase} \equiv \text{\x.<\e l.l, EraseableElement, x>,}$$

where:

- Last must be a closed λ-term with type $X \multimap \alpha$;
- Body[f,e,ft,et,t] is the body of the step function. It must be a closed λ-term with the following two features. It must have type X and the variables f, e, ft, et and t must be *sub-terms* of Body that must occur linearly in it;
- wHTStep[Body] is the step function that must have type $(A \multimap \alpha \multimap \alpha) \multimap A \multimap X \multimap X$;
- wHTBase is the base function that must have type X.

For example:

$$\text{wHeadTail[Last, Body] (\g y.g b (g a y))}$$
$$\to^* \text{\f x.Last (wHTStep[Body] f b (wHTStep[Body] f a (wHTBase x)))}$$
$$\to^* \text{\f x.Last ((\<ft, et, t>.Body[f, b, ft, et, t]) Body[f, a, \e l.l, EraseableElement, x]).} \quad (4)$$

It iterates wHTStep[Body] from wHTBase on the input. If EraseableElement is different from any possible element of the list, the rightmost occurrence of Body in (4) knows that the iteration is at its step zero and it can operate on a as consequence of this fact. In general, Body can identify a sequence of iteration steps of predetermined length, say n. Then, Body can operate on the first n elements of the list in a specific way. The invariant of the computation pattern that wHeadTail[Last,Body] develops is that Body can have simultaneous stepwise access to two consecutive elements in the list. For example, Body in (4) can use a and EraseableElement at step zero. At step one it has access to b and et and the latter may contain a or some element derived from it. This invariant is crucial to implement a bitwise forwarding mechanism of the state in the term of TFA that implements the multiplicative inverse wInv. For example, let:

$$Last \equiv \backslash<\_,\_,1>.1 \tag{5}$$
$$Body \equiv \backslash f\ e.\backslash<ft, et, t>.<f, e, ft\ et\ t>$$

We can implement a λ-term that pops the last element out of the input list and we can check this by assuming (5) in the λ-terms of (4) which yields \f x.f a x.

3 Multiplicative Inversion as a Term of **TFA**

We illustrate how to encode BEA as the term wInv which has type in TFA. The top level structure of wInv is in Fig. 3. The first step towards writing wInv in TFA is to identify the operations that BEA requires and the basic data structures they must operate on.

```
wInv[V,G1,G2,F] =
\U.GetG1 (D (\tw.wRevInit (wHeadTail[LastRevMode,BodyRevMode]
                    (wRev (wHeadTail[LastForMode,BodyForMode] tw))
              ))) (MapThread[makeThread] U V G1 G2 F B0 B1 V' G2' F')
```

Fig. 3. Definition of wInv.

On the one hand, the basic operations we must encode are: (i) add pairs of polynomials, (ii) check if the indeterminate z divides some given polynomials u and g_1, (iii) be able to divide a polynomial by the indeterminate z, (iv) check if the only bit set to 1 in u is its lsb, i.e.check $u = 1$, (v) compare the degree of two polynomials.

On the other hand, Church words, as introduced in Sect. 2, are our basic data structure. They allow to represent every polynomial on binary finite fields as the list of their binary coefficients on which we can operate by the standard and uniform iteration mechanism that λ-calculus offers.

It is worth remarking that despite the λ-calculus imposes a strictly sequential and essentially uniform access scheme to the elements of any Church word, the iterative mechanism does not add any artificial layer of difficulty as compared to the standard programming paradigms with direct data access. The reason lies in the intrinsic nature of the above operations that we aim at representing as λ-terms in TFA.

Let us focus on testing $u = 1$. Even in presence of a direct access to the components of u, the test requires to access the value of every bit of u, for example following the natural order from the lsbof u to its msb, i.e., the test

$u = 1$ is a *forward* operation. Let us now analyze the meaning of the test $u > v$. It forces to bitwise cross u and v, but from their msbto their lsb, i.e., $u > v$ is a *backward* operation. A further case is the execution of a sum such as $g_1 + f$. We forcefully have to bitwise range all over the coefficients of the Church words that represent u and g_1 without necessarily complying to the direction "lsbto msb", or vice versa. The reason is that adding two bits in a binary finite field, i.e., executing a Xor on pairs of bits, does not need any carry. So, the sum is an *undirected* operation. The final case includes the simultaneous shifting to the right of u and g_1 or $g_1 + f$. We shall see that we can complete the first half of the operation by moving leftward on our Church words and the second half by moving in the opposite direction. Therefore, we classify the shift to the right as a *bidirectional* operation.

The unique slight annoyance coming from a mandatory use of the iteration, intrinsic of the Church words, is that to operate in reverse mode on any given Church word we need to reverse it by means of wRev. Once reversed, the former msbis the current lsb. This is why wInv in Fig. 3 contains wRev (see Sect. 2) and its slight variant wRevInit we will comment later.

Figure 3 illustrates the relevant components and the main behavioral aspects of wInv.

wInv depends on the four parameters V, G1, G2 and F. They are Church words that represent the corresponding parameters of BEA. The unique argument U is the input which encodes u.

Also B0, B1, V', G2' and F' are Church words. They only contain occurrences of B. As the computation proceeds the elements of B0 and B1 will play the role of a state, while V', G2' and F' serve as support. We shall see that by setting two corresponding bits in B0 and B1 to 1 and B we keep recording that z divides both u and g_1. Instead, V', G2' and F' allow to bitwise replicate the bits of V, G2 and F. The goal is to let V, G2 and F survive the process that implements the division of u and g_1, or $g_1 + f$, by z.

All U, V, ...G2', F' are inputs of MapThread[makeThread]. Since, by definition:

$$\texttt{makeThread} - \texttt{\textbackslash u.\textbackslash v.\textbackslash g}_1.\texttt{\textbackslash g}_2.\texttt{\textbackslash f.\textbackslash b}_0.\texttt{\textbackslash b}_1.\texttt{\textbackslash v'.\textbackslash g}_2'.\texttt{\textbackslash f'.} < < u, v, g_1, g_2, f >, < b_0, b_1, v', g_2', f' > > \quad (6)$$

the output of MapThread[makeThread] is a Church word with pairs of tuples as its elements. The first component of every pair collects the bits that in U, V, G1, G2 and F occur in the same position. The second component has analogous structure but its bits belong to the Church words B0, B1, V', G2' and F'.

We call *threaded word* every Church word whose elements are pairs of tuples of bits. The notation of any element of a threaded wordis:

$$\ll u, v, g_1, g_2, f >, < b_0, b_1, v', g_2', f' \gg, \quad (7)$$

where the name of every bit recalls the Church word it comes from. In (7), u, v, $g_1, \ldots, g_2'$ and f' occupy the i-th position in the Church word they belong to.

The result of MapThread[makeThread] in wInv is the starting configuration of an iteration that uses the Church numeral D as iterator on the step function:

$$\text{\tw. wRevInit (wHeadTail[LastRightward, BodyRightward} \tag{8}$$
$$\text{(wRev (wHeadTail[LastLeftward, BodyLeftward tw)).}$$

The value of D amounts to the square of the degree of the given binary finite field. This is a point where the lack of any mechanism able to stop the computation as soon as required, which is typical of λ-calculus, takes over. Of course, when moving from the purely functional setting to the imperative one, we shall be able to exit from the iteration as soon as required.

The application of wHeadTail[LastLeftward, BodyLeftward to any threaded wordtw amounts to iterate BodyLeftward on the elements of tw. Specifically, the λ-term BodyLeftward implements the function B_L in Fig. 4, where B_L is:

$$B_L(W, S) = <W'', S'>$$

by assuming $S = <b_0, b_1, v', g_2', f'>$, for some given b_0, b_1, v', g_2', f'. The values of b_0, b_1 identify the state we are in and determine $<W'', S'>$. Specifically, b_0 *propagates* the information saying if z divides u or g_1.

$$B_L(W, <b_0, b_1, v', g_2', f'>) = \begin{cases} <<0, v', 0, g_2', f'>, <1, b_1, v, g_2, f>> & \text{if } (b_0, b_1) = (\bot, \bot), \\ & \text{and } W = <0, v, 0, g_2, f> \\ <<u, v', g_1, g_2', f'>, <1, b_1, v, g_2, f>> & \text{if } (b_0, b_1) = (1, \bot), \\ & \text{and } W = <u, v, g_1, g_2, f>, \\ \\ <<0, v', g_1 + f, g_2', f'>, <0, b_1, v, g_2, f>> & \text{if } (b_0, b_1) = (\bot, \bot), \\ & \text{and } W = <0, v, 1, g_2, f> \\ <<u, v', g_1 + f, g_2', f'>, <0, b_1, v, g_2, f>> & \text{if } (b_0, b_1) = (0, \bot), \\ & \text{and } W = <u, v, g_1, g_2, f> \\ \\ <<1, v, g_1, g_2, f>, <\bot, 0, \bot, \bot, \bot>> & \text{if } (b_0, b_1) = (\bot, \bot), \\ & \text{and } W = <1, v, g_1, g_2, f> \\ <<0, v, g_1, g_2, f>, <\bot, 0, \bot, \bot, \bot>> & \text{if } (b_0, b_1) = (\bot, 0), \\ & \text{and } W = <0, v, g_1, g_2, f> \\ <<1, v, g_1, g_2, f>, <\bot, 1, \bot, \bot, \bot>> & \text{if } (b_0, b_1) = (\bot, 0), \\ & \text{and } W = <1, v, g_1, g_2, f> \\ <W, <\bot, 1, \bot, \bot, \bot>> & \text{if } (b_0, b_1) = (\bot, 1), \\ \\ (w, (b_0, b_1, v', g_2', f')) & \text{otherwise} \end{cases}$$

Fig. 4. The function that BodyLeftward implements.

For example, let $(b_0, b_1) = (\bot, \bot)$ in S and let us focus on B_L. By definition, all the bits in W and S are the lsbsof the Church words U, V, G1, ...G2' and F'.

Under the above assumption, as a first case let both u and g_1 in W be equal to 0. This means we must propagate the information that all the bits which come from the Church words U and G1 must shift one place to their right, while all the bits that come from V, G2 and F must keep their position. To propagate such information we let $<W'', S'>$ equal to $\ll 0, v', 0, g_2', f'>, <1, b_1, v, g_2, f \gg$ in the first defining clause of B_L. We observe that v, g_2, and f, which initially are in W, get copied to W''. This is the propagation mechanism we already mentioned. It will eventually preserve the position of all the bits coming from V, G2 and F while allowing the global shifting of U and G1 to the right.

As a second case let u be 0 and g_1 be 1 in W. This time we must propagate the information that all the bits coming from U and G1+F must shift one place to their right. Like in the previous case, the bits from V, G2 and F must keep their position. To propagate such information we let $<W'', S'>$ equal to $\ll 0, v', g_1 + f, g_2', f'>, <0, b_1, v, g_2, f \gg$ in the third defining clause of B_L. Of course, "+" stands for Xor. Once more, we observe that v, g_2, and f, which initially are in W, get copied to W''.

In (9), we list the legal combinations of values of b_0 and b_1 we can find in the msbof the threaded wordthat the last application of BodyLeftward gives as its result:

$$(b_0, b_1) = \begin{cases} (1, \perp) & \text{if } z \text{ divides } u \text{ and } g_1, \\ (0, \perp) & \text{if } z \text{ divides } u \text{ but not } g_1, \\ (\perp, 0) & \text{if } u = 1, \\ (\perp, 1) & \text{if } z \text{ does not divide } u \text{ and } u \neq 1 \end{cases} \qquad (9)$$

LastLeftward implements L_L in Fig. 5 which behaves in accordance with (9) to finalize the threaded wordthat wHeadTail[LastLefward, BodyLeftward must produce.

$L_L(<u, v, g_1, g_2, f>, <b_0, b_1, v', g_2', f'>) =$

$$\begin{cases} \ll 0, 0, 0, 0, 0 >, <b_0, b_1, \perp, \perp, \perp \gg \ll u, v', g_1, g_2', f'>, <b_0, b_1, \perp, \perp, \perp \gg & \text{if } b_0 \in \{0, 1\} \\ & \text{and } b_1 = \perp \\ \\ \ll u, v', g_1, g_2', f'>, <1, 1, \perp, \perp, \perp \gg & \text{if } (b_0, b_1) = (\perp, 0) \\ \\ \ll u, v', g_1, g_2', f'>, <b_0, b_1, \perp, \perp, \perp \gg & \text{otherwise} \end{cases}$$

Fig. 5. The function that LastLeftward implements.

The first clause of L_L completes the threaded wordunder construction by adding two pairs. The rightmost one is the element that wHeadTail[LastLefward, BodyLeftward] naturally keeps separate from the rest of the threaded wordit takes as input. It serves to propagate v', g_2' and f' in the first component. On the other hand, the reason to add $\ll 0, 0, 0, 0, 0 >, <b_0, b_1, \perp, \perp, \perp \gg$ is to record the state

(b_0, b_1). As soon as L_L completes its first clause it implements the first part of *bidirectional*, i.e. the division of u and one between g_1 or $g_1 + f$ by z. The reason is that, once we will reverse the threaded word with its length increased by one unit, we can erase its msb by means of wHeadTail[LastRightward, BodyRightward. This means that erasing the lsb before the swap takes place and such an erasure is the second part of our *bidirectional* operation which completes the implementation of the division of u and g_1, or $g_1 + f$, by z.

The second and third cases of L_L complete the threaded word under construction by adding a pair. The pair is the element that wHeadTail[LastLefward, BodyLeftward] naturally keeps separate from the rest of the threaded word it takes as input. They both store v', g_2' and f' in the first component but propagate a different state. In the second case we record that $u = 1$ by setting both bits of the state to 1. This will freeze the content of the threaded word because it contains the result.

The threaded word produced which wHeadTail[LastRightward,BodyRightward] takes as its input has a state which is compliant with the list of cases in (9).

The application of wHeadTail[LastRightward, BodyRightward to a threaded word amounts to iterate BodyRightward on it. Specifically, BodyRightward implements the function B_R in Fig. 6.

The function B_R produces an output which depends on the values of some bits in W and on b_0, b_1 which keeps identifying the state we are in.

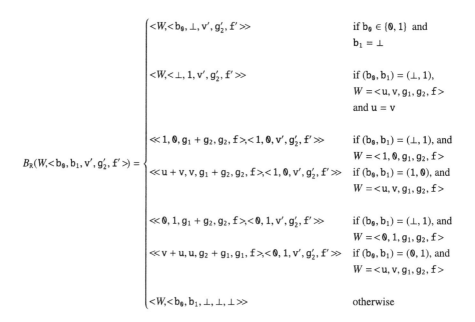

$$B_R(W, <b_0, b_1, v', g_2', f'>) = \begin{cases} <W, <b_0, \bot, v', g_2', f'>> & \text{if } b_0 \in \{0, 1\} \text{ and } \\ & b_1 = \bot \\ <W, <\bot, 1, v', g_2', f'>> & \text{if } (b_0, b_1) = (\bot, 1), \\ & W = <u, v, g_1, g_2, f> \\ & \text{and } u = v \\ \ll 1, 0, g_1 + g_2, g_2, f>, <1, 0, v', g_2', f'>\gg & \text{if } (b_0, b_1) = (\bot, 1), \text{ and } \\ & W = <1, 0, g_1, g_2, f> \\ \ll u + v, v, g_1 + g_2, g_2, f>, <1, 0, v', g_2', f'>\gg & \text{if } (b_0, b_1) = (1, 0), \text{ and } \\ & W = <u, v, g_1, g_2, f> \\ \ll 0, 1, g_1 + g_2, g_2, f>, <0, 1, v', g_2', f'>\gg & \text{if } (b_0, b_1) = (\bot, 1), \text{ and } \\ & W = <0, 1, g_1, g_2, f> \\ \ll v + u, u, g_2 + g_1, g_1, f>, <0, 1, v', g_2', f'>\gg & \text{if } (b_0, b_1) = (0, 1), \text{ and } \\ & W = <u, v, g_1, g_2, f> \\ <W, <b_0, b_1, \bot, \bot, \bot>> & \text{otherwise} \end{cases}$$

Fig. 6. The function that BodyRightward implements.

The first clause manages the cases that require to erase the msbsso to obtain the overall effect of shifting to the right the bits coming from U and G1. The erasure will take place effectively when we will apply LastRightward. This will conclude the second part of our *bidirectional* operation which we started before reversing the threaded wordthat wHeadTail[LastRightward, BodyRightward takes as input.

The last clause propagates the state (b_1, b_1) which says that $u = 1$. We select the second clause when we know we need to bitwise compare the polynomials u and v but we do not know which one has greatest degree.

The remaining clauses serve to simultaneously and bitwise execute sums and swaps, in accordance with the definition of BEA. For example, the third clause identifies the point where u shows a degree greater than v, so it switches the state (b_0, b_1) to $(1, 0)$ which is further propagated by the fourth clause.

It should be evident that all the clauses of B_R, but the last one, contribute to the completion of either the second part of our *bidirectional* operation or any of the operations we classify as *backward* or *undirected*.

In (10) below, we list the legal combinations of values of b_0 and b_1 we can find in the msbof the threaded wordthat the last application of BodyLeftward gives as result:

$$(b_0, b_1) = \begin{cases} (1, \bot) & \text{if } z \text{ divides } u \text{ and } g_1 \\ (0, \bot) & \text{if } z \text{ divides } u \text{ but not } g_1 \\ (1, 0) & \text{if } u > v \\ (0, 1) & \text{if } u < v \\ (1, 1) & \text{if } u = 1 \end{cases} \qquad (10)$$

LastRightward implements L_R in Fig. 7 which behaves in accordance with (10).

$$L_R(<u, v, g_1, g_2, f>, <b_0, b_1, v', g_2', f'>) = (\ll u, v', g_1, g_2', f'>, <b_0, b_1, \bot, \bot, \bot \gg) \qquad \text{if } b_1 \neq \bot$$

Fig. 7. The function that LastRightward implements.

L_R completes the threaded wordthat wHeadTail[LastRightward, BodyRightward has to build.

Let the state say that we must not execute any shift to the right of the bits coming from U and G1. In accordance with (10) it must be $b_1 \neq \bot$ and the clause in Fig. 7 applies. It completes the threaded wordunder construction with the element that wHeadTail[LastRightward, BodyRightward keeps separate from the rest of the threaded worditself.

If $b_1 = \bot$ we simply do not apply L_R and the element kept separate from the threaded wordgets forgotten. In the corresponding λ-term of TFA this amounts to erase such an element as explained in (5).

Summing up, L_R finalizes either the second part of our *bidirectional* operations or any of the operations we classify as *backward* or *undirected*.

Once wHeadTail[LastRightward, BodyRightward concludes, we reverse the threaded wordit produces by using wRevInit that executes its main task while resetting the bits that belong to the second component of every element of the threaded word. So, we can again start either the first part of our *bidirectional* operation or any of the operations we classify as *forward* or *undirected*.

After the last step of the iteration that D implements GetG1 iterates a step function which extracts only the bits coming from G1 from the last produced threaded word.

What have we learned? On one side, the description of wInv should convince the reader that it is a term of TFA. The reason is that all the step functions we use can have second order types which allow their iteration. On the other, we have split the operations of BEA into two groups which we apply when either in *leftward* or in *rightward* mode. By definition, we are in *leftward* mode when we can apply operations from the lsb to the msb of any threaded word; they are the first part of our *bidirectional* operation or any of the operations we classify as *forward* or *undirected*. We are in *rightward* mode when we can operate from the msb to the lsb of any threaded wordby using the second part of our *bidirectional* operation or any of the operations we classify as *backward* or *undirected*. The way to switch between the modes is to reverse the threaded words at hand.

4   An Imperative Version of wInv and Its Correctness

We introduce DCEA, the imperative version of wInv. The pseudo-code of DCEA and BEA are Table 1. The variable *mode* of DCEA flips from *leftward* to *rightward* to drive the execution of the operations in accordance with the classification, given above at the end of Sect. 3.

Proving the equivalence of DCEA and BEA amounts to showing that they behave the same, starting from identical pre-conditions. Two significant cases exist:

– Let $z \mid u$, i.e., let z divide u. BEA iterates in E in the loop that starts at line 3 until $z \nmid u$. Under the same pre-condition DCEA iterates the sequence A, D, B, D until $z \nmid u$, i.e., until z does not divide u. In both cases it should be evident that the post-conditions coincide.
– Let $u \neq 1$ and $z \nmid u$. BEA skips both E and F and execute G. DCEA skips A, D, and B to finally interpret C which has the same set of instructions of G.

As soon as DCEA and BEA check $u = 1$ they are obviously equivalent because neither of the two alter any among u, v, g_1 and g_2.

5   Experimental Results

The multiplicative inverse over a finite field is the most time-consuming operation. A high-speed implementation is frequently much more than desirable, since its running-time can have a significant impact on several cryptographic

Table 1. Algorithms for multiplicative inverse of a given binary finite field.

INPUT: $a \in \mathbb{F}_{2^m}, a \neq 0$
OUTPUT: $a^{-1} \bmod f$
 1: $u \leftarrow a, v \leftarrow f, g_1 \leftarrow 1$
 2: $g_2 \leftarrow 0$, $side \leftarrow leftward$
 3: **if** $mode = leftward$ **then**
 4:     **if** z divides u but not g_1 **then**   Ⓐ
 5:         $g_1 \leftarrow g_1 + f$
 6:     **end if**
 7:     $mode \leftarrow rightward$
 8: **else**
 9:     **if** z divides u **then**   Ⓑ
10:         $u \leftarrow u/z$; $g_1 \leftarrow g_1/z$
11:     **else**
12:         **if** $\deg(u) < \deg(v)$ **then**
13:             $u \leftrightarrow v$; $g_1 \leftrightarrow g_2$
14:         **end if**   Ⓒ
15:         $u \leftarrow u + v$; $g_1 \leftarrow g_1 + g_2$
16:     **end if**
17:     $mode \leftarrow leftward$
18: **end if**
19: **if** $u = 1$ **then**
20:     **return** g_1 Ⓓ
21: **end if**
22: **go to** 3

(a) DCEA.

INPUT: $a \in \mathbb{F}_{2^m}, a \neq 0$
OUTPUT: $a^{-1} \bmod f$
 1: $u \leftarrow a, v \leftarrow f$
 2: $g_1 \leftarrow 1, g_2 \leftarrow 0$
 3: **while** z divides u **do**
 4:     $u \leftarrow u/z$
 5:     **if** z divides g_1 **then**
 6:         $g_1 \leftarrow g_1/z$ Ⓔ
 7:     **else**
 8:         $g_1 \leftarrow (g_1 + f)/z$
 9:     **end if**
10: **end while**
11: **if** $u = 1$ **then**
12:     **return** g_1 Ⓕ
13: **end if**
14: **if** $\deg(u) < \deg(v)$ **then**
15:     $u \leftrightarrow v$; $g_1 \leftrightarrow g_2$ Ⓖ
16: **end if**
17: $u \leftarrow u + v$; $g_1 \leftarrow g_1 + g_2$
18: **go to** 3

(b) BEA.

algorithms and protocols. We present the results of a number of tests which compare the execution time of DCEA, BEA and of the inversion that the OpenSSL library [7] supplies.

Our tests are on the five different hardware architectures in Table 2. The "Core2", "Pentium4", "ARM" and "UltraSPARC" platforms are microprocessors. The "ATmega328" is a microcontroller (we used an Arduino Duemilanove[2] prototype board which integrates an ATmega328).

We compare the performances on the following binary fields adhering to recommendation of FIPS 186-3 standard [8]:

– the field $\mathbb{F}_{2^{61}}[z]/(z^{61} + z^5 + z^2 + z + 1)$,
– the field $\mathbb{F}_{2^{163}}[z]/(z^{163} + z^7 + z^6 + z^3 + 1)$,
– the field $\mathbb{F}_{2^{233}}[z]/(z^{233} + z^{74} + 1)$.

where 61, 163 and 233 are the degrees of the filed, i.e.the dimension the length n of the threaded words we uniformly manipulate with wInv in Sect. 3. The source code of DCEA and BEA are available at http://dcea.sourceforge.net/.

---

[2] http://arduino.cc/en/Main/ArduinoBoardDuemilanove

Table 2. Specifications of the test platforms.

CPU	Clock	Word size	Compiler	Optimization flags
Intel Core2 Duo P8600	2.40 GHz	64 bit	gcc 4.7.3	-O4
Sun UltraSPARC IIe	500 MHz	64 bit	gcc 4.2.1	-O4
Intel Pentium4	3.00 GHz	32 bit	gcc 4.4.5	-O4
ARM Cortex-A9 MPCore	1 GHz	32 bit	gcc 4.6.3	-O4
ATmega328	16 MHz	16 bit	avr-gcc 4.3.2	-Os

5.1   Comparing the Running-Time of **DCEA** and **BEA**

We briefly explain our findings regarding the performances of DCEA and BEA.

By "*generic* algorithm" we refer to an implementation of a multiplicative inversion which can operate on any field $\mathbb{F}_{2^n}[z]/(m(z))$, with a generic degree n and modulus $m(z)$. Instead, by "*specialized* algorithm" we mean a specific implementation that can only work on a given field $\mathbb{F}_{2^n}[z]/(m(z))$, with a fixed degree n and modulus $m(z)$. Note that fixing n and $m(z)$ *a-priori* usually allows to better optimize the code, so a specialized algorithm is typically faster than its generic counterpart.

For instance, the Listings 1.1 and 1.2 show the C code used to test the BEA and DCEA algorithms over $\mathbb{F}_{2^{61}}$ on the Core2 platform. The snippets does not precisely reflect the pseudo-code listed in Table 1a and b since several ad-hoc optimizations were applied, such as:

- elimination of the selection on the *mode* variable in the DCEA code;
- elimination of the selection in the block A of Table 1a via a Shannon expansion (lines 31–32 of Listing 1.2);
- the comparison between the polynomial degrees is computed using a simple and efficient integer comparison (line 41 of Listing 1.1 and line 37 of Listing 1.2).

In Tables 3 and 4, we compare the average running-time in microseconds (μs) that DCEA and BEA need to calculate a single inversion on a given field.

Table 3. Generic algorithms: average time in μs taken by BEA and DCEA.

Field	Core2		Pentium4		UltraSPARC		ARM		ATmega328	
	BEA	DCEA	BEA	DCEA	BEA	DCEA	BEA	DCEA	BEA	DCEA
$\mathbb{F}_{2^{61}}$	2.63	2.64	6.10	6.15	10.52	10.89	18.44	15.43	7596.13	7685.26
$\mathbb{F}_{2^{163}}$	25.14	25.43	41.77	41.48	102.11	107.29	99.69	98.12	59755.80	60160.20
$\mathbb{F}_{2^{233}}$	46.34	46.83	91.22	91.23	199.23	205.62	191.86	188.48	122471.00	123576.85

```
1   #define SHIFT(i) \
2      tmp1 = u[i] >> 1; \
3      tmp2 = (u[i + 1] & 1) << 63; \
4      tmp3 = g1[i] >> 1; \
5      tmp4 = (g1[i + 1] & 1) << 63; \
6      u[i] = tmp1 ^ tmp2; \
7      g1[i] = tmp3 ^ tmp4
8
9   #define SWAP_SUM(i) \
10     u[i] ^= v[i]; \
11     g1[i] ^= g2[i]; \
12     v[i] ^= u[i] & x1; \
13     g2[i] ^= g1[i] & x1
14
15  void bea64_61(uint64_t r[], uint64_t a[])
16  {
17     uint64_t u[2] = { a[0] };
18     uint64_t v[2] = { (11<<61)^(1<<5)^(1<<2)^(1<<1)^1};
19     uint64_t g1[2] = { 1 };
20     uint64_t g2[2] = { 0 };
21     uint64_t x0, x1;
22     uint64_t tmp1, tmp2, tmp3, tmp4;
23
24     while (TRUE)
25     {
26        while ((u[0] & 1) == 0)
27        {
28           x0 = ~((g1[0] & 11) - 11);
29           g1[0] ^= ((11<<61)^(1<<5)^(1<<2)^(1<<1)^1) & x0;
30           SHIFT(0);
31           u[1] >>= 1;
32           g1[1] >>= 1;
33        }
34
35        if (u[0] == 1 && u[1] == 0)
36        {
37           r[0] = g1[0];
38              return;
39        }
40
41        x1 = ~((u[1] < v[1] || u[0] < v[0]) - 11);
42        SWAP_SUM(0);
43        SWAP_SUM(1);
44     }
45  }
```

Listing 3.1. BEAalgorithm: specialized C code for the field $\mathbb{F}_{2^{61}}$ and the Core2 architectures.

```
1  #define SHIFT(i) \
2      tmp1 = u[i] >> 1; \
3      tmp2 = (u[i + 1] & 1) << 63; \
4      tmp3 = g1[i] >> 1; \
5      tmp4 = (g1[i + 1] & 1) << 63; \
6      u[i] = tmp1 ^ tmp2; \
7      g1[i] = tmp3 ^ tmp4
8
9  #define SUM(i) \
10     u[i] ^= v[i]; \
11     g1[i] ^= g2[i]
12
13 #define SWAP_SUM(i) \
14     u[i] ^= v[i]; \
15     g1[i] ^= g2[i]; \
16     v[i] ^= u[i]; \
17     g2[i] ^= g1[i]
18
19 void dcea61(uint64_t r[], uint64_t a[])
20 {
21     uint64_t u[2] = { a[0] };
22     uint64_t v[2] = { (11<<61)^(1<<5)^(1<<2)^(1<<1)^1 };
23     uint64_t g1[2] = { 1 };
24     uint64_t g2[2] = { 0 };
25     uint64_t x0;
26     uint64_t tmp1, tmp2, tmp3, tmp4;
27
28     do
29      if ((u[0] & 1) == 0)
30      {
31         x0 = ~((g1[0] & 11) - 11);
32         g1[0] ^= ((11<<61)^(1<<5)^(1<<2)^(1<<1)^1) & x0;
33         SHIFT(0);
34         u[1] >>= 1;
35         g1[1] >>= 1;
36      }
37      else if (u[1] < v[1] || u[0] < v[0])
38      {
39         SWAP_SUM(0);
40          SWAP_SUM(1);
41      }
42      else
43      {
44      SUM(0);
45          SUM(1);
46      }
47     while (u[0] != 1 || u[1] != 0);
48
49     r[0] = g1[0];
50 }
```

Listing 3.2. DCEAalgorithm: specialized C code for the field $\mathbb{F}_{2^{61}}$ and the Core2 architectures.

Table 4. Specialized algorithms: average time in μs taken by BEA and DCEA.

Field	Core2		Pentium4		UltraSPARC		ARM		ATmega328	
	BEA	DCEA	BEA	DCEA	BEA	DCEA	BEA	DCEA	BEA	DCEA
$\mathbb{F}_{2^{61}}$	0.70	0.78	1.45	1.47	2.99	2.58	7.18	6.23	1108.59	1159.87
$\mathbb{F}_{2^{163}}$	5.92	5.94	13.77	13.78	38.54	30.01	67.65	61.21	15250.45	15504.68
$\mathbb{F}_{2^{233}}$	10.83	10.88	30.30	30.75	86.34	82.39	129.86	136.82	36039.93	36695.22

If we exclude the UltraSPARC and ARM architectures, DCEA and BEA have essentially the same performances with a slight prevalence of the latter. However, on UltraSPARC and ARM platforms, the specialized versions of DCEA are significantly faster than the BEA ones. For instance, they achieve respectively a 1.28 and a 1.11 speedup factor over $\mathbb{F}_{2^{163}}$.

5.2 Comparing the Running-Time of DCEA and OpenSSL

OpenSSL[7] is one of the most used and widespread cryptographic toolkits for securing a network communication, especially in the open-source world. Table 5 shows the average running-times of OpenSSL 1.0.1e[3] and DCEA, both the generic and specialized versions, to calculate a single inversion on the given field on an Intel Core2 CPU.

Table 5. Average time in μs that the OpenSSL and DCEA take to compute an inversion.

Field	OpenSSL	DCEA	
		Generic	Specialized
$\mathbb{F}_{2^{61}}$	3.97	2.64	0.78
$\mathbb{F}_{2^{163}}$	13.05	25.43	5.90
$\mathbb{F}_{2^{233}}$	20.58	46.83	10.88

In Fig. 8, we graphically depicts the data in Table 5 to better emphasize the differences among the performances of OpenSSL 1.0.1e and DCEA.

We remark that OpenSSL implements MAIA (Modified Almost Inverse Algorithm) which is a generic version of BEA. The specialized versions of DCEA always outperform the OpenSSL, especially on small fields. The generic version of DCEA seems faster only on $\mathbb{F}_{2^{61}}$. In this case it is twice as fast. This is an interesting result since several algebraic structures, such as hyper-elliptic curves, can guarantee a high level of security using fields with a low order.

---

[3] We tested the `BN_GF2m_mod_inv()` function which is declared in the `openssl/bn.h` header.

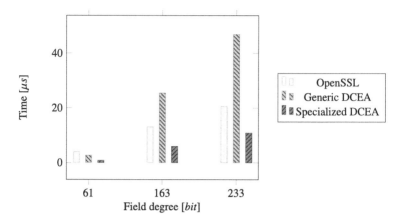

Fig. 8. Comparison of the OpenSSL and DCEA implementations.

6 Conclusions and Future Work

This paper proposes the evidence that the project started in [1] can be well founded so that we can speculate a positive answer to the title. Recall that in [1] we aimed at implementing a library of potential real interest able to supply operations over binary finite fields which can be automatically optimized, once fixed the main parameters. We have explored if a pure functional paradigm with implicit restrictions on the running-time might help when looking for a good implementation of the multiplicative inversion is the issue. Once implemented a well known implementation of the inversion as a functional term, we discovered that we can get back to a new imperative algorithm which results in a simple reorganization of the original one. The new algorithm can go relevantly faster than the original one on specific architectures.

One open problem is to fully investigate why. The conjecture, about which we have some evidence, is that the slight reorganization of the code, which we obtain from the intermediate functional and almost linear version of the inversion, heavily influences the generation of the object code in a way that the optimizer can better exploit.

A further open problem is to assess to which extent we can exploit the functional and almost linear programming patterns we use here to design a (specific domain) imperative language able to generate, as a its distinguishing feature, object code optimizations similar to the ones we obtained in DCEA. The hope is to design a language characterized by two seemingly contrasting features. It should be expressive enough in terms of programs we can write but its constructs should be limited enough to imply the application of good compilation techniques and optimizations able to fully exploit the hardware architecture of a CPU such as, for example, an ARM processor.

References

1. Cesena, E., Pedicini, M., Roversi, L.: Typing a core binary-field arithmetic in a light logic. In: Peña, R., van Eekelen, M., Shkaravska, O. (eds.) FOPARA 2011. LNCS, vol. 7177, pp. 19–35. Springer, Heidelberg (2012)
2. Bjesse, P., Claessen, K., Sheeran, M., Singh, S.: Lava: hardware design in Haskell. SIGPLAN Not. **34**(1), 174–184 (1998)
3. Baillot, P., Terui, K.: Light types for polynomial time computation in lambda calculus. I&C **207**(1), 41–62 (2009)
4. Fong, K., Hankerson, D., Lopez, J., Menezes, A.: Field inversion and point halving revisited. IEEE Trans. Comput. **53**(8), 1047–1059 (2004)
5. Asperti, A., Roversi, L.: Intuitionistic light affine logic. ACM ToCL **3**(1), 1–39 (2002)
6. Roversi, L.: A P-time completeness proof for light logics. In: Flum, J., Rodríguez-Artalejo, M. (eds.) CSL 1999. LNCS, vol. 1683, pp. 469–483. Springer, Heidelberg (1999)
7. The OpenSSL team: OpenSSL: The Open Source toolkit for SSL/TLS (2013). (http://www.openssl.org/)
8. National Institute of Standards and Technology: FIPS PUB 186-3 FEDERAL INFORMATION PROCESSING STANDARDS PUBLICATION Digital Signature Standard (DSS), June 2009

Probabilistic Analysis of Programs: A Weak Limit Approach

Alessandra Di Pierro[1] and Herbert Wiklicky[2(✉)]

[1] Dipartimento di Informatica, Università di Verona, Verona, Italy
alessandra.dipierro@univr.it
[2] Department of Computing, Imperial College, London, UK
h.wiklicky@imperial.ac.uk

Abstract. We present an approach to probabilistic analysis which is based on program semantics and exploits the mathematical properties of the semantical operators to ensure a form of optimality for the analysis. As in the algorithmic setting, where the analysis results are used the help the design of efficient algorithms, the purposes of our framework are to offer static analysis techniques usable for resource optimisation.

1 Introduction

In probabilistic analysis we can distinguish two different situations, namely the case in which the program is deterministic and the input data varies according to some probability distribution, and the case in which the program is probabilistic and we evaluate its behaviour in different executions determined by the probability distribution on the same input data.

In this paper we present a general framework for the probabilistic static analysis of quantitative properties, that can cover both aspects and in particular includes the treatment of average case analyses as a special instance of a wider range of applications centred on the quantification of resource consumption. This is similar to the algorithmic setting where probabilistic analysis, or average-case analysis, refers to the estimation of the computational complexity of an algorithm starting from an assumption about the probabilistic distribution on the set of all possible inputs; the results of such an analysis are then used for the design of efficient algorithms. The approach we follow is a semantics based analysis where the program semantics is defined formally so as to express the various resources via the observable behaviour of the program.

As the possible behaviours of a given program are often 'too many', the complexity of the analysis of the possible executions of some code often suffers from the problem of combinatorial explosion (even when un-decidability is not involved). At the centre of numerous approaches to program analysis is therefore the attempt of a "simplification" or "abstraction" of programs and their possible executions, in particular the abstraction of the concrete state space to a substantially simpler one.

© Springer International Publishing Switzerland 2014
U. Dal Lago and R. Peña (Eds.): FOPARA 2013, LNCS 8552, pp. 58–76, 2014.
DOI: 10.1007/978-3-319-12466-7_4

In previous work [1–3] we have introduced a framework for probabilistic analysis based on *least square approximation*, which achieves such a simplification. We have called the general methodology Probabilistic Abstract Interpretation (PAI) for its strong analogy with the theory of Abstract Interpretation [4]. PAI aims in constructing statistical or average estimates of program properties which are usable for resource optimisation, in the same way as in algorithmic complexity a probabilistic analysis might aim at estimating the average-case computational complexity of an algorithm to the purpose of improving its efficiency.

Contrary to the classical abstract interpretation based static analysis, PAI-based analyses are not necessarily safe, i.e. it is not guaranteed that all accepted behaviours conform a given specification. They are rather guaranteed to be as close as possible to the concrete properties. This is because the objective of a PAI based analysis is 'performance' rather than 'correctness', and applications are the optimisation of resource usage rather than the construction of bounds for the (minimal or maximal) probability that something happens. As very often probability bounds tend to be 0 or 1 they are only of limited use in a context where optimisation is the main issue.

In previous work we have studied various aspects of the PAI framework for large but still *finite* state spaces. The central contribution of this paper is to extend PAI to *infinite* state spaces, by facing the mathematical problems which arise in this case and showing how they can be overcome. In particular, we will present a weak limit construction for abstraction operators on infinite domains that will allow us to deal with the problem of the unboundedness of such operators.

Mathematical Background. For the mathematical notions and notation used in this paper we refer to the standard literature and in particular to the recent monograph by Kubrusly [5] with regard to functional analytical and operator algebraic concepts. We will only recall here some basic notions that are essential for the comprehension of the results we are going to present.

The concrete Banach and Hilbert spaces we consider here are spaces ℓ_p of infinite sequences of real numbers $(x_i)_{i \in \mathbb{N}}$ for which $(\sum_{i \in \mathbb{N}} |x_i|^p)^{1/p} < \infty$ with $p = 1$ and $p = 2$, respectively. The space ℓ_1 is the standard example of a Banach space; in particular it contains (as the set of positive normalised elements) all probability distributions on $\mathbb{N}$. The space ℓ_2 is the standard example of a real Hilbert space with inner product $\langle (x_i), (y_i) \rangle = \sum_i x_i y_i$.

We also recall the definition of the three main topologies on Hilbert spaces, namely the norm or uniform convergence, denoted $\mathbf{A}_n \to \mathbf{A}$ or $\lim_n \mathbf{A}_n = \mathbf{A}$, the strong operator topology, $\mathbf{A}_n \xrightarrow{s} \mathbf{A}$ or $s\text{-}\lim_n \mathbf{A}_n = \mathbf{A}$ and the weak topology $\mathbf{A}_n \xrightarrow{w} \mathbf{A}$ or $w\text{-}\lim_n \mathbf{A}_n = \mathbf{A}$ defined by (cf. e.g. pag. 378 and [5, Definition 4.45]):

$$\mathbf{A}_n \to \mathbf{A} \text{ iff } \|\mathbf{A}_n - \mathbf{A}\| \to 0$$
$$\mathbf{A}_n \xrightarrow{s} \mathbf{A} \text{ iff } \|(\mathbf{A}_n - \mathbf{A})(x)\| \to 0$$
$$\mathbf{A}_n \xrightarrow{w} \mathbf{A} \text{ iff } \langle (\mathbf{A}_n - \mathbf{A})(x), y \rangle \to 0$$

for all $x, y \in \mathcal{H}$. Note that the norm topology is defined in terms of the operator norm, while the strong topology in terms of the vector norm on $\mathcal{H}$. We have $\mathbf{A}_n \to \mathbf{A}$ implies $\mathbf{A}_n \xrightarrow{s} \mathbf{A}$ and $\mathbf{A}_n \xrightarrow{s} \mathbf{A}$ implies $\mathbf{A}_n \xrightarrow{w} \mathbf{A}$, but not vice versa.

Three definitions regarding linear operators on Hilbert spaces will play an important role in the next, namely those of *normally solvable*, *densely defined* and *closed* operators, which we will therefore recall here. We will write $\mathcal{L}(\mathcal{X}, \mathcal{Y})$ for the set of all linear operators between $\mathcal{X}$ and $\mathcal{Y}$, and for $\mathbf{T} \in \mathcal{L}(\mathcal{X}, \mathcal{Y})$, we will denote by $\mathcal{D}(\mathbf{T})$, $\mathcal{N}(\mathbf{T})$ and $\mathcal{R}(\mathbf{T})$ the domain, the null space and the range of $\mathbf{T}$, respectively. A linear operator $\mathbf{T} : \mathcal{X} \to \mathcal{Y}$ between two Hilbert spaces $\mathcal{X}$ and $\mathcal{Y}$ is *bounded* if $\|\mathbf{T}\| = \sup \|\mathbf{T}(x)\| / \|x\| < \infty$. For linear operators the concept of *continuity* is equivalent to the concept of *boundedness*, see, e.g. [5, Theorem 4.14]). A linear map $\mathbf{T} \in \mathcal{L}(\mathcal{X}, \mathcal{Y})$ is normally solvable if its range is closed. A necessary and sufficient condition for $\mathbf{T}$ to be normally solvable is that its range coincide with the orthogonal complement of the null space of its linear adjoint $\mathbf{T}^*$. The linear map $\mathbf{T} \in \mathcal{L}(\mathcal{X}, \mathcal{Y})$ is called *closed* if its graph $\Gamma_{\mathbf{T}} = \{(x, \mathbf{T}x) \in \mathcal{D}(\mathbf{T}) \times \mathcal{Y} \subset \mathcal{X} \times \mathcal{Y}\}$ is closed in $\mathcal{X} \times \mathcal{Y}$. Equivalently, $\mathbf{T}$ is closed if and only if for any sequence $x_n \in \mathcal{D}(\mathbf{T}) \subseteq \mathcal{X}$, with $x_n \to x$ and $\mathbf{T}(x_n) \to y$ this implies that $y = \mathbf{T}(x)$, cf. [5,6]. $\mathbf{T}$ is said to be densely defined if $\mathcal{D}(\mathbf{T})$ is dense in $\mathcal{X}$, that is $\overline{\mathcal{D}(\mathbf{T})} = \mathcal{X}$, where the notation $\overline{X}$ indicates the topological closure of the space X.

2 The Language

We will discuss our framework by referring to a simple core language. This is in essence the language used by Kozen in [7]. In this section we introduce both the syntax and the semantics for this language, which we call **pWhile**.

2.1 Syntax

In a style typical of static analysis [8], we introduce a labelled version of the **pWhile** language, where labels are used to identify the programs points that are crucial for defining our formal semantics.

$$S ::= [\texttt{skip}]^\ell \mid [x := e]^\ell \mid [x\ ? = \rho]^\ell \mid S_1;\ S_2$$
$$\mid \texttt{if } [b]^\ell \texttt{ then } S_1 \texttt{ else } S_2 \texttt{ fi} \mid \texttt{while } [b]^\ell \texttt{ do } S \texttt{ od}$$

We assume a unique labelling (by numbers $\ell \in \mathbf{Lab}$).

The statement $\texttt{skip}$ does not have any operational effect but can be used, for example, as a placeholder in conditional statements. We have the usual (deterministic) assignment $x := f(x_1, \ldots, x_n)$, sometimes also in the form $x := e$.

Then we have the random assignment $x\ ? = \rho$ where the value of a variable is set to a value according to some random distribution ρ. In [7] it is left open how to define or specify distributions ρ in detail. We will use occasionally an ad-hoc notation as sets of tuples $\{(v_i, p_i)\}$, expressing the fact that value v_i will be selected with probability p_i. It might be useful to assume that the random number generator or scheduler which implements this construct can only implement choices over finite ranges, but in principle we can also use distributions with infinite support. For the rest we have the usual sequential composition, conditional statement and loop. We leave the detailed syntax of functions f or expressions e open as well as for boolean expressions or test b in conditionals and loop statements.

2.2   Linear Operator Semantics

We will base our probabilistic analysis on a syntax-based semantics which represents the executions of a program S as a Discrete Time Markov Chain (DTMC). More precisely, we associate to S a linear operator $\mathbf{T}(S)$ corresponding to the generator of the DTMC associated to S. This is a possibly infinite matrix whose domain is the set of *probabilistic configurations*, i.e. distributions on classical configurations $(x_1, \ldots, x_v, \ell)$ as row vectors, which record the value of all variables and the current label, defined by $\mathbf{Dist}(\mathbf{Conf}) = \mathbf{Dist}(\mathbb{X}^v \times \mathbf{Lab}) \subseteq \ell_2(\mathbb{X}^v \times \mathbf{Lab})$. Using the *tensor product* (e.g. [9, Chap. 14] or [10, Chap. 2.6]) we can exploit the fact that $\ell_2(\mathbb{X}^v \times \mathbf{Lab}) = \ell_2(\mathbb{X})^{\otimes v} \otimes \ell_2(\mathbf{Lab})$. We refer to $s \in \mathbf{Var} \to \mathbb{X} = \mathbb{X}^v$ as a *classical state* and to $\sigma \in \mathbf{Dist}(\mathbf{Var} \to \mathbb{X}) \subseteq \ell_2(\mathbb{X})^{\otimes v}$ as *probabilistic state*. In this definition we assume that that variables occurring in a **pWhile** program can take values in some countable set $\mathbb{X}$ that might be finite (e.g. Booleans) or infinite (typically $\mathbb{Z}$ or $\mathbb{N}$).

The labelled version of the syntax introduced in Sect. 2.1 allows us to use labels as a kind of program counter. The control flow $\mathcal{F}(S)$ in a program S is then defined via a function $flow : \mathbf{Stmt} \to \mathcal{P}(\mathbf{Lab} \times \mathbf{Lab})$ which maps statements to sets of pairs which represent the control flow graph, e.g. [8, Sect. 2.1] or [11]. This only records that a certain control flow step is possible. For tests $[b]^\ell$ in conditionals and loops we indicate the branch corresponding to the case when the test succeeds by underlining it. As our semantics is ultimately modelling the semantics of a program via the generator of a DTMC we are also confronted with the fact that such processes never terminate. For this we will add a single final loop via a virtual label ℓ^* at the end of the program.

The construction of $\mathbf{T}(S)$ is done compositionally by using among its building blocks simple operators such as the *identity matrix* $\mathbf{I}$ and the *matrix units* $\mathbf{E}_{ij}$ containing only a single non zero entry $(\mathbf{E}_{ij})_{ij} = 1$. We also define for any Boolean expression b on $\mathbb{X}$ a diagonal *projection matrix* $\mathbf{P}(b)$ with $(\mathbf{P}(b))_{ii} = 1$ if $b(i)$ holds and 0 otherwise. The operator $\mathbf{P}(s)$ tests for a classical state s, i.e. if each variable x_i has the value $s(x_i)$, and $\mathbf{P}(e = c)$ whether an expression e evaluates to a constant c. The *update* operator $\mathbf{U}$ implements state changes. The matrix $\mathbf{U}(c)$ implements the deterministic update of a variable to a constant c via $(\mathbf{U}(c))_{nm} = 1$ if $m = c$ and 0 otherwise. The operator $\mathbf{U}(x_k \leftarrow e)$ makes sure that the kth variable x_k is assigned the value of the expression e.

The matrix $\mathbf{T}(S)$ of the DTMC representing the program's executions is then defined as the sum of the effects of the individual control flow steps, i.e. the computational effect of each (labelled) block $[B]^\ell$ – with $B = $ skip, a test b

Table 1. Elements of the LOS

$$\mathbf{P}(s) = \bigotimes_{i=1}^{v} \mathbf{P}(s(\mathbf{x}_i)) \qquad \mathbf{U}(\mathbf{x}_k \leftarrow c) = \bigotimes_{i=1}^{k-1} \mathbf{I} \otimes \mathbf{U}(c) \otimes \bigotimes_{i=k+1}^{v} \mathbf{I}$$

$$\mathbf{P}(e = c) = \sum_{\mathcal{E}(e)s=c} \mathbf{P}(s) \qquad \mathbf{U}(\mathbf{x}_k \leftarrow e) = \sum_{c} \mathbf{P}(e = c)\mathbf{U}(\mathbf{x}_k \leftarrow c)$$

$$[\![x := e]^{\ell}]\!] = \mathbf{U}(x \leftarrow e) \qquad [\![v \ ?= \rho]^{\ell}]\!] = \sum_{c \in \mathbb{X}} \rho(c)\mathbf{U}(x \leftarrow c)$$

$$[\![b]^{\ell}]\!] = \mathbf{P}(b = \mathtt{false}) \qquad [\![b]^{\ell}]\!] = \mathbf{P}(b = \mathtt{true})$$

$$[\![\mathtt{skip}]^{\ell}]\!] = \underline{[\![\mathtt{skip}]^{\ell}]\!]} = \underline{[\![x := e]^{\ell}]\!]} = \underline{[\![v \ ?= \rho]^{\ell}]\!]} = \mathbf{I}$$

or a (random) assignment – and a control flow step of the form $\mathbf{E}_{\ell\ell'}$.

$$\mathbf{T}(S) = \sum_{(\ell,\ell') \in \mathcal{F}(S)} [\![B]^{\ell}]\!] \otimes \mathbf{E}_{\ell,\ell'} + \sum_{(\ell,\underline{\ell'}) \in \mathcal{F}(S)} \underline{[\![B]^{\ell}]\!]} \otimes \mathbf{E}_{\ell,\ell'}$$

If we also consider the final loop we have to add the term $\mathbf{I} \otimes \mathbf{E}_{\ell^*,\ell^*}$. The definition of the semantics of the individual blocks is given in Table 1.

Although the operator $\mathbf{T}(S)$ is in general not bounded (e.g. consider just $\mathbf{U}(\mathbf{x} \leftarrow 1)$), we can guarantee that it converges *weakly* for any initial state and any observable (specified as vector distributions in $\ell_1 \subseteq \ell_2$). We have shown this in [11], to which we refer for a full treatment of the linear operational semantics (LOS).

3   Probabilistic Abstract Interpretation

Classically the correctness of a program analysis is asserted with respect to the semantics in terms of a correctness relation. The theory of abstract interpretation allows for constructing analyses that are automatically correct without having to prove it a posteriori. This is possible because of the conditions defining a Galois connection (the mathematical structure underlying abstract interpretation), which guarantee that we do not lose safety by going back and forth between the two lattices of the concrete and the analysis domains – although we may lose precision [4,8].

Probabilistic Abstract Interpretation was introduces in [1,12] as an alternative theory leading to analyses that are possibly not safe but that are guaranteed to be as close as possible to the concrete properties. It is concerned with probabilistic analysis, i.e. an analysis intended to return quantitative answers about a program property, rather than a 'yes/no' answer.

We have shown in a number of papers how the PAI technique can be used for performing the probabilistic analysis of many problems typical of classical program analysis, such as data-flow and pointer analyses [2], and of security problems [13]. The treatment in this previous work is restricted to the special case of finite state spaces. In this paper we generalise the theory to infinite-dimensional

Hilbert spaces, where it is necessary the consideration of some appropriate topological notions in order to correctly deal with possibly infinite abstraction operators (and their generalised inverses).

Both classical abstract interpretation and PAI are usually based on state abstraction, i.e. on the abstraction of the concrete semantical domain. If we can make sure that the final state contains information about the resource(s) we are interested in, then we can use static analysis techniques in order to perform a quantitative analysis of resources and resource consumption. In some situations the computational state already describes the resources needed; for example, if we have a loop index which determines the number of iterations, then the final state(s) will automatically encode the time complexity of the program in question. If this is not the case, then we can always introduce additional variables (e.g. counters) which extend the state so as this information becomes available for a state based analysis via classical abstract interpretation (e.g. for a worst case analysis) or PAI (e.g. for an average case analysis). As an example, we have developed a 'language-based' complexity analysis of quicksort, showing how the time behaviour of a program implementing this sorting algorithm can be analysed with PAI (see Sect. 4.2).

3.1   Basic Definitions

The theory of Probabilistic Abstract Interpretation relies on the notion of generalised (or pseudo-)inverse. This notion is well-known in mathematics where it is used for finding approximate solutions to integral and differential equations [14, Chap. 9]. The abstract concept of a generalised or pseudo-inverse was introduced by Moore in the 1920s and was then rediscovered by Penrose in the 1950s.

Definition 1. *Let $\mathcal{H}_1$ and $\mathcal{H}_2$ be two Hilbert spaces and $\mathbf{A} : \mathcal{H}_1 \mapsto \mathcal{H}_2$ a linear map between them. A linear map $\mathbf{A}^\dagger = \mathbf{G} : \mathcal{H}_2 \mapsto \mathcal{H}_1$ is the Moore-Penrose pseudo-inverse of $\mathbf{A}$ iff $\mathbf{A} \circ \mathbf{G} = \mathbf{P_A}$ and $\mathbf{G} \circ \mathbf{A} = \mathbf{P_G}$, where $\mathbf{P_A}$ and $\mathbf{P_G}$ denote orthogonal projections onto the ranges of $\mathbf{A}$ and $\mathbf{G}$.*

It is also possible to define the Moore-Penrose pseudo-inverse $\mathbf{A}^\dagger$ of an operator $\mathbf{A}$ without direct reference to orthogonal projections (cf. e.g. [15, Sect. 4.7]). For this we need the notion of the adjoint $\mathbf{A}^*$ of an operator $\mathbf{A} : \mathcal{H} \to \mathcal{H}$ on a Hilbert space; this is defined via the condition $\langle \mathbf{A}(x), y \rangle = \langle x, \mathbf{A}^*(y) \rangle$. Then the Moore-Penrose pseudo-inverse can be defined via the following four conditions: $\mathbf{AA}^\dagger\mathbf{A} = \mathbf{A}$, $\mathbf{A}^\dagger\mathbf{AA}^\dagger = \mathbf{A}^\dagger$, $(\mathbf{A}^\dagger\mathbf{A})^* = \mathbf{A}^\dagger\mathbf{A}$, and $(\mathbf{AA}^\dagger)^* = \mathbf{AA}^\dagger$. In this form it is also obvious that the Moore-Penrose pseudo-inverse (like a Galois connection) is indeed a pseudo-inverse.

If $\mathcal{C}$ and $\mathcal{D}$ are two Hilbert spaces, and $\mathbf{A} : \mathcal{C} \to \mathcal{D}$ and $\mathbf{G} : \mathcal{D} \to \mathcal{C}$ are linear operators between the concrete domain $\mathcal{C}$ and the abstract domain $\mathcal{D}$, such that $\mathbf{G}$ is the Moore-Penrose pseudo-inverse of $\mathbf{A}$, then we say that $(\mathcal{C}, \mathbf{A}, \mathcal{D}, \mathbf{G})$ forms a *probabilistic abstract interpretation*.

3.2   Correctness vs Best Solution

The Moore-Penrose pseudo-inverse plays a similar role in Probabilistic Abstract Interpretation as Galois connections in the theory of classical Abstract Interpretation in helping with the problem of combinatory explosion: it allows us to simplify the semantics $\mathbf{T}(S)$ of a program S by considering the abstract semantics $\mathbf{T}^\# = \mathbf{A}^\dagger \mathbf{T}(S)\mathbf{A}$ instead of the concrete one.

However, the properties of the Moore-Penrose pseudo-inverse (e.g. [14,16]) guarantee a different form of optimality of the abstractions (abstract semantics) we can construct via PAI. In particular, these properties ensure that PAI abstractions are the *closest* ones to the concrete semantics one can construct. Here closeness is defined via the distance induced by the norm on the Hilbert space, thus the name of '*least square approximation*' which is often used to refer to this approximation notion. As a consequence, in our probabilistic setting the main aim of the analysis is to reduce the error margin rather than to 'err on the safe side', which would lead to *safe* abstractions in the usual sense, i.e. over- or under-approximations of the concrete semantics.

The choice of the Hilbert space ℓ_2 as the domain for the LOS semantics is partly motivated by the symmetry between observables and states (we recall that ℓ_2 is self-dual) but also by the fact that it provides a simple and mathematically well understood theory of best approximations by Moore-Penrose pseudo-inverses. A similar well-behaved theory does not exist in general Banach spaces like ℓ_1 which do not have an inner product and a notion of an adjoint operator $\mathbf{A}^*$. As a result the theory of approximations in Banach spaces can, in general, not even guarantee the existence of unique optima (e.g. [17]).

3.3   Compositionality of PAI

Important for the applicability of PAI is the fact that it possesses some useful compositionality properties. These allow us to construct the abstract semantics by abstracting the single blocks of the concrete semantics $\mathbf{T}(S)$:

$$\mathbf{T}(S)^\# = \mathbf{A}^\dagger \mathbf{T}(S)\mathbf{A} = \mathbf{A}^\dagger \left(\sum [\![B]\!]^\ell \right) \mathbf{A} = \sum \left(\mathbf{A}^\dagger [\![B]\!]^\ell \mathbf{A} \right) = \sum [\![B]\!]^\ell{}^\#$$

The fact that we can work with the abstract semantics of individual blocks instead of the full operator obviously reduces the complexity of the analysis substantially.

Another important fact is that the Moore-Penrose pseudo-inverse of a tensor product can be computed as: $(\mathbf{A}_1 \otimes \mathbf{A}_2 \otimes \ldots \otimes \mathbf{A}_v)^\dagger = \mathbf{A}_1^\dagger \otimes \mathbf{A}_2^\dagger \otimes \ldots \otimes \mathbf{A}_v^\dagger$, cf [14, 2.1, Example 3]. We can therefore abstract properties of individual variables and then combine them in the global abstraction. This is also made possible by the definition of the concrete LOS semantics (cf. Sect. 2.2) which is heavily based on the use of tensor product. Typically we have $[\![B]\!]^\ell = (\bigotimes_{i=1}^v \mathbf{T}_{i\ell}) \otimes \mathbf{E}_{\ell\ell'}$ or a sum of a few of such terms. The $\mathbf{T}_{i\ell}$ represents the effect of $\mathbf{T}(S)$, and in particular of $[\![B]\!]^\ell$, on variable i at label ℓ (both labels and variables only form a finite set). For example, we can define an abstraction $\mathbf{A}$ for one variable and apply it individually to all variables (e.g. extracting their even/odd property), or use different abstractions for different variables (maybe even forgetting about some of them by using $\mathbf{A}_f = (1, 1, \ldots)^t$) and define $\mathbf{A} = \bigotimes_{i=1}^{v} \mathbf{A}_i$ such that $\mathbf{A}^\dagger = \bigotimes_{i=1}^{v} \mathbf{A}_i^\dagger$ in order to get an analysis on the full state space.

Usually we do not abstract the control step $\mathbf{E}_{\ell\ell'}$, although this would also be possible. Very often most of the $\mathbf{T}_{i\ell}$'s are just the identity matrix – expressing the fact that the variable in question is not involved in whatever happens at label ℓ. In this case we have $\mathbf{A}_i^\dagger \mathbf{IA}_i = \mathbf{I}$, where the two identity operators are of the appropriate dimensions (maybe an infinite matrix on the concrete space, but a finite matrix on the abstract property space).

The abstractions of tests $[b]^\ell$, i.e. $\mathbf{P}(b)$, provide the basis for analysing *abstract branching probabilities* [18]. This can be done by constructing $\mathbf{A}^\dagger [[b]^\ell] \mathbf{A}$ and $\mathbf{A}^\dagger [[\neg b]^\ell] \mathbf{A}$. As these operators are projections, we can exploit the fact that $[[b]^\ell]^\# = \mathbf{I} - [[\neg b]^\ell]$ and compute in practice only one of them. The abstract operator $[[\neg b]^\ell]^\#$ in effect estimates the chance of the test b succeeding in terms of the abstract properties. For example, with a parity analysis we obtain a (least square) estimate for the chance that in an conditional statement, for an even number we take the `then` branch rather than the `else` branch (cf. Example in Sect. 4). If an analytical (statistical) construction of $[[b]^\ell]^\#$ is infeasible one might consider profiling information as a replacement of the exact solution.

3.4   Abstraction Operators

In classical program analysis [8] an extraction function $\alpha : C \to D$ is a function which associates to each element c of a concrete domain C an abstract description or property $d \in D$. In our framework for probabilistic analysis, we will consider Hilbert spaces for both concrete and abstract domains $\mathcal{C}$ and $\mathcal{D}$, respectively. In particular, for an extraction function $\alpha : C \to D$ we will construct the Hilbert spaces $\mathcal{C} = \ell_2(C)$ and $\mathcal{D} = \ell_2(D)$ generated by the base vectors $\{c\}_{c \in C}$ and $\{d\}_{d \in D}$. For finite C and D we can identify the two spaces with the finite dimensional vector spaces $\mathbb{R}^{|C|}$ and $\mathbb{R}^{|D|}$. We can then define a linear operator $\mathbf{A}_\alpha = \mathbf{A} : \ell_2(C) \to \ell_2(D)$ by mapping every $x = \sum_c x_c$ to $\mathbf{A}(x) = \mathbf{A}(\sum_c x_c c) = \sum_c x_c \mathbf{A}(c)$, with $(\mathbf{A}(c))_{\alpha(c)} = 1$ and $(\mathbf{A}(c))_d = 0$ for all $d \neq \alpha(c)$. In effect, this means that we construct a matrix $\mathbf{A}$, which we refer to as *classification operator*, with rows enumerated by elements in C and columns enumerated by elements in D such that $(\mathbf{A})_{cd} = 1$ iff $\alpha(c) = d$ and 0 otherwise.

The following theorem shows that a necessary and sufficient condition for the existence of the Moore-Penrose inverse for a *bounded* linear operator $\mathbf{A} : \mathcal{H} \to \mathcal{H}$ on a Hilbert space $\mathcal{H}$ is that $\mathbf{A}$ is *normally solvable*, i.e. its range $R(\mathbf{A}) = \{\mathbf{A}x \mid x \in \mathcal{H}\}$ is closed. This implies that in particular all operators on a finite dimensional Hilbert space are Moore-Penrose invertible.

Proposition 1. *[15, Theorem 4.24] A bounded operator $\mathbf{A} \in \mathcal{B}(\mathcal{H}))$ is Moore-Penrose pseudo-invertible, i.e. a unique $\mathbf{A}^\dagger$ exists, if and only if it is normally solvable. In this case $(\mathbf{A}^*\mathbf{A} + \mathbf{P})$ is invertible and $\mathbf{A}^\dagger = (\mathbf{A}^*\mathbf{A} + \mathbf{P})^{-1}\mathbf{A}^*$ where*

$\mathbf{P}$ *is the orthogonal projection of* $\mathcal{H}$ *onto* $N(\mathbf{A}) = \{x \mid \mathbf{A}(x) = o\}$ *with* o *being the null vector.*

Typically D will be finite, but C could be countably infinite. In this case we are faced with the problem that $\mathbf{A}$ might not be bounded. Thus – though $\mathbf{A}$ represents a closed map because D is finite – we need to be more careful when we construct the Moore-Penrose pseudo-inverse.

Example 1 (Forgetful Abstraction). Let us consider the abstraction into an abstract domain containing only a single property $*$, i.e. $D = \{*\}$ and $\alpha(s) = *$ for all concrete values s. Essentially, this abstraction only tests for the existence of the system. It might seem rather pointless, but it turns out to be useful in various contexts, for example to analyse only a particular variables property ignoring other program variables, (see e.g. [3]).

The matrix $\mathbf{A}_f$ representing the forgetful abstraction in the PAI framework is a single column matrix containing only 1s. This corresponds to the map $x \mapsto (\|x\|_1) \in \mathbb{R}^1 = \ell_2(\{*\})$. This matrix represents clearly an unbounded map $\ell_2 \to \mathbb{R}$: the vector $x = (x_i)_{i=0}^{\infty} = (1, \frac{1}{2}, \frac{1}{3}, \ldots)$ is in ℓ_2 but $\mathbf{A}_f(x) = (\|x\|_1) = (\infty)$.

However, one can easily check that the operator $\mathbf{A}_f$ of Example 1 is densely defined and closed. More concretely the following holds:

- $\mathbf{A}_f$ is not bounded on ℓ_2. To see this, take the vector $x = (x_i)_{i=0}^{\infty} = (1, \frac{1}{2}, \frac{1}{3}, \ldots)$ which is in ℓ_2 but for which we have $\mathbf{A}_f(x) = (\|x\|_1) = (\infty)$.
- $\mathbf{A}_f$ is defined on a dense subspace of ℓ_2, namely ℓ_1, since for all $x \in \ell_1$ the 1-dim vector $\mathbf{A}_f(x) = (\|x\|_1) \in \mathbb{R}^1$ is defined.
- $\mathbf{A}_f$ is closed (on ℓ_1). If we have a sequence of vectors $x_n \to x$ then $\mathbf{A}_f(x_n) = (\|x_n\|_1)$ converges to $\|x\|_1$ as ℓ_1 is complete and the 1-norm is continuous.

In general, the following theorem holds, which allows us to establish the existence of a Moore-Penrose pseudo-inverse also in the case of unbounded abstraction operators provided that certain conditions are satisfied.

Theorem 1. *[6, Theorem 2.12] If* $\mathbf{A} : \mathcal{D} \subseteq \mathcal{H}_1 \to \mathcal{H}_2$ *is a closed densely defined linear operator then* $\mathbf{A}^{\dagger} : \mathcal{D}(\mathbf{A}^{\dagger}) = R(\mathbf{A}) + R(\mathbf{A})^{\perp} \to \mathcal{D}(\mathbf{A}) \cap N(\mathbf{A})^{\perp}$ *is closed and densely defined. Moreover,*

(i) $\mathbf{A}^{\dagger}$ *is bounded if and only if* $R(\mathbf{A})$ *is closed.*
(ii) $\mathbf{A}\mathbf{A}^{\dagger}(y) = \mathbf{P}_{\overline{R(\mathbf{A})}}(y)$ *for all* $y \in \mathcal{D}(\mathbf{A}^{\dagger})$.
(iii) $\mathbf{A}^{\dagger}\mathbf{A}(y) = \mathbf{P}_{N(\mathbf{A})^{\perp}}(y)$ *for all* $y \in \mathcal{D}(\mathbf{A})$.

Fortunately, for classification operators, i.e. the abstraction operators of the PAI framework, we can guarantee the existence of a unique Moore-Penrose pseudo-inverse. In fact, the following two results generalise the properties of the forgetful abstraction in Example 1 to any probabilistic abstraction.

Proposition 2. *For any countable set* C *and finite set* D *the classification operator* $\mathbf{A} : \ell_2(C) \to \ell_2(D)$ *corresponding to the extraction function* $\alpha : C \to D$ *is a densely defined closed linear operator.*

Proof. The representation of the abstraction operator $\mathbf{A}$ for any extraction function α is a (possibly infinite) *stochastic* matrix, i.e. the row sums are all 1. This matrix represents therefore a bounded operator on ℓ_1 with respect to the 1-norm on ℓ_1. This is because stochastic matrices preserve the 1-norm $\|\mathbf{A}(x)\|_1 = \|x\|_1$.

Clearly, $\mathbf{A}$ is in general not defined for all vectors in ℓ_2 (cf. the operator $\mathbf{A}_f(x)$ in Example 1). However, all abstractions $\mathbf{A}$ are well-defined on ℓ_1 which is dense in ℓ_2 (e.g. [5]). In order to show that $\mathbf{A}$ is closed, we recall that $\|x\|_2 \le \|x\|_1$ holds, cf. [19, Exercise 1.15]. Therefore, if we assume convergence of a sequence $\{x_n\}$ in the 1-norm, i.e. $\|x_n - x\|_1 \to 0$ then this implies that also $\|x_n - x\|_2 \to 0$ holds. Now, if $\mathbf{A}(x_n) \to y$ in $\mathbb{R}^d \subseteq \ell_2(D)$, because by hypothesis $\mathbf{A} \in \mathcal{B}(\ell_1, \mathbb{R}^d)$ is continuous with respect to the 1-norm, we have that $\|\mathbf{A}(x_n) - \mathbf{A}(x)\|_1 \to 0$, i.e. $\mathbf{A}(x_n) \to \mathbf{A}(x)$. Because $\mathbb{R}^d$ is a finite-dimensional Hilbert space, all norms are equivalent on it, and therefore $\mathbf{A}(x) = y$ must hold. $\qquad\square$

Proposition 3. *For any countable set C and finite set D and any extraction map $\alpha : C \to D$, the corresponding probabilistic abstraction $\mathbf{A} : \ell_2(C) \to \ell_2(D)$ has a Moore-Penrose pseudo-inverse $\mathbf{A}^\dagger : \mathcal{D} \subseteq \ell_2(D) \to \ell_2(C)$.*

Proof. This follows from the fact that $\mathbf{A}$ is densely defined and closed (from Proposition 2) and Theorem 1. $\qquad\square$

3.5   Construction of Infinite-Dimensional Abstractions

For an abstraction operator $\mathbf{A}$, i.e. a classification matrix corresponding to an extraction function α on a finite dimensional space $\ell_2(C) = \mathbb{R}^{|C|}$, we can construct the Moore-Penrose pseudo-inverse by just transposing $\mathbf{A}$ and row-normalising the resulting transposed matrix. However, we cannot use the same construction for infinite abstractions even if by Proposition 3 we are guaranteed that $\mathbf{A}^\dagger$ does exist. In Example 1, it is clear that with a concrete finite space $C = \{c_1, \ldots, c_n\}$ we can construct

$$\mathbf{A}_f = (1, 1, \ldots, 1)^t \quad \text{and} \quad \mathbf{A}_f^\dagger = (\frac{1}{n}, \frac{1}{n}, \ldots, \frac{1}{n}).$$

However, if we extend this to the case of a countable infinite concrete space, e.g. $C = \mathbb{Z}$, then clearly the row-normalised transpose of an infinite version of $\mathbf{A}_f$ must be the zero (single-row) matrix.

Example 2 (Parity Abstraction). Consider as abstract and concrete domains $C = \ell_2(\{0, \ldots, n\})$ and $\mathcal{D} = \ell_2(\{\text{even}, \text{odd}\})$. The abstraction operator $\mathbf{A}_p$ and its concretisation operator $\mathbf{G}_p = \mathbf{A}_p^\dagger$ corresponding to a *parity analysis* are represented by the following $(n+1) \times 2$ and $2 \times (n+1)$ matrices (assuming w.l.o.g. that n is odd)

$$\mathbf{A}_p = \begin{pmatrix} 1\,0\,1\,0 \ldots 0 \\ 0\,1\,0\,1 \ldots 1 \end{pmatrix}^t \qquad \mathbf{A}_p^\dagger = \begin{pmatrix} \frac{2}{n+1} & 0 & \frac{2}{n+1} & 0 & \cdots & 0 \\ 0 & \frac{2}{n+1} & 0 & \frac{2}{n+1} & \cdots & \frac{2}{n+1} \end{pmatrix}$$

The concretisation operator $\mathbf{A}_p^\dagger$ represents uniform distributions over the $\frac{n}{2}$ even numbers in the range $0, \ldots, n$ (as the first row) and the n odd numbers in the same range (in the second row). Clearly, if we increase the dimension n we encounter the same problems as with $\mathbf{A}_f$.

In the following, we address the problem of effectively constructing $\mathbf{A}^\dagger$ for any probabilistic abstraction $\mathbf{A}$. This would be essential for practical and computational purposes, not least the implementation of our analyses.

In numerical mathematics [20, Sect. 12.1], there is a general theory related to the so-called *finite sections* or *projection* methods which aims in approximating infinite dimensional operators on Hilbert spaces by means of finite-dimensional approximations. A general approximating setting for projection methods is defined in [21] for bounded linear operators $\mathbf{T} : \mathcal{X} \to \mathcal{Y}$, where $\mathcal{X}$ and $\mathcal{Y}$ are Hilbert spaces over the same field (that, for our purposes, we can assume to be $\mathbb{R}$). In this setting, let $\{X_n\}$ and $\{Y_n\}$ be sequences of closed subspaces of $\mathcal{X}$ and $\mathcal{Y}$, respectively, which satisfy $\mathbf{P}_n \xrightarrow{s} \mathbf{I}_X$ and $\mathbf{Q}_n \xrightarrow{s} \mathbf{I}_Y$, where $\mathbf{P}_n = \mathbf{P}_{X_n}$ and $\mathbf{Q}_n = \mathbf{Q}_{Y_n}$ denote the orthogonal projections from $\mathcal{X}$ and $\mathcal{Y}$ onto X_n and Y_n, respectively. A generalisation of this setting was introduced in [22] where projection methods are defined that apply to densely defined and closed operators (thus to our abstraction operators). The method consists in constructing $\{Y_n\}_{n \in \mathbb{N}}$ as an increasing sequence of subspaces of $\mathcal{R}(\mathbf{T})$ such that $\overline{\cup_{n=1}^\infty Y_n} = \mathcal{R}(\mathbf{T})$, and $\{X_n\}_{n \in \mathbb{N}}$ as an increasing sequence of subspaces of the orthogonal complement $\mathcal{N}(\mathbf{T})^\dagger$ of the null space of $\mathbf{T}$ such that $\overline{\cup_{n=1}^\infty X_n} = \mathcal{N}(\mathbf{T})^\dagger$. These two sequences must be constructed so as to satisfy some particular properties that are defined in [22, Def. 3.2] and called *admissibility* of the sequences. If we now define $\mathbf{T}_n = \mathbf{P}_n \mathbf{T} \mathbf{Q}_n$ and $\hat{\mathbf{T}}_n = \mathbf{T}_{n|X_n}$, then the method is said to be convergent wrt to a given admissible pair $\{\mathbf{P}_n, \mathbf{Q}_n\}$ if for all $y \in \mathcal{Y}$ (using post-multiplication):

$$y \cdot \mathbf{P}_n \hat{\mathbf{T}}_n^\dagger \longrightarrow y \cdot \mathbf{T}^\dagger.$$

By applying Theorem 3.4 in [22], we can show that for any abstraction operator $\mathbf{A}$, we can construct $\mathbf{A}^\dagger$ by applying the generalised projection method described above. In fact, the following proposition holds:

Proposition 4. *For any countable set C and finite set D, let $\mathbf{A} : \ell_2(C) \to \ell_2(D)$ be the classification operator corresponding to the extraction function $\alpha : C \to D$. Then the generalised projection method for $\mathbf{A}$ is convergent wrt the sequence $\{\mathbf{P}_n, \mathbf{Q}_n\}$ of projections corresponding to the subspaces $X_n = \mathcal{N}(\mathbf{A})_n^\dagger$ and $Y_n = \mathcal{R}(\mathbf{A})_n$, respectively.*

The fact that for the abstraction operators constituting the PAI framework a Moore-Penrose pseudo-inverse is always defined and that it can be constructed efficiently (e.g. [23–25]), makes the PAI theory consistent, and guarantees a solid mathematical basis to the program analysis techniques based on it.

However, for the purposes of our analysis we are actually not really interested in the limit object $\mathbf{A}^\dagger$ itself; we are rather interested in the effect of the finite approximations of the abstract semantics defined via $\mathbf{A}$ and $\mathbf{A}^\dagger$ on the abstract state of a given program with respect to the property under consideration. This is captured by the notion of weak limit: if $\mathbf{T}(S)$ is the concrete (possibly unbounded) linear operator semantics for a given program S, x is an element (distribution) in the domain of the abstract operator $\mathbf{T}^{\#}(S) = \mathbf{A}^{\dagger}\mathbf{T}(S)\mathbf{A}$, and y is an abstract property (distribution) in the same domain, we are interested in analysing the behaviour of S by observing the abstract sequence of the inner products between the n-th approximation vector $x \cdot (\mathbf{T}^{\#}(S))_n$ and the observable y, i.e. the weak limit of the sequence with respect to that observable. We will show in the following that this sequence always converges in $\mathbb{R}$, and we will take this limit to define the *effect* of property y on state $x \cdot \mathbf{T}^{\#}(S)$.

For a program S and its LOS, $\mathbf{T}(S)$, we can define the finite approximations of $\mathbf{T}(S)$ as the operators $\mathbf{T}(S)_n = \mathbf{P}_n\mathbf{T}(S)\mathbf{P}_n$, where for all $n \in \mathbb{N}$, $\mathbf{P}_n$ is a diagonal matrix with all entries zero except for the first n diagonal entries that are all equal to 1. Then, for a given abstraction operator $\mathbf{A}$, we define the finite approximations $\mathbf{T}^{\#}(S)_n$ of the abstract semantics $\mathbf{T}^{\#}(S) = \mathbf{A}^{\dagger}\mathbf{T}(S)\mathbf{A}$ as $\mathbf{A}_n^{\dagger}\mathbf{T}(S)_n\mathbf{A}_n$, where $\mathbf{A}_n$ is the finite section of $\mathbf{A}$ defined in the projection method, for which we can easily construct $\mathbf{A}_n^{\dagger}$ (it is a finite matrix).

Proposition 5. *For any countable set C and finite set D and any classification map $\alpha : C \rightarrow D$, let $\mathbf{A}$ be the corresponding linear map $\mathbf{A} : \ell_2(C) \rightarrow \ell_2(D)$. Then for any program S and its LOS operator $\mathbf{T}(S)$ and for all distributions $x, y \in \mathbf{Dist(Conf)} \subset \ell_2(D)$, we have that $\lim_{n \to \infty}\langle x \cdot \mathbf{A}_n^{\dagger}\mathbf{T}(S)_n\mathbf{A}_n, y\rangle < \infty$.*

Proof. Let $x_n = x \cdot \mathbf{T}^{\#}(S)_n$ and $y \in \mathbf{Dist(Conf)} \subset \ell_1(\mathbf{Conf}) \subset \ell_2(\mathbf{Conf})$. We need to show that $\langle x_n, y\rangle = \sum_{k=1}^{\infty}(x_n)_k \cdot y_k$ converges in $\mathbb{R}$. Since the $\mathbf{T}^{\#}(S)_n$ are (sub-)stochastic matrices and $\|x\|_1 = 1$ (because x is a distribution), we have that $\|x_n\|_1 \leq 1$ and $\langle x_n, y\rangle \leq \langle x_{n+1}, y\rangle$, i.e. the sequence of the inner products is monotone. Moreover, by the Cauchy-Schwarz inequality (e.g. [10, Prop. 2.1.1]) we have that $\langle x_n, y\rangle \leq \|x_n\|_2\|y\|_2$. Thus, as in general $\|v\|_2 \leq \|v\|_1$ holds for all v (cf. [19, Exercise 1.14]), we have that $\langle x_n, y\rangle \leq \|x_n\|_2\|y\|_2 \leq \|x_n\|_1\|y\|_1 \leq 1$, i.e. $\langle x_n, y\rangle$ is a bounded, monotone sequence of reals, which thus converges. □

Example 3 (Approximation of $\mathbf{A}_f^{\dagger}$). If we construct the weak limit of finite approximations to $\mathbf{A}_f$ and consider its effect only in the context of a concrete state σ then we get a useful result even if we do not effectively construct the norm or uniform limit of $(\mathbf{A}_f)_n$. For any probabilistic state $\sigma \in \ell_1(C)$ with $\sigma_i \geq 0$ and $\|\sigma\|_1 = 1$, i.e. a probability distribution, we get for all $x \in \ell_2(C)$

$$\lim_{n \to \infty}\langle(\mathbf{A}_f)_n(\sigma), x\rangle = \mathbf{E}(x, \sigma) \quad \text{and} \quad \lim_{n \to \infty}\langle(\mathbf{A}_f^{\dagger})_n(*), x\rangle = \mathbf{E}(x, \nu),$$

where $\mathbf{E}(x, d)$ is the expectation value of x with respect to the distribution d and ν is the uniform distribution. In other words, the weak limit $\mathbf{A}_f^{\dagger} = w\text{-}\lim(\mathbf{A}_f)_n$ represents the effect of an eventually non-existing "uniform measure" on all of C, even when C is an infinite set. In measure theoretic terms this means that we represent a uniform measure (on all of C) which per se cannot be expressed as a distribution as the limit of distributions.

4   Examples

We conclude by discussing in detail an example which illustrates how probabilistic abstraction allows us to analyse the properties of programs. We also demonstrate how the PAI framework could be used for average case complexity analysis by re-phrasing the well-known probabilistic analysis of the Quicksort algorithm in our program analysis setting. We will also discuss the efficiency of the analysis, i.e. how PAI can be deployed in order to beat the combinatorial explosion or the curse of dimensionality.

4.1   Factorial

It is easy to observe that the factorial function $n!$ "almost always" returns an even number (except for $0!$ and $1!$). If we perform a classical abstraction we cannot justify this intuition as in oder to be safe we can only obtain a guarantee that the result may be *even* or *odd*. In order to provide a formal analysis of $n!$ let us first consider the concrete semantics of the program F using labelling:

$$[m := 1]^1; \texttt{ while } [n > 1]^2 \texttt{ do } [m := m \times n]^3; [n := n - 1]^4 \texttt{ od}; [\texttt{skip}]^5$$

The flow is $\mathcal{F}(F) = \{(1,2),(2,\underline{3}),(3,4),(4,2),(2,5),(5,5)\}$ which includes a looping on the final skip statement. We then have: $\mathbf{T}(F) = \mathbf{U}(\texttt{m} \leftarrow 1) \otimes \mathbf{E}_{1,2} + \mathbf{P}((\texttt{n > 1})) \otimes \mathbf{E}_{2,3} + \mathbf{U}(\texttt{m} \leftarrow (\texttt{m * n})) \otimes \mathbf{E}_{3,4} + \mathbf{U}(\texttt{n} \leftarrow (\texttt{n - 1})) \otimes \mathbf{E}_{4,2} + \mathbf{P}((\texttt{n <= 1})) \otimes \mathbf{E}_{2,5} + \mathbf{I} \otimes \mathbf{E}_{5,5}$.

If we just consider the factorials $0!$, $1!$ and $2!$ then we can restrict ourselves to values $m, n \in \{0, 1, 2\}$. In this case the semantics of each block is given by a $3 \cdot 3 \times 3 \cdot 3 = 9 \times 9$ matrix.

For the updates in label 3 and 4 we have "empty rows", i.e. rows where we have no non-zero entries. These correspond to over- and under-flows as we are dealing only with finite values in $\mathbb{Z}$, e.g. the product for $m = 2$ and $n = 2$ is not in $\{0, 1, 2\}$. We could clarify the situation in various ways, e.g. by introducing an additional value $\perp$ for undefined (concrete) values of variables, or by introducing an $\texttt{error}$ configuration. In the analysis we present here these over- and under-flows do not play any relevant role and we therefore leave things as they are.

The full operator representing the LOS semantics of the factorial program is given by a $(3 \cdot 3 \cdot 5) \times (3 \cdot 3 \cdot 5) = 45 \times 45$ matrix.

We can construct an abstract version $\mathbf{T}^{\#}(F) = \mathbf{A}^{\dagger}\mathbf{T}(F)\mathbf{A}$ of $\mathbf{T}(F)$ by recording only the parity of m as even and odd. We will not abstract n nor the labels defining the current configuration during the execution. We thus get the $(2 \cdot 3 \cdot 5) \times (2 \cdot 3 \cdot 5) = 30 \times 30$ matrix $\mathbf{T}^{\#}(F) = (\mathbf{A}_p \otimes \mathbf{I} \otimes \mathbf{I})^{\dagger}\mathbf{T}(F)(\mathbf{A}_p \otimes \mathbf{I} \otimes \mathbf{I})$. Though this abstract semantics does have some interesting properties, it appears to be only a minor improvement with regard to the concrete semantics: We managed to reduce the dimension only from 45 to 30. However, the simplification becomes substantially more dramatic once we increase the possible values of $\texttt{m}$ and $\texttt{n}$, and combinatorial explosion really takes a hold. If we allow $\texttt{n}$ to take values between 0 and n then we must allow for $\texttt{m}$ values between 0 and $n!$. Concrete values of the dimensions of $\mathbf{T}(F)$ and $\mathbf{T}^{\#}(F)$ for $n = 1, 2, \ldots, 9$ are $\dim(\mathbf{T}(F)) = 45, 140, 625, 3630, 25235, 201640, 1814445, 18144050$ but for the abstract semantics only $\dim(\mathbf{T}^{\#}(F)) = 30, 40, 50, 60, 70, 80, 90, 100$.

The problem is that the size of $\mathbf{T}(F)$ explodes so quickly that it is impossible to simulate it for values of n much larger than 5 on a normal PC. If we want to analyse the abstract semantics, things remain much smaller. Importantly, we can construct the abstract semantics in the same way as the concrete one, just using "smaller" matrices: $\mathbf{T}^{\#}(F) = \mathbf{U}^{\#}(\mathtt{m} \leftarrow 1) \otimes \mathbf{E}_{1,2} + \mathbf{P}^{\#}((\mathtt{n} > 1)) \otimes \mathbf{E}_{2,3} + \mathbf{U}^{\#}(\mathtt{m} \leftarrow (\mathtt{m} * \mathtt{n})) \otimes \mathbf{E}_{3,4} + \mathbf{U}^{\#}(\mathtt{n} \leftarrow (\mathtt{n} - 1)) \otimes \mathbf{E}_{4,2} + \mathbf{P}^{\#}((\mathtt{n} \mathrel{<=} 1)) \otimes \mathbf{E}_{2,5} + \mathbf{I}^{\#} \otimes \mathbf{E}_{5,5}$. Fortunately, most of the operators $\mathbf{T}^{\#}(\ell, \ell')$ are very easy to construct. These matrices are $2 \cdot (n+1) \cdot 5 \times 2 \cdot (n+1) \cdot 5 = 10(n+1) \times 10(n+1)$ matrices if we consider the control transfer, and only $2(n+1) \times 2(n+1)$ matrices if we deal only with the update of the current state.

Except for label 3 only either $\mathtt{m}$ or $\mathtt{n}$ but never both are involved in each statement: We thus can express the $\mathbf{T}^{\#}(\ell, \ell')$'s as tensor products of a 2×2 and a $(n+1) \times (n+1)$ matrix. Finally, we need to construct the update for label 3. It is easy to see that for even $\mathtt{m}$ the result is again even and for odd $\mathtt{m}$ the parity of $\mathtt{n}$ determines the parity of the resulting $\mathtt{m}$. We can thus write this update at label 3 as:

$$\begin{pmatrix} 1 & 0 \\ 0 & 0 \end{pmatrix} \otimes \mathbf{I} + \begin{pmatrix} 0 & 0 \\ 1 & 0 \end{pmatrix} \otimes \mathbf{P}(\mathbf{even}) + \begin{pmatrix} 0 & 0 \\ 0 & 1 \end{pmatrix} \otimes \mathbf{P}(\mathbf{odd})$$

where $\mathbf{I}$ is the identity matrix, and $\mathbf{P}(\mathbf{even})$ and $\mathbf{P}(\mathbf{odd})$ are the indicator projections for even and odd, e.g. $(\mathbf{P}(\mathbf{even}))_{ij} = 1$ if $i = j$ is even and 0 otherwise (with $i, j \in \{0, 1, \ldots\}$).

With this we can now approximate the probabilistic properties of the factorial function. In particular, if we look at the terminal configurations with the initial abstract configuration: $x_0 = \left(\frac{1}{2} \ \frac{1}{2} \right) \otimes \left(\frac{1}{n+1} \ \cdots \ \frac{1}{n+1} \right) \otimes \left(1\ 0\ 0\ 0\ 0 \right)$ which corresponds to a uniform distribution over all possible abstract values for our variables $\mathtt{m}$ and $\mathtt{n}$ (in fact, the part describing $\mathtt{m}$ could be any other distribution), then we get as final probabilistic configuration: $x = \left(\frac{n-1}{n+1} \ \frac{2}{n+1} \right) \otimes \left(\frac{1}{n+1} \ \frac{n}{n+1} \ 0 \ldots 0 \right) \otimes \left(0\ 0\ 0\ 0\ 1 \right)$. This expresses the fact that indeed in most cases (with probability $\frac{n-1}{n+1}$) we get an even factorial – only in two cases out of $n+1$ (for 0 and 1) we get an odd result (namely 1). The final value of $\mathtt{n}$ is nearly always 1 except when we start with 0 and we always reach the final statement with label 5.

If we start with the abstract initial state x_0 above and execute $\mathbf{T}^{\#}(F)$ until we get a fixpoint x we can use abstractions not to simplify the semantics but instead in order to extract the relevant information. Concretely we use: $\mathbf{A} = \mathbf{I} \otimes \mathbf{A}_f \otimes \mathbf{A}_f$, i.e. once we reached the terminal configuration (of the abstract execution) we ignore the value of n and the final label ℓ and only concentrate on the abstract, i.e. parity, values of m. Concretely we have to compute: $(\lim_{i \to \infty} x_0 \cdot (\mathbf{T}^{\#}(F))^i) \cdot \mathbf{A}$. Note that we always reach the fixpoint after a finite number of iterations (namely at most n) so this can be computed in finite time. The concrete probabilities we get for various n are:

n	even	odd
10	0.81818	0.18182
100	0.98019	0.019802

n	even	odd
1000	0.99800	0.0019980
10000	0.99980	0.00019998

We can easily compute the final distribution on $\{\mathbf{even}, \mathbf{odd}\}$ for quite large n despite the fact that, as said, it is virtually impossible to compute the explicit representation of the concrete semantics $\mathbf{T}(F)$ already for $n = 6$.

Considering the factorial only for a limited number of inputs – here for n less than 10, 100, 1000, and 10000 – means in effect considering the finite approximations for the full factorial function F with any input $n \in \mathbb{Z}$. We are essentially computing

$$(\lim_{i \to \infty} \boldsymbol{x}_0 \cdot (\mathbf{T}_n^{\#}(F))^i) \cdot \mathbf{A} = (\lim_{i \to \infty} \boldsymbol{x}_0 \cdot (\mathbf{P}_n \mathbf{T}(F)\mathbf{P}_n)^i) \cdot \mathbf{A}$$

for $n = 10, 100, 1000,$ and 10000. Numerically the last table of results shows that for $n \to \infty$ we obviously get $P(\mathbf{even}) = 1$, and $P(\mathbf{odd}) = 0$.

We see that with a uniform distribution for n we get a vanishing probability $P(\mathbf{odd}) = 0$ for m. But we could also execute the abstract program with different initial distributions to get different estimates for $P(\mathbf{odd})$. If we take, for example, as a distribution for n something like $(\frac{1}{2}, \frac{1}{2}, 0, 0, \ldots)$ – which would mean that we only need to compute 0! and 1! – we obviously get the result $P(\mathbf{even}) = 0$ for m. A worst-case, safe analysis would thus result in $0 \leq P(\mathbf{even}) \leq 1$ – which is certainly correct but trivial – while by an average case analysis providing instead optimal estimates (for different initial distributions) we can achieve more useful results.

4.2   Quicksort

QuickSort (due to C.A.R. Hoare) is one of the best known sorting algorithms. Its complexity theoretic properties are studied in practically all mongraphs on algorithms and complexity. It is well-known that its worst case time complexity is $O(n^2)$ and average case time complexity is $O(n \log n)$, where n is the length of the list to be sorted and it is assumed a uniform distribution over all permutations. We show here how our approach to probabilistic program analysis can be used to analyse the QuickSort algorithm. Our aim is not to provide a new complexity theoretic analysis of this algorithm but to illustrate how PAI can be used to gain some understanding of the average running time of QuickSort. In order to do this we consider the following simple recursive pseudo-code for QuickSort:

```
QuickSort (list,left,right)
  if (left<right) then pivot := Partition(list,left,right);
  Quicksort(list,left,pivot-1); Quicksort(list,pivot+1,right)
```

For the purposes of the analysis we concentrate on the partitioning step. Clearly, the number of calls to `Partition` determines the overall running time of `QuickSort`. To simplify the discussion we analyse the behaviour of a function `Split` which takes as input a list and splits it in two parts based on a given element p of the list (the pivot). In our implementation we take as pivot always the first element in the list. The effect of the splitting is a partition of the original list into a list of elements strictly smaller than p and a list of elements strictly larger than p. Function `Split` always returns the longest of the two lists.

We define the concrete semantics of `Split` via the corresponding transition matrix $\mathbf{T}$ on $\mathcal{V}(\bigcup_{j=1}^{n} S_j)$ where $S_j = \{\pi_i\}_{i=1}^{j!}$ is the set of all permutations of $\{1, 2, \ldots, j\}$ enumerated in some way. We denote by π_i^j the i-th permutation of length j. We observe that `Split` can produce (as longer list) either a list π which is a permutation of all elements smaller than the pivot p – i.e. an element in S_{p-1} – or a permutation of all elements larger than p, which we can also identify with an element in S_{n-p} by dropping p from all elements in π; we denote the resulting (maybe p 'shifted') list by $\lfloor \pi \rfloor$.

Let us denote by $n!! = \sum_{i=1}^{n} i!$. Given the enumeration of elements in any S_i, we enumerate the $n!!$ permutations in $\bigcup_{i=1}^{n} S_i$ by $\iota(\pi_i^k) = (k-1)!! + i$ for $\pi_i^k \in S_k$, where we set $\iota(\pi_1^1) = 1$ for the single permutation in S_1. `Split` can now be implemented as the reduction which takes a permutation $\pi_i^k \in S_k$ to a permutation π_j^l in S_l (with $l < n$). Formally, we define this reduction via an operator on $\mathbb{R}^{n!!} = \mathcal{V}(\{\bigcup_{i=1}^{n} S_i\})$ represented by an $n!! \times n!!$ matrix with entries (in row i and column j): $(\mathbf{P}(\pi))_{i,j} = 1$ if $\pi' = \lfloor \mathtt{Split}(\pi) \rfloor$ with $i = \iota(\pi)$ and $j = \iota(\pi')$, and 0 otherwise. The operator $\mathbf{T}$, which encodes all reduction steps for lists of at most n elements under `Split`, is the linear operator $\mathbf{T} : \mathbb{R}^{n!!} \to \mathbb{R}^{n!!}$

$$\mathbf{T} = \sum_{k=2}^{n} \sum_{i=1}^{k!} \mathbf{P}(\pi_i^k) + \mathbf{E}_{1,1},$$

where the second term expresses looping on terminal states, i.e. the states where the list is reduced to a singleton, in order to stay within the framework of DTMCs. The concrete semantics of the `Split` function quickly becomes very large and difficult to understand. In order to perform our analysis we nevertheless just need to concentrate on the length of the longer list produced in the splitting process, and abstract away all the rest. This can be achieved by abstracting $\mathbf{T}$ via the operator $\mathbf{A} : \mathcal{V}(\{\bigcup_{i=1}^{n} S_n\}) \to \mathcal{V}(\{1, \ldots, n\})$ or $\mathbf{A} : \mathbb{R}^{n!!} \to \mathbb{R}^n$, represented by the $n!! \times n$ matrix with entries $(\mathbf{A})_{ij} = 1$ if $i = \iota(\pi)$ and $\pi \in S_j$, and 0 otherwise. This keeps the length and ignore the concrete permutation we get after splitting. The abstract semantics is therefore: $\mathbf{T}^{\#} = \mathbf{A}^{\dagger} \mathbf{T} \mathbf{A}$. Note that if we allow for lists of any length then $\mathbf{T}^{\#}$ is an infinite dimensional operator; its finite sections are given by restricting the space according to the maximal length of the list to which it is applied. More precisely, the n-th section of $\mathbf{T}^{\#}$ is the upper left sub-matrix of $\mathbf{T}^{\#}$ defined on $\mathbb{R}^n$. We can therefore express the average behaviour of `Split`, that is the average running time of `QuickSort`, in terms of the expectation value $\langle e_n \mathbf{T}^{\#}, e_1 \rangle$, where $e_n = (0, 0, \ldots, 0, 1) \in \mathbb{R}^n$ represents all lists of length at most n and $e_1 = (1, 0, \ldots, 0)$ is the (final) point distribution representing all singleton lists reached at the end of the splitting process.

If we define $p_{\leq l} = \langle e_n (\mathbf{T}^{\#})^l, e_1 \rangle = \langle e_n (\mathbf{T}_n^{\#})^l, e_1 \rangle$ as the probability that `Split` terminates in l steps or less, then $p_l = p_{\leq l} - p_{\leq l-1}$ is the probability that `Split` terminates in exactly l steps. The average running time for lists of length n is thus $\sum_{l=0}^{\infty} l \cdot p_l = \lim_{n \to \infty} \sum_{l=0}^{n} l \cdot p_l = \lim_{n \to \infty} \sum_{l=0}^{n} l \langle e_n (\mathbf{T}^{\#})^{l-1} (\mathbf{T}^{\#} - \mathbf{I}), e_1 \rangle..

From the numerical experiments it is easy to conjecture that a general form for the abstract operator $\mathbf{T}^{\#}$ is (verified with `octave` for $n = 1, .., 9$):

$$(\mathbf{T}^{\#})_{i,j} = \begin{cases} 1 & \text{for } i = j = 1 \\ \frac{2}{i} & \text{for } i = 2k \text{ and } k \leq j < i \text{ or for } i = 2k+1 \text{ and } k < j < i \\ \frac{1}{i} & \text{for } i = 2k+1 \text{ and } j = k \\ 0 & \text{otherwise} \end{cases}$$

Based on $\mathbf{T}^{\#}$ – more precisely its nth sections $\mathbf{T}_n^{\#}$ – we can numerically calculate the average running time (until repeated calls of `Split` terminate) for lists of length $n = 1 \ldots, 100$. It is easy to see from these figures that the average running time increases roughly logarithmically. As we have simplified the problem by considering only the longer list, the results obtained this way do, of course, only indicate the actual complexity theoretic behaviour.

5   Related Work and Conclusions

The aim of this work is to provide a mathematically sound framework for probabilistic program analysis. The two main elements for this are (i) a compositionally defined semantics, called LOS, and (ii) a way to reduce the concrete semantics in order to obtain a more manageable abstract one via PAI. The concepts of a linear operator semantics and probabilistic abstract interpretation have been used before in the setting of *finite* domains in [2,3,13] for the analysis of programs and security properties. This paper extends PAI to infinite abstract domains.

Our LOS is closely related to a number of models which are popular in, for example, performance analysis, like Stochastic Automata Networks (SAN) [26,27]. The idea of reducing the complexity of dynamical systems via least square approximations, which is at the core of our PAI approach, can also be found in various approaches ranging from Kalman filters, to model order reduction [28] and aggregation of Markov models [29]. However, to the best of our knowledge most of these models are finite dimensional.

While the theoretical framework of generalised inverses for finite-dimensional and bounded operators is well understood and relatively straight forward (e.g. [14,16]), it is less well developed for the infinite dimensional unbounded case (see e.g. [6]). In the area of program analysis the well-known semantics for probabilistic programs by Kozen [7] and the application of classical abstract interpretation [30] to probabilistic languages are perhaps the closest alternatives to our LOS and PAI approach. The main differences are however that (i) the LOS – in contrast to Kozen's semantics – is not only able to capture the input/output behaviour but rather, because it uses the generator of a Markov Chain, defines the details and intermediate steps of a computational process, and (ii) PAI provides closest estimates to probabilities rather than worst case bounds for them. This makes PAI a more useful alternative in all those cases where the expected outcomes of a static analysis is not a yes-or-no answer but some estimates on which to base a speculative optimisation (compiler design, tradeoffs and cost analysis, etc). Moreover, as we have shown in Sect. 4.2, PAI can be used to develop (semi)-automatic tools for average-case complexity analysis.

References

1. Di Pierro, A., Wiklicky, H.: Concurrent constraint programming: towards probabilistic abstract interpretation. In: PPDP'00, 127–138. ACM (2000)
2. Di Pierro, A., Hankin, C., Wiklicky, H.: A systematic approach to probabilistic pointer analysis. In: Shao, Z. (ed.) APLAS 2007. LNCS, vol. 4807, pp. 335–350. Springer, Heidelberg (2007)
3. Di Pierro, A., Sotin, P., Wiklicky, H.: Relational analysis and precision via probabilistic abstract interpretation. In: QAPL'08. Volume 220(3) of ENTCS., pp. 23–42. Elsevier (2008)
4. Cousot, P., Cousot, R.: Systematic design of program analysis frameworks. In: Proceedings of POPL'79, pp. 269–282 (1979)
5. Kubrusly, C.S.: The Elements of Operator Theory, 2nd edn. Birkhäuser, Boston (2011)
6. Groetsch, C.W.: Stable Approximate Evaluation of Unbounded Operators. Lecture Notes in Mathematics. Springer, Berlin (2007)
7. Kozen, D.: Semantics of probabilistic programs. J. Comput. Syst. Sci. **22**(3), 328–350 (1981)
8. Nielson, F., Nielson, H.R., Hankin, C.: Principles of Program Analysis. Springer, Heidelberg (1999)
9. Roman, S.: Advanced Linear Algebra, 2nd edn. Springer, New York (2005)
10. Kadison, R., Ringrose, J.: Fundamentals of the Theory of Operator Algebras: Elementary Theory. AMS (1997) reprint from Academic Press edition (1983)
11. Di Pierro, A., Wiklicky, H.: Semantics of probabilistic programs: a weak limit approach. In: Shan, C. (ed.) APLAS 2013. LNCS, vol. 8301, pp. 241–256. Springer, Heidelberg (2013)
12. Di Pierro, A., Wiklicky, H.: Measuring the precision of abstract interpretations. In: Lau, K.-K. (ed.) LOPSTR 2000. LNCS, vol. 2042, pp. 147–164. Springer, Heidelberg (2001)
13. Di Pierro, A., Hankin, C., Wiklicky, H.: Measuring the confinement of probabilistic systems. Theor. Comput. Sci. **340**(1), 3–56 (2005)
14. Ben-Israel, A., Greville, T.N.E.: Gereralized Inverses - Theory and Applications. CMS Books in Mathematics, 2nd edn. Springer, New York (2003)
15. Böttcher, A., Silbermann, B.: Introduction to Large Truncated Toeplitz Matrices. Springer, New York (1999)
16. Deutsch, F.: Best Approximation in Inner-Product Spaces. Springer, New York (2001)
17. Pinkus, A.M.: On L^1-Approximation. Cambridge University Press, London (1989)
18. Di Pierro, A., Wiklicky, H.: Probabilistic data flow analysis: a linear equational approach. In: Proceedings of GandALF'13. Volume 119 of EPTCS, pp. 150–165 (2013)
19. Fabian, M., Habala, P., Hájek, P., Montesinos, V., Zizler, V.: Banach Space Theory - The Basis for Linear and Nonlinear Analysis. Springer, New York (2011)
20. Atkinson, K., Han, W.: Theoretical Numerical Analysis - A Functional Analysis Framework, 3rd edn. Springer, New York (2009)
21. Nailin, D.: Finite-dimensional approximation settings for infinite-dimensional Moore-Penrose inverses. SIAM J. of Numer. Anal. **46**(3), 1454–1482 (2008)
22. Kulkarni, S., Ramesh, G.: Projection methods for computing Moore-Penrose inverses of unbounded operators. Indian J. Pure Appl. Math. **41**(5), 647–662 (2010)

23. Groetsch, C.: Spectral methods for linear inverse problems with unbounded operators. J. Approx. Theory **70**, 16–28 (1992)
24. Groetsch, C.: Dykstra's algorithm and a representation of the Moore-Penrose inverse. J. Approx. Theory **117**, 179–184 (2002)
25. Groetsch, C.: An iterative stabilization method for the evaluation of unbounded operators. Proc. AMS **134**, 1173–1181 (2005)
26. Plateau, B., Atif, K.: Stochastic automata network of modeling parallel systems. IEEE Trans. Softw. Eng. **17**(10), 1093–1108 (1991)
27. Fourneau, J.M., Plateau, B., Stewart, W.: Product form for stochastic automata networks. In: Proceedings of ValueTools '07, ICST, pp. 32:1–32:10 (2007)
28. Gugercin, S., Antoulas, A.: Model reduction of large-scale systems by least squares. Linear Algebra Appl. **415**, 290–321 (2006)
29. Buchholz, P., Kriege, J.: Aggregation of markovian models - an alternating least squares approach. In: QEST, pp. 43–52 (2012)
30. Cousot, P., Monerau, M.: Probabilistic abstract interpretation. In: Seidl, H. (ed.) ESOP 2012. LNCS, vol. 7211, pp. 169–193. Springer, Heidelberg (2012)

Predicative Lexicographic Path Orders
An Application of Term Rewriting to the Region of Primitive Recursive Functions

Naohi Eguchi[(✉)]

Institute of Computer Science, University of Innsbruck,
Technikerstrasse 21a, 6020 Innsbruck, Austria
naohi.eguchi@uibk.ac.at

Abstract. In this paper we present a novel termination order the *predicative lexicographic path order* (PLPO for short), a syntactic restriction of the lexicographic path order. As well as lexicographic path orders, several non-trivial primitive recursive equations, e.g., primitive recursion with parameter substitution, unnested multiple recursion, or simple nested recursion, can be oriented with PLPOs. It can be shown that the PLPO however only induces primitive recursive upper bounds on derivation lengths of compatible rewrite systems. This yields an alternative proof of a classical fact that the class of primitive recursive functions is closed under those non-trivial primitive recursive equations.

1 Introduction

As observed by E.A. Cichon and A. Weiermann [2], in order to assess the *time resources* required to compute a function, one can discuss lengths of rewriting sequences, which is known as *derivation lengths*, in a term rewrite system defining the function. More precisely, if the maximal derivation length of a given rewrite system $\mathcal{R}$ is bounded by a function in a class $\mathcal{F}$, then the function defined by $\mathcal{R}$ is elementary recursive in $\mathcal{F}$. In [3], M. Avanzini and G. Moser have sharpened this connection showing that "elementary recursive in" can be replaced with "polynomial time in" if one only considers innermost rewriting sequences starting with terms whose arguments are already normalised. Based on the clear connection between time complexity of functions and derivation lengths of term rewrite systems, *complexity analysis by term rewriting* has been developed, e.g. [4–6], also providing machine-independent logical characterisations of complexity classes related to polynomial-time computable functions.

In most known cases, those term-rewriting characterisations are more flexible than purely recursion-theoretic characterisations, and thus non-trivial closure

This is the full version of the extended abstract [1] that appeared in the proceedings of the 13th International Workshop on Termination (WST 2013). This work is generously supported by Grant-in-Aid for JSPS Fellows (Grant No. 25 · 726) and partially by the Austrian Science Fund (Project No. P25781). The JSPS fellowship is granted at Graduate School of Science, Chiba University, Japan.

© Springer International Publishing Switzerland 2014
U. Dal Lago and R. Peña (Eds.): FOPARA 2013, LNCS 8552, pp. 77–92, 2014.
DOI: 10.1007/978-3-319-12466-7_5

conditions might be deduced. In this paper we present an application of rewriting techniques to some closure conditions for primitive recursive functions. It is known that the class of primitive recursive functions is closed under a recursion schema that is not an instance of primitive recursion, e.g., primitive recursion with parameter substitution (**PRP**), unnested multiple recursion (**UMR**), or simple nested recursion (**SNR**):

$$\textbf{(PRP)} \qquad f(x+1, y) = h(x, y, f(x, p(x, y)))$$
$$\textbf{(UMR)} \ f(x+1, y+1) = h(x, y, f(x, p(x, y)), f(x+1, y))$$
$$\textbf{(SNR)} \qquad f(x+1, y) = h(x, y, f(x, p(x, y, f(x, y))))$$

In the equation of (**PRP**), in contrast to a standard equation of primitive recursion $f(x+1, y) = h(x, y, f(x, y))$, the second argument of $f(x, y)$ can be parameterised with another function p, in (**UMR**) recursive calls on multiple arguments are allowed but nested forms of recursion are forbidden, and in (**SNR**) nested recursion is allowed but substitution of recursion terms for recursion arguments is forbidden in contrast to the general form of nested recursion. Note that any of (**PRP**), (**UMR**) and (**SNR**) is an instance of (nested) multiple recursion. The proofs of these facts are traced back to R. Péter's work [7], where for each of (**PRP**), (**UMR**) and (**SNR**), a tricky recursion-theoretic reduction to the standard primitive recursion was achieved.

H. Simmons [8] provided uniform proofs of Péter's results in a higher order setting. In [2], alternative proofs of Péter's results were given employing primitive recursive number-theoretic interpretations of rewrite systems corresponding to the non-trivial primitive recursive equations mentioned above. On the other side, in order to look into the distinction between primitive recursive and Péter's non-primitive recursive multiply recursive functions, it is of interest to discuss (variants of) a termination order known as the lexicographic path order (LPO for short). As shown by Weiermann [9], the LPO induces multiply recursive upper bounds on derivation lengths of compatible rewrite systems. Note that any equation of (**PRP**), (**UMR**) and (**SNR**) can be oriented with an LPO. Hence it is natural to restrict the LPO to capture these non-trivial primitive recursive equations.

Stemming from Simmons' approach in [8] but without higher-order notions. we introduce the *predicative lexicographic path order* (PLPO for short), a syntactic restriction of the LPO. As well as LPOs, (**PRP**) (**UMR**) and (**SNR**) can be oriented with PLPOs. However, in contrast to the LPO, it can be shown that the PLPO only induces primitive recursive upper bounds on derivation lengths of compatible rewrite systems (Corollary 3.9). This yields an alternative proof of the fact that the class of primitive recursive functions is closed under (**PRP**) (**UMR**) and (**SNR**) (Corollary 4.3).

1.1   Related Work

The recursion-theoretic characterisation of primitive recursive functions given in [8] is based on a restrictive (higher order primitive) recursion that is commonly known as *predicative recursion* [10] or *ramified recursion* [11]. Predicative recursion is a syntactic restriction of the standard (primitive) recursion based on a separation of argument positions into two kinds, where the number of recursive calls is measured only by an argument occurring left to semicolon whereas results of recursion are allowed to be substituted only for arguments occurring right:

$$f(0, \boldsymbol{y}; \boldsymbol{z}) = g(\boldsymbol{y}; \boldsymbol{z}) \qquad \text{(Predicative Recursion)}$$
$$f(x + 1, \boldsymbol{y}; \boldsymbol{z}) = h(x, \boldsymbol{y}; \boldsymbol{z}, f(x, \boldsymbol{y}; \boldsymbol{z}))$$

The *polynomial path order* (POP* for short) [4] is defined to be compatible with predicative recursion: $f(s(x), \boldsymbol{y}; \boldsymbol{z}) >_{\mathsf{pop}^*} h(x, \boldsymbol{y}; \boldsymbol{z}, f(x, \boldsymbol{y}; \boldsymbol{z}))$. It is worth noting that predicative recursion does not make sense with the usual composition since argument positions can be shifted from left to right. For example, given a function $f(x; y)$, the function $f'(; x, y)$ such that $f(x; y) = f'(; x, y)$ could be defined as $f'(; x, y) = f(I_1^2(; x, y); I_2^2(; x, y))$, and thus the intended argument separation would break. To maintain the constraint on the argument separation, composition is limited to a restrictive form called *predicative composition*:

$$f(\boldsymbol{x}; \boldsymbol{y}) = h(g(\boldsymbol{x};); g'(\boldsymbol{x}; \boldsymbol{y})) \qquad \text{(Predicative Composition)}$$

An auxiliary suborder $\sqsupset_{\mathsf{pop}^*}$ of the POP* $>_{\mathsf{pop}^*}$ is defined so that $f(\boldsymbol{x}; y) \sqsupset_{\mathsf{pop}^*} g_j(\boldsymbol{x};)$ holds for each $g_j \in \boldsymbol{g}$. The POP* induces the polynomial (innermost) *runtime complexity* of compatible rewrite systems. Namely, for any rewrite system $\mathcal{R}$ compatible with an instance of POP*, there exists a polynomial such that the length of any innermost $\mathcal{R}$-rewriting sequence starting with a term whose arguments are normalised can be bounded by the polynomial in the size of the starting term. Moreover, predicative recursion can be extended to (nested) multiple recursion, e.g.,

$$f(0, \boldsymbol{y}; \boldsymbol{z}) = g(\boldsymbol{y}; \boldsymbol{z}) \qquad (1)$$
$$f(x + 1, \boldsymbol{y}; \boldsymbol{z}) = h(x, \boldsymbol{y}; \boldsymbol{z}, f(x, \boldsymbol{p}(x, \boldsymbol{y};); \boldsymbol{h}'(x, \boldsymbol{y}; \boldsymbol{z}, f(x, \boldsymbol{p}'(x, \boldsymbol{y};); \boldsymbol{z})))) .$$

Essentially, the *exponential path order* (EPO* for short) [5] is defined to be compatible with predicative multiple recursion. The EPO* induces the exponential innermost runtime complexity of compatible rewrite systems. Not surprisingly, the EPO* is too weak to orient the general form of primitive recursion. In [8] the meaning of predicative recursion is relaxed (though [8] is an earlier work than [10, 11]) in such a way that recursive calls are still restrictive for (nested) multiple recursion as in the Eq. (1) but allowed even on arguments occurring right to semicolon for the standard primitive recursion, i.e.,

$$f(; 0, \boldsymbol{y}) = g(; \boldsymbol{y}) \qquad (2)$$
$$f(; x + 1, \boldsymbol{y}) = h(; x, \boldsymbol{y}, f(; x, \boldsymbol{y})).$$

Intuitively, every primitive recursive function can be used as an initial function in the underlying function algebra.

1.2 Outline

In Sect. 2 we start with defining an auxiliary suborder $\sqsupseteq_{\mathsf{plpo}}$ of the PLPO $>_{\mathsf{plpo}}$ (Definition 2.1), which is exactly the same as $\sqsupseteq_{\mathsf{pop}^*}$. The definition of $>_{\mathsf{plpo}}$ contains three important cases: (i) Case 3 of Definition 2.2 makes it possible to orient the equation of (Predicative Composition); (ii) Case 4 makes the orientation $f(; s(x), \boldsymbol{y}) >_{\mathsf{plpo}} f(; x, \boldsymbol{y})$ possible. This together with Case 3 makes it possible to orient the Eq. (2) of primitive recursion; (iii) Case 5 makes the orientation $f(s(x), \boldsymbol{y}; \boldsymbol{z}) >_{\mathsf{plpo}} f\left(x, \boldsymbol{p}(x, \boldsymbol{y};); \boldsymbol{h}'(x, \boldsymbol{y}; z, f(x, \boldsymbol{p}'(x, \boldsymbol{y};); z)))\right)$ possible as well as $f(s(x), \boldsymbol{y}; \boldsymbol{z}) >_{\mathsf{plpo}} f\left(x, \boldsymbol{p}'(x, \boldsymbol{y};); \boldsymbol{z})\right)$. This together with Case 3 makes it possible to orient the restrictive form (1) of nested recursion. Without Case 4, the PLPO only induces elementary recursive derivation lengths.

In Sect. 3 we present a primitive recursive interpretation for the PLPO. This yields that the maximal derivation length of a rewrite system compatible with a PLPO is bounded by a primitive recursive function in the size of a starting term.

In Sect. 4 we show that the complexity result about the PLPO obtained in Sect. 3 can be used to show that the class of primitive recursive functions is closed under (**PRP**), (**UMR**) and (**SNR**).

In Sect. 5 we compare the PLPO with related termination orders to make the contribution of this work clearer.

2 Predicative Lexicographic Path Orders

Let $\mathcal{V}$ denote a countably infinite set of variables. A *signature* $\mathcal{F}$ is a finite set of function symbols. The number of argument positions of a function symbol $f \in \mathcal{F}$ is denoted as $\mathsf{arity}(f)$. We write $\mathcal{T}(\mathcal{V}, \mathcal{F})$ to denote the set of terms over $\mathcal{V}$ and $\mathcal{F}$ whereas write $\mathcal{T}(\mathcal{F})$ to denote the set of closed terms over $\mathcal{F}$, or the set of *ground* terms in other words. The signature $\mathcal{F}$ can be partitioned into the set $\mathcal{C}$ of *constructors* and the set $\mathcal{D}$ of *defined* symbols. We suppose that $\mathcal{C}$ contains at least one constant. The set $\mathcal{D}$ of defined symbols includes a (possibly empty) specific subset $\mathcal{D}_{\mathsf{lex}}$, where a term will be compared lexicographically if its root symbol belongs to $\mathcal{D}_{\mathsf{lex}}$. A *precedence* $\geqslant_{\mathcal{F}}$ on the signature $\mathcal{F}$ is a quasi-order on $\mathcal{F}$ whose strict part $>_{\mathcal{F}}$ is well-founded. We write $f \approx_{\mathcal{F}} g$ if $f \geqslant_{\mathcal{F}} g$ and $g \geqslant_{\mathcal{F}} f$ hold.

In accordance with the argument separation for predicative recursion, we assume that the argument positions of every function symbol are separated into two kinds. As in the schema (Predicative Recursion), the separation is denoted by semicolon as $f(t_1, \ldots, t_k; t_{k+1}, \ldots, t_{k+l})$, where $t_1, \ldots, t_k$ are called *normal* arguments whereas $t_{k+1}, \ldots, t_{k+l}$ are called *safe* ones. The equivalence $\approx_{\mathcal{F}}$ is extended to the term equivalence $\approx$. We write $f(s_1, \ldots, s_k; s_{k+1}, \ldots, s_{k+l}) \approx g(t_1, \ldots, t_k; s_{k+1}, \ldots, t_{k+l})$ if $f \approx_{\mathcal{F}} g$ and $s_j \approx t_j$ for all $j \in \{1, \ldots, k+l\}$.

Definition 2.1. *An auxiliary relation* $s = f(s_1, \ldots, s_k; s_{k+1}, \ldots, s_{k+l}) \sqsupseteq_{\mathsf{plpo}} t$ *holds if one of the following cases holds, where* $s \sqsupseteq_{\mathsf{plpo}} t$ *denotes* $s \sqsupseteq_{\mathsf{plpo}} t$ *or* $s \approx t$.

1. $f \in \mathcal{C}$ and $s_i \sqsupseteq_{\mathsf{plpo}} t$ for some $i \in \{1, \ldots, k+l\}$.
2. $f \in \mathcal{D}$ and $s_i \sqsupseteq_{\mathsf{plpo}} t$ for some $i \in \{1, \ldots, k\}$.
3. $f \in \mathcal{D}$ and $t = g(t_1, \ldots, t_m; t_{m+1}, \ldots, t_{m+n})$ for some g such that $f >_{\mathcal{F}} g$, and $s \sqsupseteq_{\mathsf{plpo}} t_j$ for all $j \in \{1, \ldots, m+n\}$.

Now we define the *predicative lexicographic path order* (PLPO for short) denoted as $>_{\mathsf{plpo}}$. We write $s \geqslant_{\mathsf{plpo}} t$ if $s >_{\mathsf{plpo}} t$ or $s \approx t$ holds, like the relation $\sqsupseteq_{\mathsf{plpo}}$, write $(s_1, \ldots, s_k) \geqslant_{\mathsf{plpo}} (t_1, \ldots, t_k)$ if $s_j \geqslant_{\mathsf{plpo}} t_j$ for all $j \in \{1, \ldots, k\}$, and we write $(s_1, \ldots, s_k) >_{\mathsf{plpo}} (t_1, \ldots, t_k)$ if $(s_1, \ldots, s_k) \geqslant_{\mathsf{plpo}} (t_1, \ldots, t_k)$ and additionally $s_i >_{\mathsf{plpo}} t_i$ holds for some $i \in \{1, \ldots, k\}$.

Definition 2.2. *The relation* $s = f(s_1, \ldots, s_k; s_{k+1}, \ldots, s_{k+l}) >_{\mathsf{plpo}} t$ *holds if one of the following cases holds.*

1. $s \sqsupseteq_{\mathsf{plpo}} t$.
2. $s_i \geqslant_{\mathsf{plpo}} t$ for some $i \in \{1, \ldots, k+l\}$.
3. $f \in \mathcal{D}$ and $t = g(t_1, \ldots, t_m; t_{m+1}, \ldots, t_{m+n})$ for some g such that $f >_{\mathcal{F}} g$, $s \sqsupseteq_{\mathsf{plpo}} t_j$ for all $j \in \{1, \ldots, m\}$, and $s >_{\mathsf{plpo}} t_j$ for all $j \in \{m+1, \ldots, m+n\}$.
4. $f \in \mathcal{D} \setminus \mathcal{D}_{\mathsf{lex}}$ and $t = g(t_1, \ldots, t_k; t_{k+1}, \ldots, t_{k+l})$ for some g such that $f \approx_{\mathcal{F}} g$,
   - $(s_1, \ldots, s_k) \geqslant_{\mathsf{plpo}} (t_1, \ldots, t_k)$, and
   - $(s_{k+1}, \ldots, s_{k+l}) >_{\mathsf{plpo}} (t_{k+1}, \ldots, t_{k+l})$.
5. $f \in \mathcal{D}_{\mathsf{lex}}$ and $t = g(t_1, \ldots, t_m; t_{m+1}, \ldots, t_{m+n})$ for some g such that $f \approx_{\mathcal{F}} g$, and there exists $i_0 \in \{1, \ldots, \min(k, m)\}$ such that
   - $s_j \approx t_j$ for all $j \in \{1, \ldots, i_0 - 1\}$,
   - $s_{i_0} >_{\mathsf{plpo}} t_{i_0}$,
   - $s \sqsupseteq_{\mathsf{plpo}} t_j$ for all $j \in \{i_0 + 1, \ldots, m\}$, and
   - $s >_{\mathsf{plpo}} t_j$ for all $j \in \{m+1, \ldots, m+n\}$.

Let $>_{\mathsf{plpo}}$ be the PLPO induced by a precedence $\geqslant_{\mathcal{F}}$. Then, by induction according to the definition of $>_{\mathsf{plpo}}$, it can be shown that $>_{\mathsf{plpo}} \subseteq >_{\mathsf{lpo}}$ holds for the lexicographic path order $>_{\mathsf{lpo}}$ induced by the same precedence $\geqslant_{\mathcal{F}}$. The converse inclusion does not hold in general.

Example 2.3. $\mathcal{R}_{\mathsf{PR}} = \left\{ \begin{array}{l} \mathsf{f}(; 0, y) \to \mathsf{g}(; y), \\ \mathsf{f}(; \mathsf{s}(; x), y) \to \mathsf{h}(; x, y, \mathsf{f}(; x, y)) \end{array} \right\}$.

The sets $\mathcal{C}$ and $\mathcal{D}$ are defined by $\mathcal{C} = \{0, \mathsf{s}\}$ and $\mathcal{D} = \{\mathsf{g}, \mathsf{h}, \mathsf{f}\}$. Let $\mathcal{D}_{\mathsf{lex}} = \emptyset$. Define a precedence $\geqslant_{\mathcal{F}}$ by $\mathsf{f} \approx_{\mathcal{F}} \mathsf{f}$ and $\mathsf{f} >_{\mathcal{F}} \mathsf{g}, \mathsf{h}$. Define an argument separation as indicated in the rules. Then $\mathcal{R}_{\mathsf{PR}}$ can be oriented with the PLPO $>_{\mathsf{plpo}}$ induced by $\geqslant_{\mathcal{F}}$ as follows. For the first rule $\mathsf{f}(; 0, y) >_{\mathsf{plpo}} y$ and hence $\mathsf{f}(; 0, y) >_{\mathsf{plpo}} \mathsf{g}(; y)$ by Case 3 in Definition 2.2. Consider the second rule. Since $(\mathsf{s}(; x), y) >_{\mathsf{plpo}} (x, y)$, $\mathsf{f}(; \mathsf{s}(; x), y) >_{\mathsf{plpo}} \mathsf{f}(; x, y)$ holds as an instance of Case 4. An application of Case 3 allows us to conclude $\mathsf{f}(; \mathsf{s}(; x), y) >_{\mathsf{plpo}} \mathsf{h}(; x, y, \mathsf{f}(; x, y))$.

Example 2.4. $\mathcal{R}_{\mathsf{PRP}} = \left\{ \begin{array}{l} \mathsf{f}(0; y) \to \mathsf{g}(; y), \\ \mathsf{f}(\mathsf{s}(; x); y) \to \mathsf{h}(x; y, \mathsf{f}(x; \mathsf{p}(x; y))) \end{array} \right\}$.

The sets $\mathcal{C}$ and $\mathcal{D}$ are defined as in the previous example. Define the set $\mathcal{D}_{\mathsf{lex}}$ by $\mathcal{D}_{\mathsf{lex}} = \{\mathsf{f}\}$. Define a precedence $\geqslant_{\mathcal{F}}$ by $\mathsf{f} \approx_{\mathcal{F}} \mathsf{f}$ and $\mathsf{f} >_{\mathcal{F}} \mathsf{q}$ for all $\mathsf{q} \in \{\mathsf{g}, \mathsf{q}, \mathsf{h}\}$.

Define an argument separation as indicated. Then $\mathcal{R}_{\mathsf{PRP}}$ can be oriented with the induced PLPO $>_{\mathsf{plpo}}$. We only consider the most interesting case. Namely we orient the second rule. Since $\mathsf{s}(;x) \sqsupseteq_{\mathsf{plpo}} x$, $\mathsf{f}(\mathsf{s}(;x);y) \sqsupseteq_{\mathsf{plpo}} x$ holds by the definition of $\sqsupseteq_{\mathsf{plpo}}$. This together with Case 3 yields $\mathsf{f}(\mathsf{s}(;x);y) >_{\mathsf{plpo}} \mathsf{p}(x;y)$. Hence an application of Case 5 yields $\mathsf{f}(\mathsf{s}(;x);y) >_{\mathsf{plpo}} \mathsf{f}(x;\mathsf{p}(x;y))$. Another application of Case 3 allows us to conclude $\mathsf{f}(\mathsf{s}(;x);y) >_{\mathsf{plpo}} \mathsf{h}(x;y,\mathsf{f}(x;\mathsf{p}(x;y)))$.

Example 2.5. $\mathcal{R}_{\mathsf{UMR}} = \left\{ \begin{array}{c} \mathsf{f}(0,y;) \to \mathsf{g}_0(y;), \\ \mathsf{f}(\mathsf{s}(;x),0;) \to \mathsf{g}_1(x;\mathsf{f}(x,\mathsf{q}(x;);)), \\ \mathsf{f}(\mathsf{s}(;x),\mathsf{s}(;y);) \to \mathsf{h}(x,y;\mathsf{f}(x,\mathsf{p}(x,y;);),\mathsf{f}(\mathsf{s}(;x),y;)) \end{array} \right\}.$

The sets $\mathcal{C}$ and $\mathcal{D}$ are defined as in the former two examples and the set $\mathcal{D}_{\mathsf{lex}}$ is defined as in the previous example. Define a precedence $\geqslant_{\mathcal{F}}$ by $\mathsf{f} \approx_{\mathcal{F}} \mathsf{f}$ and $\mathsf{f} >_{\mathcal{F}} \mathsf{g}$ for all $\mathsf{g} \in \{\mathsf{g}_0,\mathsf{g}_1,\mathsf{p},\mathsf{q},\mathsf{h}\}$. Define an argument separation as indicated. Then $\mathcal{R}_{\mathsf{UMR}}$ can be oriented with the induced PLPO $>_{\mathsf{plpo}}$. Let us consider the most interesting case. Namely we orient the third rule. Since $\mathsf{f} >_{\mathcal{F}} \mathsf{p}$ and $\mathsf{s}(;u) \sqsupseteq_{\mathsf{plpo}} u$ for each $u \in \{x,y\}$, $\mathsf{f}(\mathsf{s}(;x),\mathsf{s}(;y);) \sqsupseteq_{\mathsf{plpo}} \mathsf{p}(x,y;)$ holds by the definition of $\sqsupseteq_{\mathsf{plpo}}$. Hence, since $\mathsf{s}(;x) >_{\mathsf{plpo}} x$, an application of Case 5 in Definition 2.2 yields $\mathsf{f}(\mathsf{s}(;x),\mathsf{s}(;x);) >_{\mathsf{plpo}} \mathsf{f}(x,\mathsf{p}(x,y;);)$. Similarly another application of Case 5 yields $\mathsf{f}(\mathsf{s}(;x),\mathsf{s}(;y);) >_{\mathsf{plpo}} \mathsf{f}(\mathsf{s}(;x),y;)$. Clearly $\mathsf{f}(\mathsf{s}(;x),\mathsf{s}(;y);) \sqsupseteq_{\mathsf{plpo}} u$ for each $u \in \{x,y\}$. Hence an application of Case 3 allows us to conclude $\mathsf{f}(\mathsf{s}(;x),\mathsf{s}(;y);) >_{\mathsf{plpo}} \mathsf{h}(x,y;\mathsf{f}(x,\mathsf{p}(x,y;);),\mathsf{f}(\mathsf{s}(;x),y;))$.

Example 2.6. $\mathcal{R}_{\mathsf{SNR}} = \left\{ \begin{array}{c} \mathsf{f}(0;y) \to \mathsf{g}(;y), \\ \mathsf{f}(\mathsf{s}(;x);y) \to \mathsf{h}(x;y,\mathsf{f}(x;\mathsf{p}(x;y,\mathsf{f}(x;y)))) \end{array} \right\}.$

The sets $\mathcal{C}$ and $\mathcal{D}$ are defined as in the former three examples and the set $\mathcal{D}_{\mathsf{lex}}$ is defined as in the former two examples. Define a precedence $\geqslant_{\mathcal{F}}$ as in the previous example. Define an argument separation as indicated. Then $\mathcal{R}_{\mathsf{SNR}}$ can be oriented with the induced PLPO $>_{\mathsf{plpo}}$. We only orient the second rule. As we observed in the previous example, $\mathsf{f}(\mathsf{s}(;x);y) >_{\mathsf{plpo}} \mathsf{f}(x;y)$ holds by Case 5. Hence $\mathsf{f}(\mathsf{s}(;x);y) >_{\mathsf{plpo}} \mathsf{p}(x;y,\mathsf{f}(x;y))$ holds by Case 3. This together with Case 5 yields $\mathsf{f}(\mathsf{s}(;x);y) >_{\mathsf{plpo}} \mathsf{f}(x;\mathsf{p}(x;y,\mathsf{f}(x;y)))$. Thus another application of Case 3 allows us to conclude $\mathsf{f}(\mathsf{s}(;x);y) >_{\mathsf{plpo}} \mathsf{h}(x;y,\mathsf{f}(x;\mathsf{p}(x;y,\mathsf{f}(x;y))))$.

Careful readers may observe that the general form of nested recursion, e.g., the defining equations for the Ackermann function, cannot be oriented with any PLPO.

3   Primitive Recursive Upper Bounds for Predicative Lexicographic Path Orders

In this section we present a primitive recursive interpretation for the PLPO. This yields that the maximal derivation length of a rewrite system compatible with a PLPO is bounded by a primitive recursive function in the size of a starting term.

Definition 3.1. *Let ℓ be a natural such that $2 \leq \ell$. Then we define a restriction $\sqsupset^{\ell}_{\mathsf{plpo}}$ of $\sqsupset_{\mathsf{plpo}}$. The relation $s = f(s_1, \ldots, s_k; s_{k+1}, \ldots, s_{k+l}) \sqsupset^{\ell}_{\mathsf{plpo}} t$ holds if one of the following cases holds, where $s \sqsupseteq^{\ell}_{\mathsf{plpo}} t$ denotes $s \sqsupset^{\ell}_{\mathsf{plpo}} t$ or $s \approx t$.*

1. *$f \in \mathcal{C}$ and $s_i \sqsupseteq^{\ell}_{\mathsf{plpo}} t$ for some $i \in \{1, \ldots, k+l\}$.*
2. *$f \in \mathcal{D}$ and $s_i \sqsupseteq^{\ell}_{\mathsf{plpo}} t$ for some $i \in \{1, \ldots, k\}$.*
3. *$f \in \mathcal{D}$ and $t = g(t_1, \ldots, t_m; t_{m+1}, \ldots, t_{m+n})$ for some g such that $f >_{\mathcal{F}} g$, and $s \sqsupset^{\ell-1}_{\mathsf{plpo}} t_j$ for all $j \in \{1, \ldots, m+n\}$.*

We write $>^{\ell}_{\mathsf{plpo}}$ to denote the PLPO induced by $\sqsupset^{\ell}_{\mathsf{plpo}}$. The *size* of a term t, which is the number of nodes in the standard tree representation of t, is denoted as $|t|$. Note that for any two terms $s, t \in \mathcal{T}(\mathcal{F}, \mathcal{V})$, if $s \approx t$, then $|s| = |t|$ holds. Following [2, p. 214], we define a primitive recursive function F_m ($m \in \mathbb{N}$).

Definition 3.2. *Given a natural $d \geq 2$, the function F_m is defined by $F_0(x) = d^{x+1}$ and $F_{m+1}(x) = F_m^{d(1+x)}(x)$, where F_m^d denotes the d-fold iteration of F_m.*

For basic properties of the function F_m, we kindly refer readers to [2, Lemma 5.4, p. 216]. Note in particular that F_m is strictly increasing and hence $F_m(x) + y \leq F_m(x+y)$ holds for any x and y.

Definition 3.3. *Given a natural $k \geq 1$, we inductively define a primitive recursive function $F_{m,n} : \mathbb{N}^k \to \mathbb{N}$ by*

$$F_{m,0}(x_1, \ldots, x_k) = 0,$$

$$F_{m,n+1}(x_1, \ldots, x_k) = \begin{cases} F_m^{F_{m,n}(x_1,\ldots,x_k)+d(1+x_{n+1})} \left(\sum_{j=1}^k x_j \right) & \text{if } n < k, \\ F_m^{F_{m,n}(x_1,\ldots,x_k)+d} \left(\sum_{j=1}^k x_j \right) & \text{if } k \leq n. \end{cases}$$

Lemma 3.4. *For any $n \geq 1$, $F_{m,n}(x_1, \ldots, x_k) \leq F_{m+1}^n \left(\sum_{j=1}^k x_j \right)$ holds.*

Proof. By induction on $n \geq 1$. In the base case, we reason as $F_{m,1}(x_1, \ldots, x_k) = F_m^{d(1+x_1)} \left(\sum_{j=1}^k x_j \right) \leq F_m^{d\left(1+\sum_{j=1}^k x_j\right)} \left(\sum_{j=1}^k x_j \right) = F_{m+1} \left(\sum_{j=1}^k x_j \right)$. For the first induction step, suppose $n < k$. Then

$$\begin{aligned} &F_{m,n+1}(x_1, \ldots, x_k) \\ &= F_m^{F_{m,n}(x_1,\ldots,x_k)+d(1+x_{n+1})} \left(\sum_{j=1}^k x_j \right) \\ &\leq F_m^{F_{m+1}^n\left(\sum_{j=1}^k x_j\right)+d(1+x_{n+1})} \left(\sum_{j=1}^k x_j \right) \quad \text{(by induction hypothesis)} \\ &\leq F_m^{d\left(1+F_{m+1}^n\left(\sum_{j=1}^k x_j\right)\right)} \left(F_{m+1}^n \left(\sum_{j=1}^k x_j \right) \right) = F_{m+1}^{n+1} \left(\sum_{j=1}^k x_j \right). \end{aligned}$$

The last inequality holds since $dx_{n+1} \leq (d-1) \cdot F_{m+1}^n \left(\sum_{j=1}^k x_j \right)$ holds. The case that $k \leq n$ can be shown in the same way.

Definition 3.5. *Let* $2 \leq \ell$, $\mathcal{F}$ *be a signature and let* $\geqslant_\mathcal{F}$ *be a precedence on* $\mathcal{F}$. *The rank* $\mathsf{rk} : \mathcal{F} \to \mathbb{N}$ *is defined in accordance with* $\geqslant_\mathcal{F}$, *i.e.,* $\mathsf{rk}(f) \geq \mathsf{rk}(g) \Leftrightarrow f \geqslant_\mathcal{F} g$. *Let* $K := \max\{k \in \mathbb{N} \mid f \in \mathcal{F}$ *and* f *has* k *normal argument positions*\}. *Then a (monotone) primitive recursive interpretation* $\mathcal{I} : \mathcal{T}(\mathcal{F}) \to \mathbb{N}$ *is defined by*

$$\mathcal{I}(t) = d^{F_{\mathsf{rk}(f)+\ell, K+1}(\mathcal{I}(t_1),\dots,\mathcal{I}(t_k))+d} \cdot \left(\sum_{j=1}^{l} \mathcal{I}(t_{k+j}) + 1 \right),$$

where $t = f(t_1,\dots,t_k; t_{k+1},\dots,t_{k+l}) \in \mathcal{T}(\mathcal{F})$. *We write* $\mathcal{J}_n(t)$ *to abbreviate* $F_{\mathsf{rk}(f)+\ell,n}(\mathcal{I}(t_1),\dots,\mathcal{I}(t_k))$, *i.e.,* $\mathcal{I}(t) = d^{\mathcal{J}_{K+1}(t)+d} \cdot \left(\sum_{j=1}^{l} \mathcal{I}(t_{k+j}) + 1 \right)$ *holds.*

Given a function symbol $f \in \mathcal{F}$ with k normal argument positions, since $k \leq K$ holds by the definition of the constant K, $\mathcal{J}_{K+1}(t) = F_{\mathsf{rk}(f)+\ell}^{\mathcal{J}_K(t)+d} \left(\sum_{j=1}^{k} \mathcal{I}(t_j) \right)$ holds. For any ground terms $s, t \in \mathcal{T}(\mathcal{F})$, it can be shown by induction on the size $|t|$ of t that if $s \approx t$, then $\mathcal{I}(s) = \mathcal{I}(t)$ holds.

Theorem 3.6. *Let* $s, t \in \mathcal{T}(\mathcal{F}, \mathcal{V})$ *and* $\sigma : \mathcal{V} \to \mathcal{T}(\mathcal{F})$ *be a ground substitution. Suppose* $\max \left(\{\mathsf{arity}(f) + 1 \mid f \in \mathcal{F}\} \cup \{\ell \cdot (K+2)+2\} \cup \{|t|+1\} \right) \leq d$. *If* $s >_{\mathsf{plpo}}^{\ell} t$, *then, for the interpretation* $\mathcal{I}$ *induced by* ℓ *and* d, $\mathcal{I}(s\sigma) > \mathcal{I}(t\sigma)$ *holds.*

Proof. Let $s, t \in \mathcal{T}(\mathcal{F}, \mathcal{V})$ and $\sigma : \mathcal{V} \to \mathcal{T}(\mathcal{F})$ be a ground substitution. As in the assumption of the theorem, choose a constant d so that $\max \left(\{\mathsf{arity}(f) + 1 \mid f \in \mathcal{F}\} \cup \{\ell \cdot (K+2)+2\} \cup \{|t|+1\} \right) \leq d$. Suppose $s >_{\mathsf{plpo}}^{\ell} t$. Then we show that $\mathcal{I}(s\sigma) > \mathcal{I}(t\sigma)$ holds by induction according to the definition of $s >_{\mathsf{plpo}}^{\ell} t$. Let $s = f(s_1,\dots,s_k; s_{k+1},\dots,s_{k+l})$.

In the base case, $s_i \approx t$ holds for some $i \in \{1,\dots,k+l\}$. In this case, $\mathcal{I}(t\sigma) = \mathcal{I}(s_i\sigma) < \mathcal{I}(s\sigma)$ holds.

The argument to show the induction step splits into several cases depending on the final rule resulting in $s >_{\mathsf{plpo}}^{\ell} t$.

CASE. $s \sqsupset_{\mathsf{plpo}}^{\ell} t$: In the subcase that $f \in \mathcal{C}$, $s_i \sqsupseteq_{\mathsf{plpo}}^{\ell} t$ for some $i \in \{1,\dots,k+l\}$, and hence $s_i \geqslant_{\mathsf{plpo}}^{\ell} t$ holds. By IH (Induction Hypothesis), $\mathcal{I}(t\sigma) \leq \mathcal{I}(s_i\sigma) < \mathcal{I}(s\sigma)$ holds. The case that $f \in \mathcal{D}$ follows from the following claim.

Claim. Suppose that $2 \leq \ell' \leq \ell$ holds. If $f \in \mathcal{D}$ and $s \sqsupset_{\mathsf{plpo}}^{\ell'} t$, then (for the interpretation $\mathcal{I}$ induced by ℓ) the following inequality holds.

$$\mathcal{I}(t\sigma) \leq F_{\mathsf{rk}(f)+\ell}^{\ell' \cdot (K+2)} \left(\sum_{j=1}^{k} \mathcal{I}(s_j\sigma) \right). \tag{3}$$

By the assumption of the theorem, $\ell' \cdot (K+2) \leq \ell \cdot (K+2) \leq d$ holds. This implies $\mathcal{I}(t\sigma) \leq F_{\mathsf{rk}(f)+\ell}^{d} \left(\sum_{j=1}^{k} \mathcal{I}(s_j\sigma) \right) < \mathcal{I}(s\sigma)$.

Proof (of Claim). By induction according to the definition of $\sqsupset_{\mathsf{plpo}}^{\ell'}$. Write $\mathcal{H}_{\ell'}(s)$ to abbreviate $F_{\mathsf{rk}(f)+\ell}^{\ell' \cdot (K+2)} \left(\sum_{j=1}^{k} \mathcal{I}(s_j\sigma) \right)$.

CASE. $s_i \sqsupseteq_{\mathsf{plpo}}^{\ell'} t$ for some $i \in \{1,\dots,k\}$: Let us observe that $s_i \sqsupseteq_{\mathsf{plpo}}^{\ell} t$ also holds. This implies $s_i \geqslant_{\mathsf{plpo}}^{\ell} t$. Hence $\mathcal{I}(t\sigma) \leq \mathcal{I}(s_i\sigma)$ holds by IH for the theorem, and thus $\mathcal{I}(t\sigma) \leq \mathcal{H}_{\ell'}(s)$ also holds.

CASE. $t = g(t_1, \ldots, t_m; t_{m+1}, \ldots, t_{m+n})$ for some $g \in \mathcal{F}$ and $t_1, \ldots, t_{m+n} \in \mathcal{T}(\mathcal{F}, \mathcal{V})$ such that $f >_{\mathcal{F}} g$ and $s \sqsupset_{\mathsf{plpo}}^{\ell'-1} t_j$ for all $j \in \{1, \ldots, m+n\}$. By IH for the claim, $\mathcal{I}(t_j\sigma) \le \mathcal{H}_{\ell'-1}(s)$ holds for all $j \in \{1, \ldots, m+n\}$. Since $m+n = \mathsf{arity}(g) \le d$ by the assumption of the theorem, $d + \sum_{j=1}^{m+n} \mathcal{I}(t_j\sigma) \le d(1 + \cdot \mathcal{H}_{\ell'-1}(s)) \le F_{\mathsf{rk}(f)+\ell}(\mathcal{H}_{\ell'-1}(s))$ holds. This implies

$$d + \sum_{j=1}^{m+n} \mathcal{I}(t_j\sigma)$$
$$\le F_{\mathsf{rk}(f)+\ell}^{(\ell'-1)\cdot(K+2)+1}\left(\sum_{j=1}^{k}\mathcal{I}(s_j\sigma)\right) = F_{\mathsf{rk}(f)+\ell}^{\ell'\cdot(K+2)-K-1}\left(\sum_{j=1}^{k}\mathcal{I}(s_j\sigma)\right). \quad (4)$$

On the other side, since $\mathsf{rk}(g) < \mathsf{rk}(f)$ by the definition of the rank rk, we can find a natural p such that $\mathsf{rk}(g) + \ell \le p < \mathsf{rk}(f) + \ell$. Hence it holds that $\mathcal{I}(t\sigma) = d^{\mathcal{J}_{K+1}(t\sigma)+d} \cdot \left(\sum_{j=1}^{n}\mathcal{I}(t_{m+j}\sigma) + 1\right) \le d^{\mathcal{J}_{K+1}(t\sigma)+d+\sum_{j=1}^{n}\mathcal{I}(t_{m+j}\sigma)+1} \le F_p\left(\mathcal{J}_{K+1}(t\sigma) + d + \sum_{j=1}^{n}\mathcal{I}(t_{m+j}\sigma)\right)$. Thus, to conclude the claim, it suffices to show that $F_p\left(\mathcal{J}_{K+1}(t\sigma) + d + \sum_{j=1}^{n}\mathcal{I}(t_{m+j}\sigma)\right) \le \mathcal{H}_{\ell'}(s)$ holds. To show this inequality, we reason as follows.

$$F_p\left(\mathcal{J}_{K+1}(t\sigma) + d + \sum_{j=1}^{n}\mathcal{I}(t_{m+j}\sigma)\right)$$
$$\le F_p\left(F_p^{\mathcal{J}_K(t\sigma)+d}\left(\sum_{j=1}^{m}\mathcal{I}(t_j\sigma)\right) + d + \sum_{j=1}^{n}\mathcal{I}(t_{m+j}\sigma)\right)$$
$$\le F_p^{1+\mathcal{J}_K(t\sigma)+d}\left(d + \sum_{j=1}^{m+n}\mathcal{I}(t_j\sigma)\right) \quad \text{(by strict increasingness of } F_p)$$
$$\le F_p^{1+F_{p+1}^{K}\left(\sum_{j=1}^{m}\mathcal{I}(t_j\sigma)\right)+d}\left(d + \sum_{j=1}^{m+n}\mathcal{I}(t_j\sigma)\right) \quad \text{(by Lemma 3.4)}$$
$$\le F_p^{1+F_{p+1}^{K}\left(d+\sum_{j=1}^{m}\mathcal{I}(t_j\sigma)\right)}\left(d + \sum_{j=1}^{m+n}\mathcal{I}(t_j\sigma)\right)$$
$$\le F_p^{1+F_{p+1}^{K}\left(F_{p+1}^{\ell'\cdot(K+2)-K-1}\left(\sum_{j=1}^{k}\mathcal{I}(s_j\sigma)\right)\right)}\left(F_{p+1}^{\ell'\cdot(K+2)-K-1}\left(\sum_{j=1}^{k}\mathcal{I}(s_j\sigma)\right)\right)$$
$$\le F_p^{1+F_{p+1}^{\ell'\cdot(K+2)-1}\left(\sum_{j=1}^{k}\mathcal{I}(s_j\sigma)\right)}\left(F_{p+1}^{\ell'\cdot(K+2)-1}\left(\sum_{j=1}^{k}\mathcal{I}(s_j\sigma)\right)\right)$$
$$\le F_{p+1}\left(F_{p+1}^{\ell'\cdot(K+2)-1}\left(\sum_{j=1}^{k}\mathcal{I}(s_j\sigma)\right)\right) = \mathcal{H}_{\ell'}(s).$$

The fifth inequality follows from the inequality (4). $\qquad\square$

CASE. $s_i >_{\mathsf{plpo}}^{\ell} t$ holds for some $i \in \{1, \ldots, k+l\}$: In this case $\mathcal{I}(t\sigma) < \mathcal{I}(s_i\sigma)$ by IH, and hence $\mathcal{I}(t\sigma) < \mathcal{I}(s\sigma)$ holds.

CASE. $f \in \mathcal{D} \setminus \mathcal{D}_{\mathsf{lex}}$ and $t = g(t_1, \ldots, t_k; t_{k+1}, \ldots, t_{k+l})$ for some g such that $f \approx_{\mathcal{F}} g$, $(s_1, \ldots, s_k) \ge_{\mathsf{plpo}}^{\ell} (t_1, \ldots, t_k)$, and $(s_{k+1}, \ldots, s_{k+l}) >_{\mathsf{plpo}}^{\ell} (t_{k+1}, \ldots, t_{k+l})$: In this case, $\mathsf{rk}(f) = \mathsf{rk}(g)$, and by IH, $\mathcal{I}(t_j\sigma) \le \mathcal{I}(s_j\sigma)$ for all $j \in \{1, \ldots, k+l\}$ and additionally $\mathcal{I}(t_i\sigma) < \mathcal{I}(s_i\sigma)$ for some $i \in \{k+1, \ldots, k+l\}$. Hence it is easy check that $\mathcal{I}(t\sigma) < \mathcal{I}(s\sigma)$ holds.

It remains to consider Case 3 and 5 of Definition 2.2.

Claim. In Case 3 and 5 of Definition 2.2, the following two inequalities hold.

$$\mathcal{J}_K(t\sigma) + d \leq \mathcal{J}_K(s\sigma). \tag{5}$$

$$\mathcal{J}_{K+1}(t\sigma) + d \leq F_{\mathsf{rk}(f)+\ell}^{\mathcal{J}_K(s\sigma)+d-1}\left(\sum_{j=1}^{k}\mathcal{I}(s_j\sigma)\right). \tag{6}$$

Proof (of Claim). We show the inequality (5) by case analysis.

CASE. $f \in \mathcal{D}$ and $t = g(t_1, \ldots, t_m; t_{m+1}, \ldots, t_{m+n})$ for some g such that $f >_{\mathcal{F}} g$, $s \sqsupseteq_{\mathsf{plpo}}^{\ell} t_j$ for all $j \in \{1, \ldots, m\}$, and $s >_{\mathsf{plpo}}^{\ell} t_j$ for all $j \in \{m+1, \ldots, m+n\}$: Since $\mathsf{rk}(g) < \mathsf{rk}(f)$, as in the proof of the previous claim, we can find a natural p such that $\mathsf{rk}(g) + \ell \leq p < \mathsf{rk}(f) + \ell$. By auxiliary induction on $j \in \{1, \ldots, m-1\}$ we show that $\mathcal{J}_j(t\sigma) + d(1 + \mathcal{I}(t_{j+1}\sigma)) \leq \mathcal{J}_j(s\sigma)$ holds. By the inequality (3) and the assumption $\ell \cdot (K+1) + 2 \leq d$, for any $j \in \{1, \ldots, m\}$, $\sum_{i=1}^{m}\mathcal{I}(t_i\sigma) + d(1 + \mathcal{I}(t_j\sigma)) \leq (K+1)F_{p+1}^{d-2}(\sum_{i=1}^{k}\mathcal{I}(s_j\sigma)) + d \leq d(1 + F_{p+1}^{d-2}(\sum_{i=1}^{k}\mathcal{I}(s_j\sigma))) \leq F_{p+1}^{d-1}(\sum_{i=1}^{k}\mathcal{I}(s_j\sigma))$. For the base case we reason as follows.

$$
\begin{aligned}
\mathcal{J}_1(t\sigma) + d(1 + \mathcal{I}(t_2\sigma)) &\leq F_p^{d(1+\mathcal{I}(t_1\sigma))}\left(\sum_{i=1}^{m}\mathcal{I}(t_i\sigma)\right) + d(1 + \mathcal{I}(t_2\sigma)) \\
&\leq F_p^{d(1+\mathcal{I}(t_1\sigma))}\left(\sum_{i=1}^{m}\mathcal{I}(t_i\sigma) + d(1 + \mathcal{I}(t_2\sigma))\right) \\
&\leq F_p^{d\left(1+F_{p+1}^{d-1}\left(\sum_{i=1}^{k}\mathcal{I}(s_j\sigma)\right)\right)}\left(F_{p+1}^{d-1}\left(\sum_{i=1}^{k}\mathcal{I}(s_j\sigma)\right)\right) \\
&= F_{p+1}^{d}\left(\sum_{i=1}^{k}\mathcal{I}(s_j\sigma)\right) \leq \mathcal{J}_1(s\sigma).
\end{aligned}
$$

The induction step can be shown accordingly. By similar induction on $j \in \{m, \ldots, K\}$ one can show that $\mathcal{J}_j(t\sigma) + d \leq \mathcal{J}_j(s\sigma)$ holds, and thus in particular, $\mathcal{J}_K(t\sigma) + d \leq \mathcal{J}_K(s\sigma)$ holds.

CASE. $f \in \mathcal{D}_{\mathsf{lex}}$ and $t = g(t_1, \ldots, t_m; t_{m+1}, \ldots, t_{m+n})$ for some $g \in \mathcal{F}$ such that $f \approx_{\mathcal{F}} g$: In this case there exists $i_0 \leq \min\{k, m\}$ such that $s_j \approx t_j$ for all $j \in \{1, \ldots, i_0 - 1\}$, $s_{i_0} >_{\mathsf{plpo}}^{\ell} t_{i_0}$, $s \sqsupseteq_{\mathsf{plpo}}^{\ell} t_j$ for all $j \in \{i_0 + 1, \ldots, m\}$, and $s >_{\mathsf{plpo}}^{\ell} t_j$ for all $j \in \{m+1, \ldots, m+n\}$. Write p to denote $\mathsf{rk}(f) + \ell$. Then $p = \mathsf{rk}(g) + \ell$ since $\mathsf{rk}(f) = \mathsf{rk}(g)$. Clearly $\mathcal{J}_j(t\sigma) = \mathcal{J}_j(s\sigma)$ for all $j < i_0$. Since $\mathcal{I}(t_{i_0}\sigma) < \mathcal{I}(s_{i_0}\sigma)$ holds by IH for the theorem, $\mathcal{J}_{i_0-1}(t\sigma) = \mathcal{J}_{i_0-1}(s\sigma)$ implies

$$\mathcal{J}_{i_0-1}(t\sigma) + d(1 + \mathcal{I}(t_{i_0}\sigma)) \leq \mathcal{J}_{i_0-1}(s\sigma) + d \cdot \mathcal{I}(s_{i_0}\sigma). \tag{7}$$

By auxiliary induction on $j \in \{i_0, \ldots, m-1\}$ we show that $\mathcal{J}_j(t\sigma) + d(1 + \mathcal{I}(t_{j+1}\sigma)) \leq \mathcal{J}_j(s\sigma)$ holds. From the inequalities (3), $\mathcal{I}(t_{i_0}\sigma) < \mathcal{I}(s_{i_0}\sigma)$ and $\ell \cdot (K+2) + 1 \leq d$, as in the previous case, for any $j \in \{1, \ldots, m\}$, one can show that $\sum_{i=1}^{m}\mathcal{I}(t_i\sigma) + d(1 + \mathcal{I}(t_j\sigma)) \leq F_p^{d}\left(\sum_{i=1}^{k}\mathcal{I}(s_i\sigma)\right)$. Assuming this inequality, for the base case we reason follows.

$$
\begin{aligned}
&\mathcal{J}_{i_0}(t\sigma) + d(1 + \mathcal{I}(t_{i_0+1}\sigma)) \\
&\leq F_p^{\mathcal{J}_{i_0-1}(t\sigma)+d(1+\mathcal{I}(t_{i_0}\sigma))}\left(\sum_{i=1}^{m}\mathcal{I}(t_i\sigma)\right) + d(1 + \mathcal{I}(t_{i_0+1}\sigma)) \\
&\leq F_p^{\mathcal{J}_{i_0-1}(s\sigma)+d\cdot\mathcal{I}(s_{i_0}\sigma)}\left(\sum_{i=1}^{m}\mathcal{I}(t_i\sigma)\right) + d(1 + \mathcal{I}(t_{i_0+1}\sigma)) \text{ (by the inequality (7))}
\end{aligned}
$$

$$\leq F_p^{\mathcal{J}_{i_0}-1(s\sigma)+d\cdot\mathcal{I}(s_{i_0}\sigma)}\left(\sum_{i=1}^m \mathcal{I}(t_i\sigma) + d(1+\mathcal{I}(t_{i_0+1}\sigma))\right)$$

$$\leq F_p^{\mathcal{J}_{i_0}-1(s\sigma)+d\cdot\mathcal{I}(s_{i_0}\sigma)}\left(F_p^d\left(\sum_{i=1}^k \mathcal{I}(s_i\sigma)\right)\right)$$

$$\leq F_p^{\mathcal{J}_{i_0}-1(s\sigma)+d(1+\mathcal{I}(s_{i_0}\sigma))}\left(\sum_{i=1}^k \mathcal{I}(s_i\sigma)\right) = \mathcal{J}_{i_0}(s\sigma).$$

The induction step can be shown in the same way but employing the induction hypothesis instead of (7). A similar induction on $j \in \{m,\ldots,K\}$ allows one to deduce $\mathcal{J}_j(t\sigma) + d \leq \mathcal{J}_j(s\sigma)$. Thus, in particular, $\mathcal{J}_K(t\sigma) + d \leq \mathcal{J}_K(s\sigma)$ holds.

Let $t = g(t_1,\ldots,t_m;t_{m+1},\ldots,t_{m+n})$ and $p = \mathsf{rk}(f) + \ell$. Then the inequality (6) is shown employing the inequality (5) as follows.

$$\mathcal{J}_{K+1}(t\sigma) + d$$
$$\leq F_p^{\mathcal{J}_K(t\sigma)+d}\left(\sum_{j=1}^m \mathcal{I}(t_j\sigma)\right) + d$$
$$\leq F_p^{\mathcal{J}_K(s\sigma)}\left(\sum_{j=1}^m \mathcal{I}(t_j\sigma)\right) + d \qquad \text{(by the inequality (5))}$$
$$\leq F_p^{\mathcal{J}_K(s\sigma)}\left(\sum_{j=1}^m \mathcal{I}(t_j\sigma) + d\right)$$
$$\leq F_p^{\mathcal{J}_K(s\sigma)}\left(F_p^{d-1}\left(\sum_{j=1}^k \mathcal{I}(s_j\sigma)\right)\right) = F_p^{\mathcal{J}_K(s\sigma)+d-1}\left(\sum_{j=1}^k \mathcal{I}(s_j\sigma)\right).$$

Note that the last inequality follows from the inequality (3).   □

Let us turn back to the proof of the theorem. In the remaining two cases, instead of showing $\mathcal{I}(t\sigma) < \mathcal{I}(s\sigma)$ directly, by subsidiary induction on the size $|t|$ of the term t, we show the following inequality holds.

$$\mathcal{I}(t\sigma) \leq d^{|t|\cdot\left(1+F_{\mathsf{rk}(f)+\ell}^{\mathcal{J}_K(s\sigma)+d-1}\left(\sum_{j=1}^k \mathcal{I}(s_j\sigma)\right)\right)} \cdot \left(\sum_{j=1}^l \mathcal{I}(s_{k+j}\sigma) + 1\right). \qquad (8)$$

Write p to denote $\mathsf{rk}(f) + \ell$. Since $|t| < d$ holds by the assumption of the theorem and $d(1 + x) \leq F_p(x)$ holds for any x, the inequality (8) allows us to conclude that $\mathcal{I}(t\sigma) < d^{F_p\left(F_p^{\mathcal{J}_K(s\sigma)+d-1}\left(\sum_{j=1}^k \mathcal{I}(s_j\sigma)\right)\right)+d} \cdot \left(\sum_{j=1}^l \mathcal{I}(s_{k+j}\sigma) + 1\right) = \mathcal{I}(s\sigma)$. Case 3 and 5 of Definition 2.2 can be reduced to the following case.

CASE. $t = g(t_1,\ldots,t_m;t_{m+1},\ldots,t_{m+n})$ for some $g \in \mathcal{D}$ and $t_1,\ldots,t_{m+n} \in \mathcal{T}(\mathcal{F},\mathcal{V})$ such that $s >_{\mathsf{plpo}}^\ell t_j$ holds for all $j \in \{m+1,\ldots,m+n\}$: Since $|t_{m+j}| \leq |t| - 1$, subsidiary induction hypothesis together with the assumption that $\max\{\mathsf{arity}(f) + 1 \mid f \in \mathcal{F}\} \leq d$ yields

$$\sum_{j=1}^n \mathcal{I}(t_{m+j}\sigma) + 1$$
$$\leq d \cdot d^{(|t|-1)\cdot\left(1+F_p^{\mathcal{J}_K(s\sigma)+d-1}\left(\sum_{i=1}^k \mathcal{I}(s_i\sigma)\right)\right)} \cdot \left(\sum_{i=1}^l \mathcal{I}(s_{k+i}\sigma) + 1\right)$$
$$= d^{(|t|-1)\cdot F_p^{\mathcal{J}_K(s\sigma)+d-1}\left(\sum_{i=1}^k \mathcal{I}(s_i\sigma)\right)+|t|} \cdot \left(\sum_{i=1}^l \mathcal{I}(s_{k+i}\sigma) + 1\right). \qquad (9)$$

This enables us to reason as follows.

$$\mathcal{I}(t\sigma) = d^{J_{K+1}(t\sigma)+d} \cdot \left(\sum_{j=1}^{n} \mathcal{I}(t_{m+j}\sigma) + 1 \right)$$

$$\leq d^{F_p^{J_K(s\sigma)+d-1}(\sum_{j=1}^{k} \mathcal{I}(s_j\sigma))} \cdot \left(\sum_{j=1}^{n} \mathcal{I}(t_{m+j}\sigma) + 1 \right) \quad \text{(by the inequality (6))}$$

$$\leq d^{F_p^{J_K(s\sigma)+d-1}(\sum_{j=1}^{k} \mathcal{I}(s_j\sigma))} \cdot$$
$$d^{(|t|-1)F_p^{J_K(s\sigma)+d-1}(\sum_{j=1}^{k} \mathcal{I}(s_j\sigma))+|t|} \cdot \left(\sum_{j=1}^{l} \mathcal{I}(s_{k+j}\sigma) + 1 \right) \quad \text{(by (9))}$$

$$= d^{|t| \cdot \left(1 + F_p^{J_K(s\sigma)+d-1}(\sum_{j=1}^{k} \mathcal{I}(s_j\sigma)) \right)} \cdot \left(\sum_{j=1}^{l} \mathcal{I}(s_{k+j}\sigma) + 1 \right).$$

This finalises the proof of the theorem   □

Lemma 3.7. *Let $s, t \in \mathcal{T}(\mathcal{F})$ be ground terms and $C(\square) \in \mathcal{T}(\mathcal{F} \cup \{\square\})$ be a (ground) context. If $\mathcal{I}(s) > \mathcal{I}(t)$, then $\mathcal{I}(C(s)) > \mathcal{I}(C(t))$ holds.*

Proof. By induction on the size $|C|$ of the given context $C \in \mathcal{T}(\mathcal{F} \cup \{\square\})$.

For a rewrite system $\mathcal{R}$, we write $\mathcal{R} \subseteq >_{\mathsf{plpo}}$ (or $\mathcal{R} \subseteq >_{\mathsf{plpo}}^{\ell}$) if $l >_{\mathsf{plpo}} r$ (or $l >_{\mathsf{plpo}}^{\ell} r$ respectively) holds for each rewriting rule $l \to r \in \mathcal{R}$.

Theorem 3.8. *Let $\mathcal{R}$ be a rewrite system over a signature $\mathcal{F}$ such that $\mathcal{R} \subseteq >_{\mathsf{plpo}}^{\ell}$ for some $\ell \geq 2$ and $s, t \in \mathcal{T}(\mathcal{F})$ be ground terms. Suppose $\max \left(\{ \mathsf{arity}(f) + 1 \mid f \in \mathcal{F} \} \cup \{ \ell \cdot (K+2) + 2 \} \cup \{ |r| + 1 \mid \exists l(l \to r \in \mathcal{R}) \} \right) \leq d$. If $s \to_{\mathcal{R}} t$, then, for the interpretation induced by ℓ and d, $\mathcal{I}(s) > \mathcal{I}(t)$ holds.*

Proof. By induction according to the rewriting relation $\to_{\mathcal{R}}$ resulting in $s \to_{\mathcal{R}} t$. The base case follows from Theorem 3.6 and the induction step follows from Lemma 3.7.

Corollary 3.9. *For any rewrite system $\mathcal{R}$, if $\mathcal{R} \subseteq >_{\mathsf{plpo}}$ holds for some PLPO $>_{\mathsf{plpo}}$, then the length of any rewriting sequence in $\mathcal{R}$ starting with a ground term is bounded by a primitive recursive function in the size of the starting term.*

Proof. Given a rewrite system $\mathcal{R}$, suppose that $\mathcal{R} \subseteq >_{\mathsf{plpo}}$ holds for some PLPO $>_{\mathsf{plpo}}$. Let $\ell \geq \max\{ |r| \mid \exists l(l \to r \in \mathcal{R}) \}$. Then it can be seen that even $\mathcal{R} \subseteq >_{\mathsf{plpo}}^{\ell}$ holds. Choose a constant d so that $\max \left(\{ \mathsf{arity}(f) + 1 \mid f \in \mathcal{F} \} \cup \{ \ell \cdot (K+2) + 2 \} \right) \leq d$. Then, for any rewriting rule $l \to r \in \mathcal{R}$, $|r| + 1 \leq \ell \cdot (K+2) + 2 \leq d$. Hence by Theorem 3.8, for any ground term t, the maximal length of rewriting sequences starting with t is bounded by $\mathcal{I}(t)$ for the interpretation $\mathcal{I}$ induced by ℓ and d. It is not difficult to observe that $\mathcal{I}(t)$ is bounded by $F(|t|)$ for a primitive recursive function F. This observation allows us to conclude.   □

4   Application to Non-trivial Closure Conditions for Primitive Recursive Functions

In this section we show that Corollary 3.9 can be used to show that the class of primitive recursive functions is closed under primitive recursion with parameter substitution (**PRP**), unnested multiple recursion (**UMR**) and simple nested recursion (**SNR**).

Lemma 4.1. *For any primitive recursive function f there exists a rewrite system $\mathcal{R}$ defining f such that $\mathcal{R} \subseteq >_{\mathsf{plpo}}$ for some PLPO $>_{\mathsf{plpo}}$, where the argument positions of every function symbol are safe ones only.*

Proof. By induction along the primitive recursive definition of f. We always assume that set $\mathcal{C}$ of constructors consists only of a constant 0 and a unary constructor s, where 0 is interpreted as the least natural 0 and s as the numerical successor function.

CASE. f is one of the initial functions: First consider the subcase that f is the k-ary constant function $(x_1, \ldots, x_k) \mapsto 0$. In this subcase f is defined by a single rule $\mathsf{o}^k(x_1, \ldots, x_k) \to 0$. Defining a precedence $\geqslant_{\mathcal{F}}$ by $\mathsf{o}^k \approx \mathsf{o}^k$ and $\mathsf{o}^k >_{\mathcal{F}} 0$, we can see that for the PLPO induced by $\geqslant_{\mathcal{F}}$, $\mathsf{o}^k(; x_1, \ldots, x_k) >_{\mathsf{plpo}} 0$ holds by Case 3 of Definition 2.2. Consider the subcase that f is a k-ary projection function $(x_1, \ldots, x_k) \mapsto x_j$ $(j \in \{1, \ldots, k\})$. In this subcase f is defined by a single rule $\mathsf{i}_j^k(x_1, \ldots, x_k) \to x_j$. An application of Case 2 of Definition 2.2 allow us to see that $\mathsf{i}_j^k(; x_1, \ldots, x_k) >_{\mathsf{plpo}} x_j$ holds.

CASE. f is defined from primitive recursive functions $\boldsymbol{g} = g_1, \ldots, g_l$ and h by composition as $f(x_1, \ldots, x_k) = h(g_1(\boldsymbol{x}), \ldots, g_l(\boldsymbol{x}))$: By IH each of the functions $\boldsymbol{g}$ and h can be defined by a rewrite system which can be oriented with a PLPO. Define a rewrite system $\mathcal{R}$ by expanding those rewrite systems obtained from IH with such a new rule as $\mathsf{f}(x_1, \ldots, x_k) \to \mathsf{h}(\mathsf{g}_1(\boldsymbol{x}), \ldots, \mathsf{g}_l(\boldsymbol{x}))$. Then the function f is defined by the rewrite system $\mathcal{R}$. Extend the precedences obtained from IH so that $\mathsf{f} \approx_{\mathcal{F}} \mathsf{f}$ and $\mathsf{f} >_{\mathcal{F}} \mathsf{g}$ for all $\mathsf{g} \in \{\mathsf{g}_1, \ldots, \mathsf{g}_l, \mathsf{h}\}$. Then, for the induced PLPO $>_{\mathsf{plpo}}$, we have that $\mathsf{f}(; \boldsymbol{x}) >_{\mathsf{plpo}} \mathsf{g}_j(; \boldsymbol{x})$ for all $j \in \{1, \ldots, l\}$ by an application of Case 3 of Definition 2.2. Hence another application of Case 3 allows us to conclude $\mathsf{f}(; x_1, \ldots, x_k) >_{\mathsf{plpo}} \mathsf{h}(; \mathsf{g}_1(; \boldsymbol{x}), \ldots, \mathsf{g}_l(; \boldsymbol{x}))$.

CASE. f is defined by primitive recursion: In this case it can be seen that the assertion holds as in Example 2.3. □

Theorem 4.2. *If a function f is defined from primitive recursive functions by an instance of* (**PRP**), (**UMR**) *or* (**SNR**), *then there exists a rewrite system $\mathcal{R}$ defining f such that $\mathcal{R} \subseteq >_{\mathsf{plpo}}$ for some PLPO $>_{\mathsf{plpo}}$.*

Proof. To exemplify the theorem, suppose that f is defined from primitive recursive functions g, p and h by (**SNR**) as $f(0, y) = g(y)$ and $f(x + 1, y) = h(x, y, f(x, p(x, y, f(x, y))))$. Let g, p and h denote function symbols corresponding respectively to the functions g, p and h. From Lemma 4.1 one can find rewrite systems defining g, p and h all of which can be oriented with some PLPO with the argument separation $\mathsf{s}(; x)$, $\mathsf{g}(; y)$, $\mathsf{p}(; x, y, z)$ and $\mathsf{h}(; x, y, z)$. We expand the signatures for g, p and h with new function symbols p', h' and f. Define a rewrite system $\mathcal{R}$ by expanding those rewrite systems for g, p and h with the following four rules.

(i) $\mathsf{p}'(x; y, z) \to \mathsf{p}(; x, y, z)$ (iii) $\mathsf{f}(0; y) \to \mathsf{g}(; y)$

(ii) $\mathsf{h}'(x; y, z) \to \mathsf{h}(; x, y, z)$ (iv) $\mathsf{f}(\mathsf{s}(; x); y) \to \mathsf{h}'(x; y, \mathsf{f}(x; \mathsf{p}'(x; y, \mathsf{f}(x; y))))$

Clearly, f is defined by the rewrite system $\mathcal{R}$. Expand the precedences for g, p and h so that $\mathsf{q}' >_{\mathcal{F}} \mathsf{q}$ for each $\mathsf{q} \in \{\mathsf{p}, \mathsf{h}\}$, $\mathsf{f} \approx_{\mathcal{F}} \mathsf{f}$ and $\mathsf{f} >_{\mathcal{F}} \mathsf{q}$ for all $\mathsf{q} \in \{\mathsf{g}, \mathsf{p}', \mathsf{h}'\}$.

Finally, we expand the separation of argument positions as indicated in the new rules (i)–(iv). Then, as observed in Example 2.6, the rule (iii) and (iv) can be oriented with the induced PLPO $>_{\mathsf{plpo}}$. For the rule (i), since $\mathsf{p}' >_{\mathcal{F}} \mathsf{p}$ and $\mathsf{p}'(x; y, z) >_{\mathsf{plpo}} u$ for all $u \in \{x, y, z\}$, $\mathsf{p}'(x; y, z) >_{\mathsf{plpo}} \mathsf{p}(; x, y, z)$ holds as an instance of Case 3 of Definition 2.2. The rule (ii) can be oriented in the same way. □

Corollary 4.3. *The class of primitive recursive functions is closed under primitive recursion with parameter substitution, unnested multiple recursion and simple nested recursion.*

Proof. Suppose that a function $f : \mathbb{N}^k \to \mathbb{N}$ is defined by an instance of either primitive recursion with parameter substitution, unnested multiple recursion, or simple nested recursion. Then by Theorem 4.2 we can find a rewrite system $\mathcal{R}$ defining f such that $\mathcal{R} \subseteq >_{\mathsf{plpo}}$ for some PLPO $>_{\mathsf{plpo}}$. We can assume that the underlying set $\mathcal{C}$ of constructors consists only of 0 and s. For each natural m let $\underline{m} \in \mathcal{T}(\mathcal{C})$ denote a ground term defined by $\underline{0} = 0$ and $\underline{m+1} = \mathsf{s}(\underline{m})$. Then by definition $|\underline{m}| = m$ for any m. Suppose that a function symbol f can be interpreted as the function f. Then by Corollary 3.9 there exists a primitive recursive function F such that the maximal length of rewriting sequences in $\mathcal{R}$ starting with $\mathsf{f}(\underline{m_1}, \ldots, \underline{m_k})$ is bounded by $F\left(\sum_{j=1}^{k} m_j\right)$. As observed in [2], one can find elementary recursive functions G, H_0 and H_1 such that $G(0, \boldsymbol{x}) = H_0(\boldsymbol{x})$, $G(y+1, \boldsymbol{x}) = H_1(y, \boldsymbol{x}, G(y, \boldsymbol{x}))$, and f is elementary recursive in the function $\boldsymbol{x} \mapsto G\left(F\left(\sum_{j=1}^{k} x_j\right), \boldsymbol{x}\right)$, where $\boldsymbol{x} = x_1, \ldots, x_k$. Essentially, the stepping function H_1 simulates one step of rewriting in $\mathcal{R}$ (assuming a suitable rewriting strategy). Obviously, the function $\boldsymbol{x} \mapsto G\left(F\left(\sum_{j=1}^{k} x_j\right), \boldsymbol{x}\right)$ is primitive recursive, and thus so is f. □

5   Comparison to Related Path Orders and Limitations of Predicative Lexicographic Path Orders

The definition of PLPO is strongly motivated by path orders based on the normal/safe argument separation [4–6]. On one hand, due to allowance of multiset comparison in the polynomial path order POP* [4], PLPO and POP* are incomparable. On the other hand, the PLPO is an extension of the exponential path order EPO* [5] though the EPO* only induces the exponential (innermost) runtime complexity. By induction according to the inductive definition of EPO* $>_{\mathsf{epo*}}$, it can be shown that $>_{\mathsf{epo*}} \subseteq >_{\mathsf{plpo}}$ holds with the same precedence and the same argument separation. In general, none of (**PRP**), (**UMR**) and (**SNR**) can be oriented with POP*s or EPO*s.

Readers also might be interested in comparison to the *ramified lexicographic path order* RLPO [12], which covers (**PRP**) and (**UMR**) but cannot handle (**SNR**). The contrast to POP*, EPO* and RLPO can be found in Fig. 1, where "runtime complexity" means innermost one. Very recently, the *generalised ramified lexicographic path order* GRLPO, which is an extension of the RLPO, has

	POP*	EPO*	RLPO	PLPO	LPO
runtime complexity	polynomial	exponential	primitive recursive		multiply recursive
(PRP)	—	—	✓	✓	✓
(UMR)	—	—	✓	✓	✓
(SNR)	—	—	—	✓	✓

(—: not orientable, ✓: orientable)

Fig. 1. Comparison to related path orders

been considered by A. Weiermann in a manuscript [13]. In contrast to the RLPO, the GRLPO can even handle (**SNR**). The GRLPO only induces the primitive recursive runtime complexity like the PLPO, but seems incomparable with the PLPO.

We mention that the PLPO can also handle a slight extension of simple nested recursion with more than one recursion parameters, known as *general* simple nested recursion [2, p. 221]. For example, consider the following two equations of general simple nested recursion:

$$f(x + 1, y + 1; z) = h(x, y; z, f(x, p(x, y;); f(x + 1, y; z))) \tag{10}$$

$$f(x + 1, y + 1; z) = h(x, y; z, f(x, p(x, y; z); f(x + 1, y; z))) \tag{11}$$

The Eq. (10) can be oriented with a PLPO, but the Eq. (11) cannot be oriented with any PLPO due to an additional occurrence of z in a safe argument position of $p(x, y; z)$.

6   Concluding Remarks

We introduced a novel termination order, the predicative lexicographic path order PLPO. As well as the lexicographic path order LPO, any instance of primitive recursion with parameter substitution (**PRP**), unnested multiple recursion (**UMR**) and simple nested recursion (**SNR**) can be oriented with a PLPO. On the other side, in contrast to the LPO, the PLPO only induces primitive recursive upper bounds on derivation lengths of compatible rewrite systems. Relying on the connection between time complexity of functions and runtime complexity of rewrite systems, this yields a uniform proof of the classical fact that the class of primitive recursive functions is closed under (**PRP**), (**UMR**) and (**SNR**).

It can be seen that the primitive recursive interpretation presented in Sect. 3 is not affected by allowing permutation of safe argument positions in Case 4 of Definition 2.2. Namely, Case 4 can be replaced with a slightly stronger condition: $f \in \mathcal{D} \setminus \mathcal{D}_{\mathsf{lex}}$, $t = g(t_1, \ldots, t_k; t_{k+1}, \ldots, t_{k+l})$ *for some g such that $f \approx_{\mathcal{F}} g$,*

- $(s_1, \ldots, s_k) \geqslant_{\mathsf{plpo}} (t_1, \ldots, t_k)$, *and*
- $(s_{k+1}, \ldots, s_{k+l}) >_{\mathsf{plpo}} (t_{\pi(k+1)}, \ldots, t_{\pi(k+l)})$ *for some permutation* $\pi : \{k + 1, \ldots, k + l\} \to \{k + 1, \ldots, k + l\}$.

Allowance of permutation of normal argument positions is not clear. One would recall that, as shown by D. Hofbauer in [14], the *multiset path order* only induces primitive recursive upper bounds on derivation lengths of compatible rewrite systems. Allowance of multiset comparison is not clear even for safe arguments.

References

1. Eguchi, N.: Predicative lexicographic path orders: towards a maximal model for primitive recursive functions. In: Waldmann, J. (ed.): Proceedings of 13th International Workshop on Termination (WST 2013), pp. 41–45 (2013)
2. Cichon, E.A., Weiermann, A.: Term rewriting theory for the primitive recursive functions. Ann. Pure Appl. Logic **83**(3), 199–223 (1997)
3. Seiffertt, J., Wunsch, D.C.: An application of unified computational intelligence. In: Seiffertt, J., Wunsch, D.C. (eds.) Unified Computational Intell. for Complex Sys. ALO, vol. 6, pp. 33–48. Springer, Heidelberg (2010)
4. Avanzini, M., Moser, G.: Complexity analysis by rewriting. In: Garrigue, J., Hermenegildo, M.V. (eds.) FLOPS 2008. LNCS, vol. 4989, pp. 130–146. Springer, Heidelberg (2008)
5. Avanzini, M., Eguchi, N., Moser, G.: A path order for rewrite systems that compute exponential time functions. In: Proceedings of 22nd International Conference on Rewriting Techniques and Applications (RTA 2011), vol. 10, pp. 123–138. Leibniz International Proceedings in Informatics (2011)
6. Avanzini, M., Eguchi, N., Moser, G.: A new order-theoretic characterisation of the polytime computable functions. In: Jhala, R., Igarashi, A. (eds.) APLAS 2012. LNCS, vol. 7705, pp. 280–295. Springer, Heidelberg (2012)
7. Péter, R.: Recursive Functions. Academic Press, New York (1967). (The 3rd revised edn., Translated from the German)
8. Simmons, H.: The realm of primitive recursion. Arch. Math. Logic **27**, 177–188 (1988)
9. Weiermann, A.: Termination proofs for term rewriting systems by lexicographic path ordering imply multiply recursive derivation lengths. Theoret. Comput. Sci. **139**(1–2), 355–362 (1995)
10. Bellantoni, S., Cook, S.A.: A new recursion-theoretic characterization of the polytime functions. Comput. Complex. **2**(2), 97–110 (1992)
11. Leivant, D.: Ramified recurrence and computational complexity I: word recurrence and poly-time. In: Clote, P., Remmel, J.B. (eds.) Feasible Mathematics II, Progress in Computer Science and Applied Logic, vol. 13, pp. 320–343. Birkhäuser, Boston (1995)
12. Cichon, E.A.: Termination orderings and complexity characterizations. In: Aczel, P., Simmons, H., Wainer, S.S. (eds.) Proof Theory, pp. 171–193. Cambridge University Press, Cambridge (1992)
13. Weiermann, A.: A termination ordering for primitive recursive schemata, 20 p. (2013, Preprint)
14. Hofbauer, D.: Termination proofs by multiset path orderings imply primitive recursive derivation lengths. Theoret. Comput. Sci. **105**(1), 129–140 (1992)

A Hoare Logic for Energy Consumption Analysis

Rody Kersten[1]([✉]), Paolo Parisen Toldin[2], Bernard van Gastel[1,3],
and Marko van Eekelen[1,3]

[1] Institute for Computing and Information Sciences, Radboud University Nijmegen,
Nijmegen, The Netherlands
{r.kersten,m.vaneekelen}@cs.ru.nl
[2] Department of Computer Science and Engineering, University of Bologna,
Bologna, Italy
parisent@cs.unibo.it
[3] Faculty of Management, Science and Technology, Open University of the
Netherlands, Heerlen, The Netherlands
{bernard.vangastel,marko.vaneekelen}@ou.nl

Abstract. Energy inefficient software implementations may cause battery drain for small systems and high energy costs for large systems. Dynamic energy analysis is often applied to mitigate these issues. However, this is often hardware-specific and requires repetitive measurements using special equipment.

We present a static analysis deriving upper-bounds for energy consumption based on an introduced energy-aware Hoare logic. Software is considered together with models of the hardware it controls. The Hoare logic is parametric with respect to the hardware. Energy models of hardware components can be specified separately from the logic. Parametrised with one or more of such component models, the analysis can statically produce a sound (over-approximated) upper-bound for the energy-usage of the hardware controlled by the software.

1 Introduction

Power consumption and green computing are nowadays important topics in IT. From small systems such as wireless sensor nodes, cell-phones and embedded devices to big architectures such as data centers, mainframes and servers, energy consumption is an important factor. Small devices are often powered by a battery, which should last as long as possible. For larger devices, the problem lies mostly with the costs of powering the device. These costs are often amplified by inefficient power-supplies and cooling of the system.

Obviously, power consumption depends not only on hardware, but also on the software *controlling* the hardware. Currently, most of the methods available to programmers to analyse energy consumption caused by software use dynamic analysis: measuring while the software is running. Power consumption measurement of a system and especially of its individual components is not a trivial task.

This work is partially financed by the IOP GenCom GoGreen project, sponsored by the Dutch Ministry of Economic Affairs, Agriculture and Innovation.

© Springer International Publishing Switzerland 2014
U. Dal Lago and R. Peña (Eds.): FOPARA 2013, LNCS 8552, pp. 93–109, 2014.
DOI: 10.1007/978-3-319-12466-7_6

A designated measuring set-up is required. This means that most programmers currently have no idea how much energy their software consumes. A static analysis of energy consumption would be a big improvement, potentially leading to more energy-efficient software. Such a static analysis is presented in this paper.

Since the software interacts with multiple components (software and hardware), energy consumption analysis needs to incorporate different kinds of analysis. Power consumption may depend on hardware state, values of variables and bounds on the required number of clock-cycles.

Related Work. There is a large body of work on energy-efficiency of software. Most papers approach the problem on a high level, defining programming and design patterns for writing energy-efficient code (see e.g. [1–3]). In [4], a modular design for energy-aware software is presented that is based on a series of rules on UML schemes. In [5,6], a program is divided into "phases" describing similar behaviour. Based on the behaviour of the software, design level optimisations are proposed to achieve lower energy consumption. A lot of research is dedicated to building compilers that optimize code for energy-efficiency, e.g. in GCC [7] or in an *iterative* compiler [8]. Petri-net based energy modelling techniques for embedded systems are proposed in [9,10]. Analyses for consumption of generic resources are built using recurrence relation solving [11], amortized analysis [12], amortization and separation logic [13] and a Vienna Development Method style program logic [14]. The main differences with our work are that we include an explicit hardware model and a context in the form of component states. This context enables the inclusion of state-dependent energy consumption. Relatively close to our approach are [15,16], in which energy consumption of embedded software is analysed for specific architectures ([15] for SimpleScalar, [16] for XMOS ISA-level models), while our approach is hardware-parametric.

Our Approach. Contrary to the approaches above, we are interested in statically deriving bounds on energy-consumption using a novel, generic approach that is parametrised with hardware models. Energy consumption analysis is an instance of resource consumption analysis. Other instances are worst-case execution time [17], size [18], loop bound [19,20] and memory [20] analysis). The focus of this paper is on energy analysis. Energy consumption models of hardware components are input for our analysis. The analysis requires information about the software, such as dependencies between variables and information about the number of loop iterations. For this reason we assume that a previous analysis (properly instantiated for our case) has been made deriving loop bounds (e.g. [20,21]) and variable dependency information (e.g. [22]).

Our approach is essentially an energy-aware Hoare logic that is proven sound with respect to an energy-aware semantics. Both the semantics and the logic assume energy-aware component models to be present. The central control is however assumed to be in the software. Consequently, the analysis is done on a hybrid system of software and models of hardware components. The Hoare logic yields an upper bound on the energy consumption of a system of hardware components that are controlled by software.

Our Contribution. The main contributions of this paper are:

- A novel hardware-parametric energy-aware software semantics.
- A corresponding energy-aware Hoare logic that enables formal reasoning about energy consumption such as deriving an upper-bound for the energy consumption of the system.
- A soundness proof of the derived upper-bounds with respect to the semantics.

The basic modelling and semantics are presented in Sect. 2. Energy-awareness is added and the logic is presented in Sect. 3. An example is given in Sect. 4 and the soundness proof is outlined in Sect. 5. The paper is concluded in Sect. 6.

2   Modelling Hybrid Systems

Most modern electronic systems consist of hardware and software. In order to study the energy consumption of such hybrid systems we will consider both hardware and software in one single modelling framework. This section defines a hybrid logic in which software plays a central role controlling hardware components. The hardware components are modelled in such a way that only the relevant information for the energy consumption analysis is present. In this paper, the controlling software is assumed to be written in a small language designed just for illustrating the analysis.

2.1   Language

Our analysis is performed on a 'while' language. The grammar for our language is defined as follows (where $\boxdot \in \{+, -, *, >, \geq, \equiv, \neq, \leq, <, \wedge, \vee\}$.):

$$c \in \mathrm{CONST} = n \in \mathbb{N}$$
$$x \in \mathrm{VAR} = \text{`A'} \mid \text{`B'} \mid \text{`C'} \mid \ldots$$
$$e \in \mathrm{EXPR} = c \mid x \mid x = e_1 \mid e_1 \boxdot e_2 \mid C_i :: f(e_1) \mid f(e_1) \mid S, e_1$$
$$S \in \mathrm{STATEMENT} = \textbf{skip} \mid S_1; S_2 \mid e \mid \textbf{if } e \textbf{ then } S_1 \textbf{ else } S_2 \textbf{ end if}$$
$$\mid \textbf{while } e \textbf{ do } S \textbf{ end while} \mid F\, S_1$$
$$F \in \mathrm{FUNC} = \textbf{function } f(x) \textbf{ begin } e \textbf{ end}$$

This language is used just for illustration purposes, so the only supported type in the language is unsigned integer. There are no explicit booleans. The value 0 is handled as a **False** value, while all the other values are handled as a **True** value. There are no global variables and parameters are passed by-value, so functions do not have side-effects on the program state. while loops are supported but recursion is not. Functions are statically scoped. There are explicit statements for operations on hardware components, like the processor, memory, storage or network devices. By explicitly introducing these statements it is easier to reason about those components, as opposed to, for instance, using conventions about certain memory regions that will map to certain hardware devices. Functions on components have a fixed number of arguments and always return a value. The notation $C_i :: f$ will refer to a function f of a component C_i.

2.2 Modelling Components

To reason about hybrid systems we need a way to model hardware components (e.g. memory, harddisk, network controller) that captures the behaviour of those components with respect to resource consumption. Hence, we introduce a *component model* that consists of a state and a set of functions that can change the state: *component functions*. A component state $C_i :: s$ is a collection of variables of any type. They can signify e.g. that the component is on, off or in stand-by.

A component function is modelled by a function that produces the return value (rv_f) and a function that updates the internal state of the component (δ_f). Both functions are functions over the state variables. The update function $C_i :: \delta_f$ and the return value function $C_i :: rv_f$ take the state s and the arguments $args$ passed to the component function and return respectively the new state of the component and the return value. Each component C_i may have multiple component functions. All the state changes in components must be explicit in the source code as an operation, a *component function*, on that specific component.

2.3 Semantics

Standard, non-energy-aware semantics can be defined for our language. Full semantics are given in a technical report [23]. Below, the assignment rule (*sAssign*) and the component function call rule (*sCallCmpF*) are given to illustrate the notation and the way of handling components.

$$\frac{\Delta \vdash \langle e, \sigma, \Gamma \rangle \Downarrow^e \langle n, \sigma', \Gamma' \rangle}{\Delta \vdash \langle x_1 = e, \sigma, \Gamma \rangle \Downarrow^e \langle n, \sigma'[x_1 \leftarrow n], \Gamma' \rangle} \text{ (sAssign)}$$

$$\frac{\Delta \vdash \langle e, \sigma, \Gamma \rangle \Downarrow^e \langle a, \sigma', \Gamma' \rangle \ C_i :: rv_f(C_i^\Gamma :: s, a) = n \ \Gamma' = \Gamma[C_i :: s \leftarrow C_i :: \delta_f(C_i^\Gamma :: s, a)]}{\Delta \vdash \langle C_i :: f(e), \sigma, \Gamma \rangle \Downarrow^e \langle n, \sigma, \Gamma' \rangle} \text{ (sCallCmpF)}$$

The rules are defined over a triple $\langle e, \sigma, \Gamma \rangle$ with respectively a program expression e (or statement S), the program state function σ and the component state environment Γ. The *program* state function returns for every variable its actual value. Δ is an environment of function definitions. We use the following notation for substitution: $\sigma[x_I \leftarrow n]$. The reduction symbol $\Downarrow^e$ is used for expressions, which evaluate to a value and a new state function. We use $\Downarrow^s$ for statements, which only evaluate to a new state function.

In the following sections we will define energy-aware semantics and energy analysis rules. We used a consistent naming scheme for the different variants of the rules (e.g. sAssign, eAssign and aAssign for the Assignment rule in respectively the standard non-energy-aware semantics, the energy aware semantics and the energy analysis rules).

3 Energy Analysis of Hybrid Systems

In this section we extend our hybrid logic in order to reason about the energy consumption of programs. We distinguish two kinds of energy usage: *incidental* and *time-dependent*. The former represents an operation that uses a constant amount of energy, disregarding any time aspect. The latter signifies a change in the state of the component; while a component is in a certain state it is assumed to draw a constant amount of energy *per time unit*.

3.1   Energy-Aware Semantics

As energy consumption can be based on time, we first need to extend our semantics to be time-aware. We effectively extend all the rules of the semantics with an extra argument, a global timestamp t. Using this timestamp we are able to model and analyse time-dependent energy usage.

We track energy usage for each component individually, by using an accumulator $\mathfrak{e}$ that is added to the component model. For time-dependent energy usage, with each component state change, the energy used while the component was in the previous state is added to the accumulator. To enable calculation of the time spent in the current state, we add τ to the component model, signifying the timestamp at which the component entered the current state. We assume that each component has a constant *power draw* while in a state. Therefore, the component model function $C_i :: \phi(s)$ maps component states onto the corresponding power draw, independent of time. To calculate the power consumed while in a certain state we define the *td* function, with as arguments the component and the current timestamp:

$$td(C_i, t) = C_i :: \phi(s) \cdot (t - C_i :: \tau)$$

We model *incidental energy usage* associated with a component function f with the constant $C_i :: \mathfrak{E}_f$. For each call to a component function we add this constant to the energy accumulator.

A component function call can influence energy consumption in two ways: through its associated incidental energy consumption and by changing the state, thereby influencing time-dependent energy usage. This is expressed by the energy-aware semantic rule $(eCallCmpF)$ for component functions as defined below, with $C_i :: \mathfrak{T}_f$ representing the time it costs to execute this component function.

$$\frac{\Delta \vdash \langle e, \sigma, \Gamma, t \rangle \Downarrow^e \langle a, \sigma', \Gamma', t' \rangle \qquad C_i :: rv_f(C_i^{\Gamma'} :: s, a) = n}{\Gamma'' = \Gamma[C_i :: \mathfrak{e} \mathrel{+}= C_i :: \mathfrak{E}_f + td(C_i^{\Gamma'}, t), C_i :: s \leftarrow C_i :: \delta_f(C_i^{\Gamma'} :: s, a), C_i :: \tau \leftarrow t']}{\Delta \vdash \langle C_i :: f(e), \sigma, \Gamma, t \rangle \Downarrow^e \langle n, \sigma, \Gamma'', t' + C_i :: \mathfrak{T}_f \rangle} \text{ (eCallCmpF)}$$

Note the addition of the incidental and time dependent energy usages ($C_i :: \mathfrak{E}_f$ and $td(C_i^{\Gamma}, t)$ respectively) to the energy accumulator $C_i :: \mathfrak{e}$, the incrementation of the global time with $C_i :: \mathfrak{T}_f$ and the update of the component timestamp $C_i :: \tau$. Evaluation by $\Downarrow$ in the energy-aware semantics extends the original semantics with a timestamp and an energy accumulator, which are used to calculate the total energy consumption of the evaluation ($\mathfrak{e}_{system}$ as defined below). The full energy-aware semantics are given in Fig. 1.

The energy accumulator of the components is not always up to date with respect to the current time, as it is only updated in the $(eCallCmpF)$ rule.

This is done for simplicity; otherwise each rule that adjusts the global time needs to update the energy accumulator of all components.

To calculate the total actual energy usage, the time the components are in their current state should still be accounted for. This means we have to add the result of the td function for each component. The total energy consumption of the system can be calculated at any time as follows:

$$\mathfrak{e}_{system}(\Gamma, \mathfrak{t}) = \sum_i C_i^\Gamma :: \mathfrak{e} + td(C_i^\Gamma, \mathfrak{t})$$

We can now make the distinction between non-energy-aware component state $C_i :: s$, and energy-aware component state, which also includes the time-stamp τ and the energy accumulator $\mathfrak{e}$.

Most energy consuming actions are explicit in our language: $C_i :: consume()$. However, basic language features, such as evaluation of arithmetic expressions, also implicitly consume energy. We capture this behaviour in the C_{imp} component. This component is an integral part of our energy-aware semantics and logic. The C_{imp} component should at least have resource consumption constants defined for the following operations:

- $C_{imp} :: \mathfrak{E}_e$ and $C_{imp} :: \mathfrak{T}_e$ for expression evaluation.
- $C_{imp} :: \mathfrak{E}_a$ and $C_{imp} :: \mathfrak{T}_a$ for assignment.
- $C_{imp} :: \mathfrak{E}_w$ and $C_{imp} :: \mathfrak{T}_w$ for while loops.
- $C_{imp} :: \mathfrak{E}_{ite}$ and $C_{imp} :: \mathfrak{T}_{ite}$ for conditionals.

To capture the resource consumption of these basic operations, we extend the associated rules in the semantics. The energy-aware rule for assignment ($eAssign$) is listed below, with $C_{imp} :: \mathfrak{E}_a$ for the incidental energy usage of an assignment and $C_{imp} :: \mathfrak{T}_a$ for the time it takes to perform an assignment.

$$\frac{\Delta \vdash \langle e, \sigma, \Gamma, \mathfrak{t} \rangle \Downarrow^e \langle n, \sigma', \Gamma', \mathfrak{t}' \rangle \qquad \Gamma'' = \Gamma'[C_{imp} :: \mathfrak{e} \mathrel{+}= C_{imp} :: \mathfrak{E}_a]}{\Delta \vdash \langle x = e, \sigma, \Gamma, \mathfrak{t} \rangle \Downarrow^e \langle n, \sigma'[x \leftarrow n], \Gamma'', \mathfrak{t}' + C_{imp} :: \mathfrak{T}_a \rangle} \quad (eAssign)$$

All computations of resource consumption and new component states are done symbolically. In the logic, these values are added, multiplied and subtracted or their `max` is taken. Hence, every $\mathfrak{t}$, $\mathfrak{e}$ and τ, as well as the values in component states, are polynomial expressions, extended with the `max` operator, over program variables. Additionally, symbolic states are used, both as input for the program and as start state for the components. The aforementioned polynomials also range over the symbols used in these symbolic states.

3.2   Energy-Aware Modelling

Energy-aware models will be used to derive upper-bounds for energy consumption of the modelled system. In order for the energy-aware model to be suited for the analysis the model should reflect an upper-bound on the actual consumption. This can be based on detailed documentation or on actual energy measurements.

$$\frac{}{\Delta \vdash \langle c, \sigma, \Gamma, t \rangle \Downarrow^e \langle c, \sigma, \Gamma, t \rangle}(\text{eConst}) \qquad \frac{}{\Delta \vdash \langle x, \sigma, \Gamma, t \rangle \Downarrow^e \langle \sigma(x), \sigma, \Gamma, t \rangle}(\text{eVar})$$

$$\frac{\Delta \vdash \langle e_1, \sigma, \Gamma, t \rangle \Downarrow^e \langle n, \sigma', \Gamma', t' \rangle \qquad C_{imp} :: \Box(n, m) = p}{\Delta \vdash \langle e_2, \sigma', \Gamma', t' \rangle \Downarrow^e \langle m, \sigma'', \Gamma'', t'' \rangle \quad \Gamma''' = \Gamma''[C_{imp} :: \mathfrak{e} \mathrel{+}= C_{imp} :: \mathfrak{E}_e]}{\Delta \vdash \langle e_1 \Box e_2, \sigma, \Gamma, t \rangle \Downarrow^e \langle p, \sigma'', \Gamma''', t'' + C_{imp} :: \mathfrak{T}_e \rangle}(\text{eBinOp})$$

$$\frac{\Delta \vdash \langle e, \sigma, \Gamma, t \rangle \Downarrow^e \langle n, \sigma', \Gamma', t' \rangle \quad \Gamma'' = \Gamma'[C_{imp} :: \mathfrak{e} \mathrel{+}= C_{imp} :: \mathfrak{E}_a]}{\Delta \vdash \langle x = e, \sigma, \Gamma, t \rangle \Downarrow^e \langle n, \sigma'[x \leftarrow n], \Gamma'', t' + C_{imp} :: \mathfrak{T}_a \rangle}(\text{eAssign})$$

$$\frac{\Delta \vdash \langle e, \sigma, \Gamma, t \rangle \Downarrow^e \langle a, \sigma', \Gamma', t' \rangle \quad C_i :: rv_f(C_i^{\Gamma'} :: s, a) = n}{\Gamma'' = \Gamma[C_i :: \mathfrak{e} \mathrel{+}= C_i :: \mathfrak{E}_f + td(C_i^{\Gamma'}, t), C_i :: s \leftarrow C_i :: \delta_f(C_i^{\Gamma'} :: s, a), C_i :: \tau \leftarrow t']}{\Delta \vdash \langle C_i :: f(e), \sigma, \Gamma, t \rangle \Downarrow^e \langle n, \sigma, \Gamma'', t' + C_i :: \mathfrak{T}_f \rangle}(\text{eCallCmpF})$$

$$\frac{\Delta(f) = (e_1, \Delta', x)}{\Delta \vdash \langle e, \sigma, \Gamma, t \rangle \Downarrow^e \langle a, \sigma', \Gamma', t' \rangle \quad \Delta' \vdash \langle e_1, [x \leftarrow a], \Gamma', t' \rangle \Downarrow^e \langle n, \sigma'', \Gamma'', t'' \rangle}{\Delta \vdash \langle f(e), \sigma, \Gamma, t \rangle \Downarrow^e \langle n, \sigma', \Gamma'', t'' \rangle}(\text{eCallF})$$

$$\frac{\Delta \vdash \langle S, \sigma, \Gamma, t \rangle \Downarrow^s \langle \sigma', \Gamma', t' \rangle \quad \Delta \vdash \langle e, \sigma', \Gamma', t' \rangle \Downarrow^e \langle n, \sigma'', \Gamma'', t'' \rangle}{\Delta \vdash \langle S, e, \sigma, \Gamma, t \rangle \Downarrow^e \langle n, \sigma'', \Gamma'', t'' \rangle}(\text{eExprConcat})$$

$$\frac{\Delta \vdash \langle e_1, \sigma, \Gamma, t \rangle \Downarrow^e \langle n, \sigma', \Gamma', t' \rangle}{\Delta \vdash \langle e_1, \sigma, \Gamma, t \rangle \Downarrow^s \langle \sigma', \Gamma', t' \rangle}(\text{eExprAsStmt}) \qquad \frac{}{\Delta \vdash \langle \mathbf{skip}, \sigma, \Gamma, t \rangle \Downarrow^s \langle \sigma, \Gamma, t \rangle}(\text{eSkip})$$

$$\frac{\Delta \vdash \langle S_1, \sigma, \Gamma, t \rangle \Downarrow^s \langle \sigma', \Gamma', t' \rangle \quad \Delta \vdash \langle S_2, \sigma', \Gamma', t' \rangle \Downarrow^s \langle \sigma'', \Gamma'', t'' \rangle}{\Delta \vdash \langle S_1; S_2, \sigma, \Gamma, t \rangle \Downarrow^s \langle \sigma'', \Gamma'', t'' \rangle}(\text{eStmtConcat})$$

$$\frac{\Delta \vdash \langle S_2, \sigma', \Gamma', t' \rangle \Downarrow^s \langle \sigma'', \Gamma'', t'' \rangle}{\Delta \vdash \langle e, \sigma, \Gamma, t \rangle \Downarrow^e \langle 0, \sigma', \Gamma', t' \rangle \quad \Gamma''' = \Gamma''[C_{imp} :: \mathfrak{e} \mathrel{+}= C_{imp} :: \mathfrak{E}_{ite}]}{\Delta \vdash \langle \mathbf{if}\ e\ \mathbf{then}\ S_1\ \mathbf{else}\ S_2\ \mathbf{end\ if}, \sigma, \Gamma, t \rangle \Downarrow^s \langle \sigma'', \Gamma''', t'' + C_{imp} :: \mathfrak{T}_{ite} \rangle}(\text{eIf-False})$$

$$\frac{n \neq 0 \qquad \Delta \vdash \langle S_1, \sigma', \Gamma', t' \rangle \Downarrow^s \langle \sigma'', \Gamma'', t'' \rangle}{\Delta \vdash \langle e, \sigma, \Gamma, t \rangle \Downarrow^e \langle n, \sigma', \Gamma', t' \rangle \quad \Gamma''' = \Gamma''[C_{imp} :: \mathfrak{e} \mathrel{+}= C_{imp} :: \mathfrak{E}_{ite}]}{\Delta \vdash \langle \mathbf{if}\ e\ \mathbf{then}\ S_1\ \mathbf{else}\ S_2\ \mathbf{end\ if}, \sigma, \Gamma, t \rangle \Downarrow^s \langle \sigma'', \Gamma''', t'' + C_{imp} :: \mathfrak{T}_{ite} \rangle}(\text{eIf-True})$$

$$\frac{\Delta \vdash \langle e, \sigma, \Gamma, t \rangle \Downarrow^e \langle 0, \sigma', \Gamma', t' \rangle \quad \Gamma'' = \Gamma'[C_{imp} :: \mathfrak{e} \mathrel{+}= C_{imp} :: \mathfrak{E}_w]}{\Delta \vdash \langle \mathbf{while}\ e\ \mathbf{do}\ S_1\ \mathbf{end\ while}, \sigma, \Gamma, t \rangle \Downarrow^s \langle \sigma', \Gamma'', t' + C_{imp} :: \mathfrak{T}_w \rangle}(\text{eWhile-False})$$

$$\frac{\Gamma'' = \Gamma'[C_{imp} :: \mathfrak{e} \mathrel{+}= C_{imp} :: \mathfrak{E}_w] \quad \Delta \vdash \langle e, \sigma, \Gamma, t \rangle \Downarrow^e \langle n, \sigma', \Gamma', t' \rangle}{\Delta \vdash \langle S_1; \mathbf{while}\ e\ \mathbf{do}\ S_1\ \mathbf{end\ while}, \sigma', \Gamma'', t' + C_{imp} :: \mathfrak{T}_w \rangle \Downarrow^s \langle \sigma'', \Gamma''', t'' \rangle \quad n \neq 0}{\Delta \vdash \langle \mathbf{while}\ e\ \mathbf{do}\ S_1\ \mathbf{end\ while}, \sigma, \Gamma, t \rangle \Downarrow^s \langle \sigma'', \Gamma''', t'' \rangle}(\text{eWhile-True})$$

$$\frac{\Delta[f \leftarrow (e, \Delta, x)] \vdash \langle S, \sigma, \Gamma, t \rangle \Downarrow^s \langle \sigma', \Gamma', t' \rangle}{\Delta \vdash \langle \mathbf{function}\ f(x)\ \mathbf{begin}\ e\ \mathbf{end}\ S, \sigma, \Gamma, t \rangle \Downarrow^s \langle \sigma', \Gamma', t' \rangle}(\text{eFuncDef})$$

Fig. 1. Energy-aware semantics.

To provide a sound analysis, we need to assume that components are modelled in such a way that the component states reflect different power-levels and are partially ordered. Greater states should imply greater power draw. We will use finite state models only to enable fixpoint calculation in our analysis of while loops. The modelling should be such that the following properties hold (in the context of the full soundness proof in [23] these properties are axioms):

– *Components states form a finite lattice* with a partial order based on the ordering of polynomials (extended with max) over symbolic variables. Within the lattice each pair of component states has a least upper-bound.

$$\frac{}{\{\Gamma;\mathfrak{t};\rho\}n\{\Gamma;\mathfrak{t};\rho\}}(\text{aConst}) \qquad \frac{}{\{\Gamma;\mathfrak{t};\rho\}x\{\Gamma;\mathfrak{t};\rho\}}(\text{aVar})$$

$$\frac{\{\Gamma;\mathfrak{t};\rho\}e_1\{\Gamma_1;\mathfrak{t}_1;\rho_1\} \quad \{\Gamma_1;\mathfrak{t}_1;\rho_1\}e_2\{\Gamma_2;\mathfrak{t}_2;\rho_2\} \quad \Gamma_3 = \Gamma_2[C_{imp}::\mathfrak{e} \mathrel{+}= C_{imp}::\mathfrak{E}_e]}{\{\Gamma;\mathfrak{t};\rho\}e_1 \boxdot e_2\{\Gamma_3;\mathfrak{t}_2 + C_{imp}::\mathfrak{T}_e;\rho_2\}}(\text{aBinOp})$$

$$\frac{\{\Gamma;\mathfrak{t};\rho\}e\{\Gamma_1;\mathfrak{t}_1;\rho_1\} \quad \Gamma_2 = \Gamma_1[C_{imp}::\mathfrak{e} \mathrel{+}= C_{imp}::\mathfrak{E}_a]}{\{\Gamma;\mathfrak{t};\rho\}x = e\{\Gamma_2;\mathfrak{t}_1 + C_{imp}::\mathfrak{T}_a;\rho_2\}}(\text{aAssign})$$

$$\frac{\Gamma_1 = \Gamma[C_i::s \leftarrow C_i::\delta_f(C_i::s), C_i::\tau \leftarrow \mathfrak{t}, C_i::\mathfrak{e} \mathrel{+}= C_i::\mathfrak{E}_f + td(C_i,\mathfrak{t})]}{\{\Gamma;\mathfrak{t};\rho\}C_i::f(args)\{\Gamma_1;\mathfrak{t} + C_i::\mathfrak{T}_f;\rho\}}(\text{aCallCmpF})$$

$$\frac{\Delta(f) = (e_1, x) \qquad \{\Gamma;\mathfrak{t};\rho\}e\{\Gamma_1;\mathfrak{t}_1;\rho_1\}}{e = a \in \rho \quad \{\Gamma_1;\mathfrak{t}_1;\rho_1[x' \leftarrow a]\}e_1[x \leftarrow x']\{\Gamma_2;\mathfrak{t}_2;\rho_2\} \quad x' \text{ fresh in } e_1}{\{\Gamma;\mathfrak{t};\rho\}f(e)\{\Gamma_2;\mathfrak{t}_2;\rho_2\}}(\text{aCallF})$$

$$\frac{}{\{\Gamma;\mathfrak{t};\rho\}\mathbf{skip}\{\Gamma;\mathfrak{t};\rho\}}(\text{aSkip}) \qquad \frac{\{\Gamma;\mathfrak{t};\rho\}S_1\{\Gamma_1;\mathfrak{t}_1;\rho_1\} \quad \{\Gamma_1;\mathfrak{t}_1;\rho_1\}S_2\{\Gamma_2;\mathfrak{t}_2;\rho_2\}}{\{\Gamma;\mathfrak{t};\rho\}S_1;S_2\{\Gamma_2;\mathfrak{t}_2;\rho_2\}}(\text{aConcat})$$

$$\frac{\{\Gamma;\mathfrak{t};\rho\}e\{\Gamma_1;\mathfrak{t}_1;\rho_1\} \qquad \{\Gamma_2;\mathfrak{t}_1 + C_{imp}::\mathfrak{T}_{ite};\rho_1\}S_1\{\Gamma_3;\mathfrak{t}_2;\rho_2\}}{\Gamma_2 = \Gamma_1[C_{imp}::\mathfrak{e} \mathrel{+}= C_{imp}::\mathfrak{E}_{ite}] \quad \{\Gamma_2;\mathfrak{t}_1 + C_{imp}::\mathfrak{T}_{ite};\rho_1\}S_2\{\Gamma_4;\mathfrak{t}_3;\rho_3\}}{\{\Gamma;\mathfrak{t};\rho\}\mathbf{if}\ e\ \mathbf{then}\ S_1\ \mathbf{else}\ S_2\ \mathbf{end\ if}\{\text{lub}(\Gamma_3,\Gamma_4);\max\{\mathfrak{t}_2,\mathfrak{t}_3\};\rho_4\}}(\text{aIf})$$

$$\frac{\Gamma_1 = \mathbf{process\text{-}td}(\Gamma,\mathfrak{t}) \qquad \Gamma_3 = \Gamma_2[C_{imp}::\mathfrak{e} \mathrel{+}= C_{imp}::\mathfrak{E}_w]}{\{\mathbf{wci}(\Gamma_1,e;S);\mathfrak{t};\rho\}e\{\Gamma_2;\mathfrak{t}_1;\rho_1\} \quad \{\Gamma_3;\mathfrak{t}_1 + C_{imp}::\mathfrak{T}_w;\rho_1\}S\{\Gamma_4;\mathfrak{t}_2;\rho_2\}}{\{\Gamma;\mathfrak{t};\rho\}\mathbf{while}_{ib}\ e\ \mathbf{do}\ S\ \mathbf{end\ while}\{\mathbf{oe}(\Gamma_1,\mathfrak{t},\Gamma_4,\mathfrak{t}_2,ib);\rho_3\}}(\text{aWhile})$$

Fig. 2. Energy analysis rules.

– *Energy-aware component states are partially ordered.* This ordering extends the ordering on component states in a natural way by adding an energy accumulator and a timestamp. The timestamp stores the time of the latest change to the component state. So, the earliest timestamp reflects the highest energy usage. Therefore, with respect to timestamps the energy-aware component state ordering should be defined such that smaller timestamps lead to bigger energy-aware component states.
– *Power draw functions preserve the ordering,* i.e. larger states consume more energy than smaller states.
– *Component state update functions δ preserve the ordering.* For this reason, δ_f cannot depend on the arguments of f. To signify this, we will use $\delta(s)$ instead of $\delta(s, args)$ in the logic. As a result, component models cannot influence each other. Our soundness proof (Theorem 2 in Sect. 5) requires this assumption.

Severeness of Model Restrictions. There are several restrictions to the modelling that may seem far from reality.

1. *Component state functions take up a constant amount of time and incidental energy.* This is needed for the soundness proof. For instance, when a radio component sends a message, the duration of the function call cannot directly depend on the number of bytes in the message. In most cases this can be dealt with by using a different way of modelling. First, one can use an overestimation. Second, such dependencies can be removed by distributing the costs

over multiple function calls. For instance, the radio component can have a function to send a fixed number of bytes. If it internally keeps a queue, the additional costs of sending the full queue can be modelled by distributing it over separate queueing operations. energy consumption of components must remain fixed per component state.

2. *With each component state a constant power draw is associated.* However, some hardware may accumulate heat over time incurring increasing energy consumption over time. Such a 'heating' problem can be modelled e.g. by changing state to a higher energy level with every call of a component function. This is still an approximation of course. In the future, we want to study models with time driven state change or with time-dependent power draw.

3. *Component model must be finite state machines.* Modelling systems with finite state machines is not uncommon, e.g. using model checking and the right kind of abstraction for the property that is studied. In our models the abstraction should be such that the energy consumption is modelled as close as possible.

4. *The effect of component state functions on the component states cannot depend on the arguments of the function.* Also, component models cannot influence each other. Both restrictions are needed for soundness guarantee of our analysis. This restricts the modelling. Using multiple component state functions instead of dynamic arguments and cross-component calls is a way of modelling that can mitigate these restrictions in certain cases. Relieving these restrictions in general is part of future work.

3.3   A Hoare Logic for Energy Analysis

This section treats the definition of an energy-aware logic with energy analysis rules that can be used to bound the energy consumption of the analysed system. The full set of rules is given in Fig. 2. These rules are deterministic; at each moment only one rule can be applied.

Our energy consumption analysis depends on external symbolic analysis of variables and loop analysis. The results of this external analysis are assumed to be accessible in our Hoare Logic in two ways.

Firstly, we restrict the scope of our analysis to programs that are bound in terms of execution. We assume that all loops and component functions terminate on any input. Each loop is annotated with a bound: $\textbf{while}_{ib}$. The bound is a polynomial over the input variables, which expresses an upper-bound on the number of iterations of the loop. We have added the ib to the while rule in the energy analysis rules to make this assumption explicit. Derivation of bounds is considered out of scope for our analysis. We assume that an external analysis has produced a sound bound.

Secondly, the symbolic state environment ρ gives us a symbolic state of every variable for each line of code, e.g., $\{x_1 = e_1\}x_1 = x_1 + x_2 + x_3\{x_1 = e_1 + x_2 + x_3\}$, plus other non-energy related properties invariants that have already been proven. In Fig. 2 we included this prerequisite by explicitly denoting it as $\rho, \rho_1, \ldots$.

All the judgements in the rules have the following shape: $\{\Gamma; \mathsf{t}; \rho\}S\{\Gamma'; \mathsf{t}'; \rho'\}$, where Γ is the set of all energy aware component states, t is the global time and ρ represents the symbolic state environment retrieved from the earlier standard analysis. The notation $\Gamma[n \mathrel{+}= m]$ is a shorthand for $\Gamma[n \leftarrow n+m]$. As (energy-aware) component states are partially ordered, we can take a least upper bound of states $\mathbf{lub}(s_1, s_2)$ and sets of energy-aware component states $\mathbf{lub}(\Gamma_1, \Gamma_2)$.

We will highlight the most relevant aspects of the rules. The ($aCallCmpF$) rule uses the $td(C_i, t)$ function to estimate the time-dependent energy consumption of component function calls. The (aIf) rule takes the least upper bound of the energy-aware component states and the maximum of the time estimates.

Special attention is warranted for the ($aWhile$) rule. We study the body of the while loop in isolation. This requires processing the time-dependent energy consumption that occurred before the loop (**process-td**). An over-estimation (**oe**) of the energy consumption of the loop will be calculated by taking the product of the bound on the number of iterations and an over-estimation of the energy consumption of a single iteration, i.e. the worst-case iteration (**wci**). The worst-case-iteration is determined by taking the least upper-bound of the set of all states that can occur during the execution of the loop. As there are a finite number of states for each component, this set can be determined via a fix point construction (**fix**). The fixpoint is calculated by iterating the component iteration function (**ci**).

In order to support the analysis of statements after the loop, also an over-estimation of the component states after the loop has to be calculated. For brevity in Fig. 2, this is dealt with in the calculation of **oe**.

Five calculations are needed:

1. Component iteration function **ci**. The component iteration function $\mathbf{ci}_i(S)$ aggregates the (possibly overestimated) effects of S on C_i. It performs the analysis on S, then considers only the effects on C_i. overestimated in the same manner as in the rest of the analysis. By $\mathbf{ci}_i^n(S)$ we mean the component iteration function applied n times: $\mathbf{ci}_i(S) \circ \mathbf{ci}_i^{n-1}(S)$, with $\mathbf{ci}_i^1(S) = \mathbf{ci}_i(S)$.

2. Fixpoint function **fix**. Because component states are finite, there is an iteration after which a component is in a state that it has already been in, earlier in the loop (unless the loop is already finished before this point is reached). Since components are independent, the behaviour of the component will be identical to its behaviour the first time it was in this state. This is a fix-point on the set of component states that can be reached in the loop. It can be found using the $\mathbf{fix}_i(S)$ function, which finds the smallest n for which $\exists k.\mathbf{ci}_i^{n+1}(S) = \mathbf{ci}_i^k(S)$. The number of possible component states is an upper bound for n.

3. Worst-Case Iteration function **wci**. To make a sound overestimation of the energy consumption of a loop, we need to find the iteration that consumes the most. As our analysis is non-decreasing with respect to component states, this is the iteration which starts with the largest component state in the precondition. For this purpose, we introduce the worst-case iteration function $\mathbf{wci}_i(S)$, which computes the least-upper bound of all the states up to the

fixpoint: $\mathbf{wci}_i(S) = \mathbf{lub}(\mathbf{ci}_i^0(S), \mathbf{ci}_i^1(S), \ldots, \mathbf{ci}_i^{\mathbf{fix}_i(S)}(S))$. The global version $\mathbf{wci}(\Gamma, S)$ is defined by iteratively applying the $\mathbf{wci}_i(S)$ function to each component C_i in Γ.

4. Overestimation function **oe**. This function overestimates the energy-aware output states of the loop. It needs to do three things: find the largest non-energy-aware output states, find the minimal timestamps and add the resource consumption of the loop itself. This function gets as input: the start state of the loop Γ_{in}, the start time t, the output state from the analysis of the worst-case iteration Γ_{out}, the end time from the analysis of the worst-case iteration t' and the iteration bound ib. It returns an overestimated energy-aware component state and an overestimated global time.

   Because component state update functions δ preserve the ordering, the analysis of the worst-case iteration results in the maximum output state for any iteration. This, however, does not yet address the case where the loop is not entered at all. Therefore, we need to take the least-upper bound of the start state and the result of the analysis of the worst-case iteration.

   To overestimate time-dependent energy usage, we must revert component timestamps to the time of entering the loop. So, if a component is switched to a greater state at some point in the loop, the analysis assumes it has been in this state since entering the loop. Note that the least-upper bound of energy-aware component states does exactly this: maximise the non-energy-aware component state and minimise the timestamp. Taking $\Gamma_{base} = \mathbf{lub}(\Gamma_{in}, \Gamma_{out})$ we find both the maximum output states and the minimum timestamps.

   Now, we can add the consumption of the loop itself. We perform the following calculation for each component: $C_i^{\Gamma_{base}} :: \mathfrak{e} = C_i^{\Gamma_{in}} :: \mathfrak{e} + (C_i^{\Gamma_{out}} :: \mathfrak{e} - C_i^{\Gamma_{in}} :: \mathfrak{e}) \cdot ib$. We do something similar for the time consumption: $t_{ret} = t + ((t' - t) \cdot ib)$.

5. Processing time-dependent energy function **process-td**. When analysing an iteration of a loop, we must take care not to include any energy consumption outside of the iteration. This would lead to a large overestimation, since it would be multiplied by the (possibly overestimated) number of iterations. Therefore, before analysing the body, we add the time-dependent energy consumption to the energy accumulator for each component and set all timestamps to the current time. Otherwise, the time-dependent consumption before entering the loop would also be included in the analysis of the iteration. We introduce the function **process-td**(Γ, t), which adds $td(C_i, t)$ to $C_i :: \mathfrak{e}$ and sets $C_i :: \tau$ to t, for each component C_i in Γ.

Applying the rules overestimates the sum of the incidental energy consumption and the time-dependent energy consumption. However, the time-dependent energy consumption is only added to the accumulator at changes of component states. So, as for the energy-aware semantics, the time the components are in their current state should still be accounted for by calculating $\mathfrak{e}_{system}(\Gamma_{end}, t_{end})$.

4   Example: Wireless Sensor Node

To illustrate our analysis, we model a wireless sensor node, which has a sensor C_s and a radio C_r. Furthermore, it has a basic C_{imp} component for the implicit

```
while_n  n > 0  do
      C_s :: on();
         ... some code taking 10 seconds ...
      x = C_s :: off();
      C_r :: send(x);
      n = n - 1;
end while;
```

Fig. 3. Example program.

resource consumption. We analyse the energy usage of a program that repeatedly measures the sensor for 10 s, then sends the measurement over the radio, shown in Fig. 3. The example illustrates both *time-dependent* (sensor) and *incidental* (radio) energy usage. We choose a highly abstract modelling to keep the example brief and simple. A more elaborate example can be found in [23], in which a less abstract modelling is used and two algorithms are compared.

Modelling. The sensor component C_s has two states: s_{on} and s_{off}. It does not have any incidental energy consumption. It has a power draw (thus time-dependent consumption) only when on. For this power draw we introduce the constant $\mathfrak{e}_{\mathrm{on}}$. There are two component functions, namely on and off, which switch between the two component states.

The radio component C_r only has incidental energy consumption. It does not have a state. Its single component function is send, which uses $C_r :: \mathfrak{T}_{send}$ time and $C_r :: \mathfrak{E}_{send}$ energy.

The C_{imp} component models the *implicit* resource consumption by various language constructs. For the sake of presentation, we choose a very simple model here, in which only assignment consumes time and energy. We set both the associated constants $C_{imp} :: \mathfrak{T}_a$ and $C_{imp} :: \mathfrak{E}_a$. The other six constants in the C_{imp} model (see Sect. 3.1 for a list) are set to 0.

Application of the energy-aware semantics from Fig. 1 on the loop body results in a time consumption $\mathfrak{t}_{\mathrm{body}}$ of $10 + C_r :: \mathfrak{T}_{send} + 2 \cdot C_{imp} :: \mathfrak{T}_a$ and an energy consumption $\mathfrak{e}_{\mathrm{body}}$ of $10 \cdot \mathfrak{e}_{\mathrm{on}} + C_r :: \mathfrak{E}_{send} + 2 \cdot C_{imp} :: \mathfrak{E}_a$. Intuitively, the time and energy consumptions of the whole loop are $n(\mathfrak{t}_{\mathrm{body}})$ and $n(\mathfrak{e}_{\mathrm{body}})$.

Energy Consumption Analysis. The analysis (Fig. 2) always starts with a symbolic state. Note that only the sensor component C_s has a state. We introduce the symbol $\mathbf{on}_0^s$ for the symbolic start-state (on or off) of the sensor.

We start the analysis with the while loop. So, we apply the (*aWhile*) rule:

$$\Gamma_1 = \textbf{process-td}(\Gamma_0, t_0)$$

$$\frac{\{\textbf{wci}(\Gamma_1, n > 0; S_{\mathrm{body}}); t_0; \rho_0\}n > 0\{\Gamma_2; t_1; \rho_1\} \qquad \{\Gamma_2; t_1; \rho_1\}S_{\mathrm{body}}\{\Gamma_{it}; t_{it}; \rho_{it}\}}{\{\Gamma_0; t_0; \rho_0\}\textbf{while}_n\ n > 0\ \textbf{do}\ S_{it}\ \textbf{end while}\{\textbf{oe}(\Gamma_1, t_0, \Gamma_{it}, t_{it}, \rho(n)); \rho_{end}\}} \text{(aWhile)}$$

Since $C_{imp} :: \mathfrak{E}_w$ and $C_{imp} :: \mathfrak{T}_w$ are 0, we omit them here. We will first solve the **process-td** and **wci** functions, then analyse the loop guard and body (i.e. the part above the line), then determine the final results with the **oe** function.

We first add time-dependent energy consumption and set timestamps to t_0 for all components using the **process-td** function. If we would not do this, the time-dependent energy consumption *before* the loop would be included in the calculation of the resource consumption of the worst-case iteration. As this would be multiplied by the number of iterations, it would lead to a large overestimation. C_r and C_{imp} do not have a state, so we only need to add the time-dependent consumption of C_s: $td(C_s, t_0) = C_s :: \phi(\mathbf{on_0^s}) \cdot (t_0 - C_s :: \tau_0)$, where $C_s :: \tau_0$ is the symbolic value of the sensor timestamp before starting the analysis.

We must now find the worst-case iteration, using the **wci** function. For the C_s component we need the $\mathbf{ci}_s(n > 0; S_{\mathrm{body}})$ function. As the other components do not have a state, $\mathbf{ci}_{imp}(n > 0; S_{\mathrm{body}})$ and $\mathbf{ci}_r(n > 0; S_{\mathrm{body}})$ are simply the identity function. The loop body sets the state of the sensor to s_{off}, independent of the start state. So, $\mathbf{ci}_s(n > 0; S_{\mathrm{body}})$ always results in s_{off}. Now we can find the fixpoint. In the first iteration, we enter the loop with symbolic state $\mathbf{on_0^s}$. In the second iteration, the loop is entered with state s_{off}. In the third iteration, the loop is again entered with state s_{off}. We have thus found the fixpoint. The worst-case iteration can now be calculated by $\mathbf{wci}_s(n > 0; S_{\mathrm{body}}) = \mathbf{lub}(\mathbf{ci}_s^0(n > 0; S_{\mathrm{body}}), \mathbf{ci}_s^{bib1}(n > 0; S_{\mathrm{body}})) = \mathbf{on_0^s}$. Intuitively this means that, since after any number of iterations the sensor is off, the symbolic start state, in which it is unknown whether the sensor is on or off, yields the worst-case.

As there are no costs associated with the evaluation of expressions, the analysis of $n > 0$ using the $(aBinOp)$ rule does not have any effect on the state. We continue with analysis of the loop body, which starts with a call to component function **on**. We apply the $(aCallCmpF)$ rule:

$$\frac{\Gamma_3 = \Gamma_2[C_s :: s \leftarrow C_s :: \delta_{on}(C_s :: s), C_s :: \tau \leftarrow t_1, C_s :: \mathbf{e} \mathrel{+}= td(C_s, t_1)]}{\{\Gamma_2; t_1; \rho_1\} C_s :: on()\{\Gamma_3; t_1; \rho_2\}} \text{(aCallCmpF)}$$

There is no incidental energy consumption or time consumption associated with the call. We must however add the time-dependent energy consumption to the energy accumulator, by adding $td(C_s, t)$. Since we have just set $C_s :: \tau$ to t_0 and the evaluation of $n > 0$ costs 0 time, hence $t_1 = t_0$, $td(C_s, t_1)$ results in 0. The function $C_r :: \delta_{on}$ produces new component state s_{on}. It also saves the current timestamp to the component state, in order to know when the last state transition happened. For simplicity, we omit the application of the concatenation rule $(aConcat)$ in the following.

After ten seconds of executing other statements (which we assume only cost time, not energy), the sensor is turned off. The call to the function *off* returns the measurement, which is assigned to x. We must therefore first apply the $(aAssign)$ rule. This adds $C_{imp} :: \mathfrak{T}_a$ to the global time and $C_{imp} :: \mathfrak{E}_a$ to the energy accumulator. We now apply the $(aCallCmpF)$ rule to the right-hand side of the assignment, i.e. the call to $C_s :: off$. This updates the state of the component to s_{off}. It also executes the $td(C_s, t_2)$ function in order to determine the energy cost of the component being on for ten seconds. Because $t_2 = C_s :: \tau + 10$ and our model specifies a power draw of $\mathfrak{e}_{\mathbf{on}}$ for s_{on}, this results in $10 \cdot \mathfrak{e}_{\mathbf{on}}$. We add this to the energy accumulator of the sensor component.

We apply the $(aCallCmpF)$ rule again, this time to the *send* function of the C_r component. As the transmission costs a fixed amount of energy, all time-dependent constants associated with transmitting are set to zero. So, the $(aCall\text{-}CmpF)$ rule will only add the incidental energy usage specified by $C_s :: \mathfrak{E}_{send}$ and the constant time usage $C_s :: \mathfrak{T}_{send}$. Finally, we apply the $(aBinOp)$ rule, which has no costs, and the $(aAssign)$ rule, which again adds $C_{imp} :: \mathfrak{E}_a$ and $C_{imp} :: \mathfrak{T}_a$.

Analysis of the worst-case iteration results in global time t_{it} and energy-aware component state environment Γ_{it}. We can now apply the overestimation function $\mathbf{oe}(\Gamma_1, t_0, \Gamma_{it}, t_{it}, \rho(n))$. This takes as base the least-upper bound of Γ_1 and Γ_{it}, which in this case is exactly Γ_1 (note that the state of the sensor is overestimated as $\mathbf{on}_0^s$). It then adds the consumption of the worst-case iteration, multiplied by the number of iterations. The worst-case iteration results in a global time of $t_0 + 10 + C_r :: \mathfrak{T}_{send} + 2 \cdot C_{imp} :: \mathfrak{T}_a$. So, $\mathbf{oe}$ results in a global time t_{end} of $t_0 + n \cdot (10 + C_r :: \mathfrak{T}_{send} + 2 \cdot C_{imp} :: \mathfrak{T}_a)$. Note that this is equal to the time consumption resulting from the energy-aware semantics.

A similar calculation is made for energy consumption, for each component. Then, we can calculate $\mathfrak{e}_{system}$. In total, the $\mathbf{oe}$ function results in an energy usage of $\mathfrak{e}_0 + n \cdot (10 \cdot \mathfrak{e}_{on} + C_r :: \mathfrak{E}_{send} + 2 \cdot C_{imp} :: \mathfrak{E}_a)$. However, we still need to add the time-dependent energy consumption for each component. This is where potential overestimation occurs in this example. Since C_r and C_{imp} do not have a state, we only need to add the time-dependent consumption of C_s. After the analysis of the loop, the state of the sensor is overestimated as $\mathbf{on}_0^s$. We must therefore add a consumption of $td(C_s, t_{end}) = C_s :: \phi(\mathbf{on}_0^s) \cdot (t_{end} - t_0) = C_s :: \phi(\mathbf{on}_0^s) \cdot n \cdot (10 + C_r :: \mathfrak{T}_{send} + 2 \cdot C_{imp} :: \mathfrak{T}_a)$. This leads to an overestimation only in case $\mathbf{on}_0^s = s_{on}$ and $n > 0$. Otherwise, the result of the analysis is equal to that of the energy-aware semantics.

5   Soundness

In this section we outline a proof of the soundness of the energy-aware Hoare logic with respect to the energy-aware semantics. Intuitively, this means we prove that the analysis over-estimates the actual energy consumption. Here, we present only the fundamental theorems. The reader is referred to [23] for the full proof. Soundness of the annotations (loop bounds and symbolic states) is assumed in order to guarantee soundness of the final result.

We first show that the logic over-estimates time consumption. In order to establish soundness of the analysis of the energy consumption of the program, we need to establish first soundness of the timing analysis.

Theorem 1 (Timing over-estimation). *If $\langle S, \sigma, \Gamma, t \rangle \Downarrow^s \langle \sigma', \Gamma', t' \rangle$, then for any derivation $\{\Gamma; t; \rho\} S \{\Gamma_1; t_1; \rho_1\}$ holds that $t_1 \geq t'$.*

Proof. Theorem 1 derives from the property that the analysis does not depend on the timestamp in the precondition. For $\{\Gamma_1; t_1; \rho_1\} S \{\Gamma_2; t_2; \rho_2\}$, the duration $t_2 - t_1$ always over-estimates the duration of every possible real execution of the statement S. Theorem 1 is proved by induction on the energy-aware semantics and the energy analysis rules. The only source of any over-estimation are the rules (aIf) and $(aWhile)$. The (aIf) rule computes a max between the final timestamps of then-branch and the else-branch. In the $(aWhile)$ rule, the execution time of one iteration of the loop is over-estimated and multiplied by the loop bound, which is an over-estimation of the number of iterations of the loop.   □

Over-estimating the component state is fundamental for over-estimating the total energy consumption. A larger component state requires more power and hence consumes more energy.

Theorem 2 (Component state over-estimation). *If* $\{\Gamma; t; \rho\} S \{\Gamma_1; t_1; \rho_1\}$ *and* $\langle S, \sigma, \Gamma, t \rangle \Downarrow^s \langle \sigma', \Gamma', t' \rangle$ *then* $\Gamma_1 \geq \Gamma'$.

Proof. Induction on the energy-aware semantics and the energy analysis rules, yields that the update function δ preserves the ordering on component states (see Sect. 3.2).   □

Now, we can formulate and prove the main soundness theorem:

Theorem 3 (Soundness). *If* $\{t; \Gamma; \rho\} S \{t_1; \Gamma_1; \rho_1\}$ *and* $\langle S, \sigma, \Gamma, t \rangle \Downarrow^s \langle \sigma', \Gamma', t' \rangle$ *then* $\mathfrak{e}_{system}(\Gamma_1; t_1) \geq \mathfrak{e}_{system}(\Gamma'; t')$.

Proof. By induction on the energy-aware semantics and the energy analysis rules. Theorem 1 ensures that the final timestamp is an over-estimation of the actual time-consumption, hence the calculation of energy usage is based on an over-estimated period of time. Theorem 2 ensures (given that the analysis is non-decreasing with respect to component states, a larger input state means a larger output state) that we find the maximum state (including incidental energy-usage) that can result from an iteration of a loop body with the logic. This depends on the **wci** function determining the maximal initial state for any iteration. It follows, by the definition of $\mathfrak{e}_{system}$ that $\mathfrak{e}_{system}(\Gamma_1; t_1) \geq \mathfrak{e}_{system}(\Gamma'; t')$. The total energy consumption resulting from the analysis is larger than that of every possible execution of the analysed program.   □

6 Conclusion and Future Work

We presented a hybrid, energy-aware Hoare logic for reasoning about energy consumption of systems controlled by software. The logic comes with an analysis which is proven to be sound with respect to the semantics. To our knowledge, our approach is the first attempt at bounding energy-consumption statically in a way which is parametric with respect to hardware models. This is a first step towards a hybrid approach to energy consumption analysis in which the software is analysed automatically together with the hardware it controls.

Future Work. Many future research directions can be envisioned: e.g. providing an implementation of an automatic analysis for a real programming language[1],

---

[1] A proof-of-concept implementation for our While language is described in [24] and available at http://resourceanalysis.cs.ru.nl/energy.

performing energy measurements for defining component models, modelling of software components and enabling the development of tools that can automatically derive energy consumption bounds for large systems, finding the most suited tool(s) to provide the right loop bounds and annotations for our analysis and study energy usage per time unit on systems that are always running, removing certain termination restrictions.

Acknowledgements. We would like to thank the anonymous referees for their extensive feedback which helped us to considerably improve the paper.

References

1. Albers, S.: Energy-efficient algorithms. Commun. ACM **53**(5), 86–96 (2010)
2. Saxe, E.: Power-efficient software. Commun. ACM **53**(2), 44–48 (2010)
3. Ranganathan, P.: Recipe for efficiency: principles of power-aware computing. Commun. ACM **53**(4), 60–67 (2010)
4. te Brinke, S., Malakuti, S., Bockisch, C., Bergmans, L., Akşit, M.: A design method for modular energy-aware software. In: Proceedings of the 28th Annual ACM Symposium on Applied Computing, pp. 1180–1182. ACM, New York (2013)
5. Cohen, M., Zhu, H.S., Senem, E.E., Liu, Y.D.: Energy types. SIGPLAN Not. **47**(10), 831–850 (2012)
6. Sampson, A., Dietl, W., Fortuna, E., Gnanapragasam, D., Ceze, L., Grossman, D.: EnerJ: approximate data types for safe and general low-power computation. SIGPLAN Not. **46**(6), 164–174 (2011)
7. Zhurikhin, D., Belevantsev, A., Avetisyan, A., Batuzov, K., Lee, S.: Evaluating power aware optimizations within GCC compiler. In: GROW-2009: International Workshop on GCC Research Opportunities (2009)
8. Gheorghita, S.V., Corporaal, H., Basten, T.: Iterative compilation for energy reduction. J. Embed. Comput. **1**(4), 509–520 (2005)
9. Junior, M.N.O., Neto, S., Maciel, P.R.M., Lima, R., Ribeiro, A., Barreto, R.S., Tavares, E., Braga, F.: Analyzing software performance and energy consumption of embedded systems by probabilistic modeling: an approach based on coloured petri nets. In: Donatelli, S., Thiagarajan, P.S. (eds.) ICATPN 2006. LNCS, vol. 4024, pp. 261–281. Springer, Heidelberg (2006)
10. Nogueira, B., Maciel, P., Tavares, E., Andrade, E., Massa, R., Callou, G., Ferraz, R.: A formal model for performance and energy evaluation of embedded systems. EURASIP J. Embed. Syst. **2011**, 2:1–2:12 (2011)
11. Albert, E., Arenas, P., Genaim, S., Puebla, G., Zanardini, D.: COSTA: design and implementation of a cost and termination analyzer for Java bytecode. In: de Boer, F.S., Bonsangue, M.M., Graf, S., de Roever, W.-P. (eds.) FMCO 2007. LNCS, vol. 5382, pp. 113–132. Springer, Heidelberg (2008)
12. Hoffmann, J., Aehlig, K., Hofmann, M.: Multivariate amortized resource analysis. In: POPL'11, pp. 357–370. ACM (2011)
13. Atkey, R.: Amortised resource analysis with separation logic. In: Gordon, A.D. (ed.) ESOP 2010. LNCS, vol. 6012, pp. 85–103. Springer, Heidelberg (2010)
14. Aspinall, D., Beringer, L., Hofmann, M., Loidl, H.W., Momigliano, A.: A program logic for resources. Theor. Comput. Sci. **389**(3), 411–445 (2007)

15. Jayaseelan, R., Mitra, T., Li, X.: Estimating the worst-case energy consumption of embedded software. In: RTAS'06, pp. 81–90. IEEE (2006)
16. Kerrison, S., Liqat, U., Georgiou, K., Mena, A.S., Grech, N., Lopez-Garcia, P., Eder, K., Hermenegildo, M.V.: Energy consumption analysis of programs based on XMOS ISA-level models. In: LOPSTR'13, September 2013. Springer (2013)
17. Wilhelm, R., Engblom, J., Ermedahl, A., Holsti, N., Thesing, S., Whalley, D.B., Bernat, G., Ferdinand, C., Heckmann, R., Mitra, T., Mueller, F., Puaut, I., Puschner, P.P., Staschulat, J., Stenström, P.: The worst-case execution-time problem-overview of methods and survey of tools. ACM Trans. Embed. Comput. Syst. **7**(3), 1–53 (2008)
18. Shkaravska, O., van Eekelen, M.C.J.D., van Kesteren, R.: Polynomial size analysis of first-order shapely functions. Log. Methods Comput. Sci. **5**(2), 1–35 (2009)
19. Shkaravska, O., Kersten, R., Van Eekelen, M.: Test-based inference of polynomial loop-bound functions. In: PPPJ'10: Proceedings of the 8th International Conference on the Principles and Practice of Programming in Java, pp. 99–108. ACM (2010)
20. Kersten, R., van Gastel, B.E., Shkaravska, O., Montenegro, M., van Eekelen, M.: ResAna: a resource analysis toolset for (real-time) JAVA. Concurrency Comput.: Pract. Exper. **26**(14), 2432–2455 (2013)
21. Podelski, A., Rybalchenko, A.: A complete method for the synthesis of linear ranking functions. In: Steffen, B., Levi, G. (eds.) VMCAI 2004. LNCS, vol. 2937, pp. 239–251. Springer, Heidelberg (2004)
22. Hunt, J.J., Tonin, I., Siebert, F.: Using global data flow analysis on bytecode to aid worst case execution time analysis for real-time Java programs. In: Bollella, G., Locke, C.D. (eds.) JTRES. ACM International Conference Proceeding Series, vol. 343, pp. 97–105. ACM (2008)
23. Parisen Toldin, P., Kersten, R., van Gastel, B., van Eekelen, M.: Soundness proof for a Hoare logic for energy consumption analysis. Technical report ICIS-R13009, Radboud University Nijmegen, October 2013
24. Schoolderman, M., Neutelings, J., Kersten, R., van Eekelen, M.: ECAlogic: hardware-parametric energy-consumption analysis of algorithms. In: FOAL '14, pp. 19–22. ACM (2014)

Reasoning About Resources in the Embedded Systems Language Hume

Hans-Wolfgang Loidl[(✉)] and Gudmund Grov

School of Mathematical and Computer Sciences,
Heriot-Watt University, EH14 4AS, Edinburgh, UK
{H.W.Loidl,G.Grov}@hw.ac.uk

Abstract. In this paper we present an instrumented program logic for
the embedded systems language Hume, suitable to reason about resource
consumption. Matching the structure of Hume programs, it integrates
two logics, a VDM-style program logic for the functional language and
a TLA-style logic for the coordination language of Hume. We present
a soundness proof of the program logic, and demonstrate the usability
of these logics by proving resource bounds for a Hume program. Both
logics, the soundness proof and the example have been fully formalised
in the Isabelle/HOL theorem prover.

1 Introduction

Typically resources on embedded systems, such as memory, are very scarce.
Thus, an important property of an embedded program is to execute within these
limited resources. The Hume embedded systems language achieves a high degree
of predictability of resource consumption by defining two language layers: a
strict, higher-order functional language at the expression layer, and a restricted
language of interacting boxes at the coordination layer. With this design the
full computational power of a modern programming language can be used at
the expression layer. Where verification and analysis of an expression become
intractable, the code can be decomposed into a network of boxes. This language
is far more restricted, but easier to analyse and verify.

The different layers require different formalisms for proving (resource) properties. At the expression layer we apply standard techniques from program verification based on a deep embedding of the expression language, which facilitates
accurate resource modelling. We develop a Vienna Development Method (VDM)-
style [12] program logic to reason about programs. At the coordination layer we
find a network of boxes defining their interactions. The properties of interest for
this layer can often be described as system invariants. We therefore mechanise a
Temporal Logic of Actions (TLA) [14] on this layer. Both layers have been fully
formalised in the Isabelle/HOL theorem prover. In this paper, we build a shallow
embedding of the coordination layer of Hume on top of an existing, shallow TLA
embedding [8] and integrate it with the VDM-style logic.

© Springer International Publishing Switzerland 2014
U. Dal Lago and R. Peña (Eds.): FOPARA 2013, LNCS 8552, pp. 110–126, 2014.
DOI: 10.1007/978-3-319-12466-7_7

While these two kinds of logics, and their formalisations, have been studied in isolation, this paper makes three contributions in (i) proving soundness for the VDM-style program logic in Isabelle/HOL; (ii) combining both logics into an integrated Isabelle/HOL formalisation; and (iii) demonstrating the usability of the combined logics by proving, in Isabelle/HOL, bounded heap consumption of a simple Hume program.

2   The Hume Language

Hume [9] is designed as a layered language where the *coordination layer* is used to construct reactive systems using a finite-state-automata based notation, representing a static system of interconnecting *boxes*; while the *expression layer* describes the behaviour of a box using a strict, higher-order, purely functional rule-based notation. A central design goal of Hume is predictability of resource consumption, so that each expression-layer program can execute within bounded time and space constraints. Thus, we are mainly interested in proving resource bounds for Hume programs.

The *expression layer* of Hume corresponds to a strict, higher-order language with general algebraic datatypes. To accurately model resource consumption, we formalise the expression layer of Hume in the form that is used as an intermediate language in the compiler, distinguishing between first- and higher-order function calls for performance reasons. This language makes some structural restrictions on the source code, most notably it is in let-normal-form, and uses general algebraic data-types:

$$\text{Patt} \ni p ::= x \mid v \mid c\,x_1 \ldots x_n \mid \_$$

$$\text{Expr} \ni e ::= x \mid v \mid c\,x_1 \ldots x_n \mid f\,x_1 \ldots x_n \mid x\,x_1 \ldots x_n \mid \texttt{if } x \texttt{ then } e_1 \texttt{ else } e_2 \mid$$
$$x_1 \oplus x_2 \mid \texttt{let } x = e_1 \texttt{ in } e_2 \mid \texttt{case } x \texttt{ of } p_1 \rightarrow e_1 \texttt{ otherwise } e_2$$

A pattern p is either a variable $x \in \text{Var}$, a value $v \in \text{Val}$, a constructor application $c\,x_1 \ldots x_n$ ($c \in \text{Constr}$) or a wildcard $\_$. An expression e is either a variable x, a value v, a constructor application $c\,x_1 \ldots x_n$, a first-order function call of f or a higher-order function call of x with arguments $x_1 \ldots x_n$, a conditional, a binary primitive operation $\oplus$, a let-expression, or a case expression. The latter is a one-step matching expression, with a default branch to be used if the match was unsuccessful. The entire program is represented by a table funTab, which maps a function name (f) to its formal arguments ($args_f$) and to its body ($body_f$).

The *coordination layer* of Hume comprises of a set of concurrent, asynchronous boxes, scheduled in an alternating sequence of execute and super-step phases. In the *execute* phase any box with sufficient available inputs will be executed. In the following *super-step* phase, the results of the boxes will be copied to single-buffer wires, provided they are free. Boxes are defined through pattern-matching rules, of the form $p \rightarrow e$, using the syntax of the expression language above. The semantics of these rules is similar to the one of expression-layer pattern matching, but additionally accounts for possibly missing input values.

```
box copy
  in(i::[int 16])
  out( o1::[int 16], o2::[int 16])
  match  x -> copy(x)

box fuse
  in(i::[int 16],i2::[int 16])
  out(o::[int 16])
  match (x,y) -> fuse(x,y)
```

Fig. 1. The Running Hume Example

To illustrate, Fig. 1, shows a configuration of two connected boxes, copy followed by fuse, which will be our running example in this paper: Here, both boxes work on lists of 16-bit integers as input value, and calls two respective functions which we will return to later. In general, the body of a box is comprised of a sequence of rules, with the left hand side being matched against the input data, and first successful match enabling execution of its right hand side. The two output wires of copy are the inputs of fuse, and we will in this discussion ignore the source input of copy and the destination output of fuse.

3 A VDM-style Program Logic for the Expression Layer

3.1   Operational Semantics

Figure 2 summarises the domains used in the formalisation. The sets of identifiers for variables ($x \in$ Var), functions ($f \in$ Funs), and data constructors ($c \in$ Constr) are disjoint. We represent heaps ($h \in$ Heap) by finite mappings from locations to values (written $\leadsto_f$), and environments ($E \in$ Env) by total functions of variables to values (written $\Rightarrow$). A location $l \in$ Locn is either a natural number (representing an address in the heap), or the constant nil. We write Locn* for the domain of sequences of elements in Locn, $E \star \vec{xs}$ for mapping E over the sequence $\vec{xs}$, prefix $\#$ for the length of a sequence and $++$ for append of sequences. We model heap usage of h as the size of its domain, i.e. $|\text{dom } h|$. Other resources, such as time, are modelled in the *resource vector* $p \in$ Resources and $\smile$ combines these.

$$
\begin{array}{llll}
l,a,r \in \text{Locn} & = \mathbb{N} \uplus \{\text{nil}\} & E, E' \in \text{Env} & = \text{Var} \Rightarrow \text{Val} \\
h,h' \in \text{Heap} & = \text{Locn} \leadsto_f \text{Val} & G \in \text{Ctxt} & = \mathcal{P}\{(\text{Expr, Assn})\} \\
v \in \text{Val} & = \{\bot\} \uplus \mathbb{Z} \uplus \mathbb{B} \uplus \text{Locn} \uplus (\text{Constr, Locn}^*) \uplus (\text{Funs, } \mathbb{N}, \text{Locn}^*) \\
P,Q,A \in \text{Assn} & = \text{Env} \Rightarrow \text{Heap} \Rightarrow \text{Heap} \Rightarrow \text{Val} \Rightarrow \text{Resources} \Rightarrow \mathbb{B} \\
p \in \text{Resources} & = (clock :: \mathbb{Z}, \; callc :: \mathbb{Z}, maxstack :: \mathbb{Z})
\end{array}
$$

Fig. 2. Basic Domains

We obtain costs for basic operations from a parameterised table $\mathcal{R}$. The operation freshloc has the property: freshloc $s \notin s$, for all s.

A judgement of the big-step operational semantics, shown in Fig. 3, has the form $E, h \vdash e \Downarrow_m (v, h', p)$ and is read as follows: given a variable environment, E, and a heap, h, e evaluates in m steps to the value v, yielding the modified heap,

$$\frac{}{E, h \vdash v \Downarrow_1 (v, h, \mathcal{R}^{\text{const}})} \text{ (Value)} \qquad \frac{E\ x = v}{E, h \vdash x \Downarrow_1 (v, h, \mathcal{R}^{\text{var}})} \text{ (Var)}$$

$$\frac{l = \text{freshloc (dom } h)}{E, h \vdash c\ \vec{xs} \Downarrow_1 (l, h', \mathcal{R}^{\text{constr}}\ ^{\#\vec{xs}})} \text{ (Constr)} \qquad \frac{\begin{array}{cc} v_1 = E\ x_1 & v_2 = E\ x_2 \\ v = v_1 \oplus v_2 \end{array}}{E, h \vdash x_1 \oplus x_2 \Downarrow_1 (v, h, \mathcal{R}^{\oplus})} \text{ (PrimBin)}$$

$$\frac{E\ x = \text{true} \qquad E, h \vdash e_1 \Downarrow_n (v, h', p')}{E, h \vdash \text{if } x \text{ then } e_1 \text{ else } e_2 \Downarrow_{n+1} (v, h', p' \smallfrown \mathcal{R}^{\text{if true}})} \text{ (IfTrue)}$$

$$\frac{E\ x = \text{false} \qquad E, h \vdash e_2 \Downarrow_n (v, h', p')}{E, h \vdash \text{if } x \text{ then } e_1 \text{ else } e_2 \Downarrow_{n+1} (v, h', p' \smallfrown \mathcal{R}^{\text{if false}})} \text{ (IfFalse)}$$

$$\frac{E, h \vdash e_1 \Downarrow_m (v, h', p') \qquad E(x := v), h' \vdash e_2 \Downarrow_n (v'', h'', p'')}{E, h \vdash \text{let } x = e_1 \text{ in } e_2 \Downarrow_{m+n} (v'', h'', p' \smallfrown p'' \smallfrown \mathcal{R}^{\text{let}})} \text{ (Let)}$$

$$\frac{l = E\ x \quad \text{MATCH } E, h \vdash p \text{ at } l \Downarrow (E', v') \quad v' \neq \bot \quad E', h \vdash e_1 \Downarrow_n (v, h', p')}{E, h \vdash \text{case } x \text{ of } p \to e_1 \text{ otherwise } e_2 \Downarrow_{n+1} (v, h', p' \smallfrown \mathcal{R}^{\text{case true}})}$$
$$\text{(CaseTrue)}$$

$$\frac{l = E\ x \quad \text{MATCH } E, h \vdash p \text{ at } l \Downarrow (E', v') \quad v' = \bot \quad E, h \vdash e_2 \Downarrow_n (v, h', p')}{E, h \vdash \text{case } x \text{ of } p \to e_1 \text{ otherwise } e_2 \Downarrow_{n+1} (v, h', p' \smallfrown \mathcal{R}^{\text{case false}})}$$
$$\text{(CaseFalse)}$$

$$\frac{E' = E(args_f := E \star \vec{xs}) \qquad E', h \vdash body_f \Downarrow_n (v, h', p)}{E, h \vdash f\ \vec{xs} \Downarrow_{n+1} (v, h', p \smallfrown \mathcal{R}^{f\ \#\vec{xs}})} \text{ (CallFun)}$$

$$\frac{\begin{array}{ccc} l = E\ x & \text{Some } (f, i, \vec{rs}) = h\ l & i + \#\vec{xs} < \#args_f \\ l' = \text{freshloc (dom } h) & h' = h(l' \mapsto (f, (i + \#\vec{xs}), (\vec{rs} + \!\!+ (E \star \vec{xs})))) \end{array}}{E, h \vdash x\ \vec{xs} \Downarrow_1 (l', h', \mathcal{R}^{\text{ap false}\ \#\vec{xs}})}$$
$$\text{(CallVarUnderApp)}$$

$$\frac{\begin{array}{cc} l = E\ x \quad \text{Some } (f, i, \vec{rs}) = h\ l \quad i + \#\vec{xs} = \#args_f \\ E' = E(args_f := \vec{rs} + \!\!+ (E \star \vec{xs})) \qquad E', h \vdash body_f \Downarrow_n (v, h', p) \end{array}}{E, h \vdash x\ \vec{xs} \Downarrow_{n+1} (v, h', p \smallfrown \mathcal{R}^{\text{ap true}\ \#\vec{xs}})}$$
$$\text{(CallVarExact)}$$

Fig. 3. Operational Semantics of Expression-layer Hume

h', and consumes resources p. A value v is itself the result (VALUE). For a variable x a lookup is performed in E (VAR). For a constructor application $c\ \vec{xs}$ the heap is extended with a fresh location, mapped to c and its argument values (CONSTR). For primitive operations a shallow embedding is used so that the operator $\oplus$ can be directly applied to the values of its variables (PRIMBIN). A conditional returns the value of the then branch e_1 or the else branch e_2, depending on the value of x. A let binds the result of e_1 to the variable x and returns the value of the body e_2 (LET). The judgement of the pattern-matching semantics, MATCH $E, h \vdash p$ at $l \Downarrow$ (E', l'), matches the value at location l against pattern p, returning a modified environment and l on success, or the same environment and $\bot$ on failure. A case is a one-step matching expression, that matches a variable x against a pattern p; if successful its value is that of e_1 (CASETRUE), if unsuccessful its value is that of e_2 (CASEFALSE). In first-order function calls, we bind the values in the arguments to the formal parameters ($args_f$), and use the modified environment to evaluate the body ($body_f$) of the function f (CALLFUN). For higher-order function calls, with function closures represented as triples $(f, i, \vec{rs})$ of function name, number of arguments and their values, we have to distinguish two cases. If we have fewer than the required number of arguments, the result will be a new closure consisting of f, the number of arguments supplied so far and their values. If we have precisely the number of arguments that the function requires, the values in the closure and the those of the arguments ($\vec{xs}$) are bound to the formal parameters ($args_f$) of the function, before the function body is evaluated using these new bindings (CALLVAREXACT).

3.2   Program Logic

We use a VDM-style of assertions [12] to model properties of programs. This means that rather than using the more common Hoare-triples of pre-condition, program and post-condition, we use a judgement of the following form, $G \rhd e :$ P, meaning that expression e fulfils the assertion P in a context G. As shown in Fig. 2, an *assertion* is a predicate over the components of the operational semantics, and a context is a set of pairs of program expression $e \in$ Expr and assertion $P \in$ Assn. See [13] for a comparison of VDM- and Hoare-style logics.

The rules in Fig. 4 define the program logic for expression-layer Hume. A value w is the result value, and the heap is unchanged (VDMVALUE). A variable x requires a lookup in the environment, and the heap is unchanged (VDMVAR). In a constructor application, the newly allocated location is existentially quantified, and the heap is updated with a binding to this location (VDMCONSTR). The two possible control flows in the conditional are encoded in the logic as implications, based on the boolean contents of variable x (VDMIF). In the let rule (VDMLET), the intermediate value, heap and resources are existentially quantified, and the environment for executing e_2 is updated accordingly. The control flows in the case construct are encoded as implications, based on the result from the pattern match (VDMCASE). In a first order call (VDMCALLFUN), the assertion to be proven for f is added with the call into the context, and the function body has

$$\frac{}{G \,\triangleright\, w \;:\; \lambda E\ h\ h'\ v\ p.\ v = w \ \wedge\ h = h' \ \wedge\ p = \mathcal{R}^{\mathtt{const}}} \quad (\text{VDM}\textsc{Value})$$

$$\frac{}{G \,\triangleright\, x \;:\; \lambda E\ h\ h'\ v\ p.\ v = E\ x \ \wedge\ h = h' \ \wedge\ p = \mathcal{R}^{\mathtt{var}}} \quad (\text{VDM}\textsc{Var})$$

$$\frac{}{\begin{array}{l} G \,\triangleright\, c\ \vec{xs} \;:\; \lambda E\ h\ h'\ v\ p.\ \exists l\ \vec{rs}.\ l = \mathrm{freshloc(dom}\ h) \ \wedge\ \vec{rs} = E \star \vec{xs} \ \wedge \\ \qquad\qquad v = l \ \wedge\ h' = h(l \mapsto (c,\ \vec{rs})) \ \wedge p = \mathcal{R}^{\mathtt{constr}\ \#\vec{xs}} \end{array}} \quad (\text{VDM}\textsc{Constr})$$

$$\frac{}{\begin{array}{l} G \,\triangleright\, x_1 \oplus x_2 \;:\; \lambda E\ h\ h'\ v\ p.\ \exists v_1\ v_2.\ E\ x_1 = v_1 \ \wedge\ E\ x_2 = v_2 \ \wedge \\ \qquad\qquad v = v_1 \oplus v_2 \ \wedge\ h = h' \ \wedge\ p = \mathcal{R}^{\oplus} \end{array}} \quad (\text{VDM}\textsc{PrimBin})$$

$$\frac{G \,\triangleright\, e_1 \;:\; P_1 \qquad G \,\triangleright\, e_2 \;:\; P_2}{\begin{array}{l} G \,\triangleright\, \mathtt{if}\ x\ \mathtt{then}\ e_1\ \mathtt{else}\ e_2 \;:\; \lambda E\ h\ h'\ v\ p. \\ (E\ x = \mathrm{true} \ \longrightarrow\ \exists p'.\ P_1\ E\ h\ h'\ v\ p' \ \wedge\ p = p' \smile \mathcal{R}^{\mathtt{if\ true}}) \wedge \\ (E\ x = \mathrm{false} \ \longrightarrow\ \exists p'.\ P_2\ E\ h\ h'\ v\ p' \ \wedge\ p = p' \smile \mathcal{R}^{\mathtt{if\ false}}) \end{array}} \quad (\text{VDM}\textsc{If})$$

$$\frac{G \,\triangleright\, e_1 \;:\; P_1 \qquad G \,\triangleright\, e_2 \;:\; P_2}{\begin{array}{l} G \,\triangleright\, \mathtt{let}\ x\ =\ e_1\ \mathtt{in}\ e_2 \;:\; \lambda E\ h\ h'\ v\ p.\ \exists v'\ h''\ p'\ p''. \\ (P_1\ E\ h\ h''\ v'\ p' \ \wedge\ P_2\ E(x := v')\ h''\ h'\ v\ p'' \ \wedge\ p = p' \smile p'' \smile \mathcal{R}^{\mathtt{let}}) \end{array}} \quad (\text{VDM}\textsc{Let})$$

$$\frac{G \,\triangleright\, e_1 \;:\; P_1 \qquad G \,\triangleright\, e_2 \;:\; P_2}{\begin{array}{l} G \,\triangleright\, \mathtt{case}\ x\ \mathtt{of}\ p_1 \to e_1\ \mathtt{otherwise}\ e_2 \;:\; \lambda E\ h\ h'\ v\ p.\ \forall l.\ l = E\ x \ \longrightarrow\ \forall E'\ v'. \\ \mathtt{MATCH}\ E,\ h \vdash\ p_1\ \mathtt{at}\ l \Downarrow (E', v') \ \longrightarrow \\ ((v' = \bot \ \longrightarrow\ \exists p'.\ P_2\ E\ h\ h'\ v\ p' \ \wedge\ p = p' \smile \mathcal{R}^{\mathtt{case\ false}}) \ \wedge \\ (v' \neq \bot \ \longrightarrow\ \exists p'.\ P_1\ E'\ h\ h'\ v\ p' \ \wedge\ p = p' \smile \mathcal{R}^{\mathtt{case\ true}})) \end{array}} \quad (\text{VDM}\textsc{Case})$$

$$\frac{\{(f\ \vec{xs}, P)\} \cup G \,\triangleright\, body_f \;:\; \lambda E\ h\ h'\ v\ p.\ \forall E'.\ E = E'(args_f := E' \star \vec{xs}) \ \longrightarrow \\ \qquad\qquad\qquad\qquad P\ E'\ h\ h'\ v\ (p \smile \mathcal{R}^{f\ \#\vec{xs}})}{G \,\triangleright\, f\ \vec{xs} \;:\; P} \quad (\text{VDM}\textsc{CallFun})$$

$$\frac{\begin{array}{l} \forall E\ h\ h'\ v.\ \Phi_{x,\vec{xs}}\ E\ h\ h'\ v \ \longrightarrow\ P\ E\ h\ h'\ v\ \mathcal{R}^{\mathtt{ap\ false}\ \#\vec{xs}} \\ (\forall f.\ \{(x\ \vec{xs}, P)\} \cup G \,\triangleright\, body_f \;:\; \lambda E\ h\ h'\ v\ p.\ \forall E'.\ (\exists \vec{rs}.\ \Psi_{x,\vec{xs}}\ E'\ h\ h'\ v\ f\ \vec{rs} \ \wedge \\ E = E'(args_f := \vec{rs} \mathbin{+\!\!+} (E' \star \vec{xs})) \ \longrightarrow\ P\ E'\ h\ h'\ v\ (p \smile \mathcal{R}^{\mathtt{ap\ true}\ \#\vec{xs}})) \end{array}}{G \,\triangleright\, x\ \vec{xs} \;:\; P} \quad (\text{VDM}\textsc{CallVar})$$

$$\frac{(e, P) \in G}{G \,\triangleright\, e \;:\; P} \ (\text{VDM}\textsc{Ax}) \qquad \frac{\forall E\ h\ h'\ v\ p.\ P\ E\ h\ h'\ v\ p \ \longrightarrow\ Q\ E\ h\ h'\ v\ p \qquad G \,\triangleright\, e \;:\; P}{G \,\triangleright\, e \;:\; Q} \ (\text{VDM}\textsc{Conseq})$$

$$\begin{array}{l} \Phi_{x,\vec{xs}} \equiv \lambda E\ h\ h'\ v.\ \exists l\ l'\ f\ i\ \vec{rs}.\ E\ x = l \ \wedge\ h\ l = \mathrm{Some}(f,\ i,\ \vec{rs}) \ \wedge\ i + \#\vec{xs} < \#args_f \ \wedge \\ \qquad\qquad l' = \mathrm{freshloc\ (dom}\ h) \ \wedge\ v = l' \ \wedge\ h' = h(l' \mapsto (f,\ (i + \#\vec{xs}),\ (\vec{rs} \mathbin{+\!\!+} (E \star \vec{xs})))) \\ \Psi_{x,\vec{xs}} \equiv \lambda E'\ h\ h'\ v\ f\ \vec{rs}.\ \exists l\ i\ .\ E'\ x = l \ \wedge\ h\ l = \mathrm{Some\ } (f,\ i,\ \vec{rs}) \ \wedge\ i + \#\vec{xs} = \#args_f \end{array}$$

Fig. 4. Program Logic for Expression-layer Hume

to fulfil the assertion, after modifying environment and resources. The higher-order function call (VDMCALLVAR) directly encodes the preconditions of the two cases of under application (Φ) and of exact application (Ψ) from the operational semantics. Thus, the definition of Φ reads as follows: for the pre-state E, h we find in variable x a closure with i arguments, and the total number of arguments is smaller than the function's arity ($i + \#\vec{xs} < \#args_f$). In this case, the result state v, h', p is constructed such that the result value is a new closure, containing all arguments, and the result heap is updated accordingly. The definition of Ψ reads as follows: For the pre-state E', h we find in variable x a closure with i arguments, and the total number of arguments matches the function's arity ($i + \#\vec{xs} = \#args_f$). In this case, the second premise in rule VDMCALLVAR demands that the body of f ($body_f$) fulfils the assertion P, with the environment adjusted for parameter passing and a modified resource vector to account for the costs of the function call. Note that Ψ has to be parameterised over the function f and the argument values $\vec{rs}$ captured in its closure, so that the VDMCALLVAR rule can quantify over f and $\vec{rs}$. In particular, the quantification over f scopes over the entire second judgement in the premise of VDMCALLVAR, because it is needed to retrieve the function's body via $body_f$. Finally, the quantification over $\vec{rs}$ scopes over the entire pre-condition inside the assertion. The environment E is constructed out of E' by binding the formal parameters to the values in the closure ($\vec{rs}$) and those retrieved from the arguments $\vec{xs}$. The final two rules, VDMAX and VDMCONSEQ, are the standard rules for using an axiom, present in the context, and for logical consequence in the meta-language.

3.3   Soundness

We define (relativised) semantic validity of an assertion for an expression in a context as follows.

Definition 1 (validity). *Assertion P is valid for expression e ($\models_n e : P$) iff*

$$\forall m \leq n.\ \forall E\ h\ h'\ v\ p.\ (E,\ h\ \vdash\ e\ \Downarrow_m\ (v, h', p)) \ \longrightarrow\ P\ E\ h\ h'\ v\ p$$

Assertion P is valid for expression e in context G ($G\ \models e : P$) iff

$$\forall n.\ (\forall (e', P') \in G.\ \models_n\ e'\ :\ P')\ \longrightarrow\ \models_n\ e\ :\ P$$

Based on these simple definitions of validity, exploiting the shallow nature of our embedding of assertions, the soundness theorem can be stated as follows.

Theorem 1 (soundness). *For all contexts G, expressions e, assertions P*

$$G \rhd e : P \Longrightarrow G \models e : P$$

Proof structure: By induction over the rules of the program logic. In the case of function calls, induction over the index n in the semantics relation[1].   □

---

[1] This is theorem `soundness` in the Isabelle/HOL theory `GRUMPY.thy`.

Our approach to proving *mutually recursive functions*, building on [1], is to define a predicate *goodContext*. In the first-order case, it requires context elements to be function calls associated to entries in the function specification table $\mathcal{F}$, and, informally, the context must be powerful enough to prove all of its assertions. This means that it has to encode information about all functions called in the body of the function under consideration. Note the universal quantification over the arguments $\vec{ys}$ of the function. This allows us to adapt the function arguments to the concrete values provided at the call site.

Definition 2. *A context G is called a good context w.r.t. specification table $\mathcal{F}$, written goodContext $\mathcal{F}$ G, iff*

$$\forall e\ P\ .\ (e, P) \in G \longrightarrow$$
$$\exists f\ \vec{xs}.\ e = f\ \vec{xs}\ \wedge\ P = \mathcal{F}\ f\ \vec{xs}\ \wedge$$
$$\forall \vec{ys}.\ G \rhd body_f\ :$$
$$\lambda E\ h\ h'\ v\ p.\ \forall E'.\ E = E'(args_f := E' \star \vec{ys}) \longrightarrow$$
$$(\mathcal{F}\ f\ \vec{ys})\ E'\ h\ h'\ v\ (p \smallsmile \mathcal{R}^{f\ \#\vec{ys}})$$

$$\frac{G \rhd e : P}{G \cup G' \rhd e : P}\ (\text{CTXTWEAK}) \qquad \frac{G \rhd e' : P' \qquad (\{(e', P')\} \cup G) \rhd e : P}{G \rhd e : P}\ (\text{CUT})$$

$$\frac{\text{finite } G \qquad |\,G\,| = n \qquad goodContext\ \mathcal{F}\ G \qquad (e, P) \in G}{\emptyset \rhd e : P}\ (\text{MUTREC})$$

$$\frac{goodContext\ \mathcal{F}\ G \qquad \text{finite } G \qquad (f\ \vec{xs}, \mathcal{F}\ f\ \vec{xs})\ \in G}{\emptyset \rhd f\ \vec{ys}\ :\ \mathcal{F}\ f\ \vec{ys}}\ (\text{VDMADAPT})$$

Fig. 5. Admissible Rules

Figure 5 shows a set of *admissible rules* that are useful in proving concrete program properties. The rules CTXTWEAK and CUT are proven by induction over the derivation of $G \rhd e : P$. Rule MUTREC is proven by induction over the size of G. Finally, VDMADAPT, which is used when proving a property on a function call, follows directly from MUTREC. Note that VDMADAPT reduces the proof to one of the above good context predicate that has to be constructed for the function under consideration. Thus, proving *goodContext $\mathcal{F}$ G*, for a specially constructed context, becomes the main step in proving a property for (mutually) recursive functions. Section 5 gives an example.

4   Incorporating the Coordination Layer Using TLA

While VDM is suitable for the expression layer, it is not a natural way of reasoning about properties of the coordination layer. This is a stateful layer, where boxes communicate over single-buffered wires. Here, we are interested in invariance properties for the overall program, expressed using the wires. For such networks and properties, a logic such as TLA [14], originally developed to reason about concurrent systems, is more suitable, and has been formalised in Isabelle/HOL [8]. A TLA specification contains a set of variables, and invariants are predicates over these variables, preceded by the temporal $\Box$ (always) operator. The behaviour of the system is written in what is known as the *action level*, which logically is a predicate over two states: a before state and an after state, separated by priming all variables in the after state. Let $\mathcal{N}$ be such an action predicate, for a specification with variables v. Moreover, let I be a state predicate (i.e. a predicate over a single state), which represents the initial state of all variables. A specification of this system is then written $I \wedge \Box[\mathcal{N}]_v$, meaning that I holds initially and every step henceforth is either a step by $\mathcal{N}$ or a stuttering step, leaving v unchanged (such stuttering a step enables internal steps which are useful when refining a program which is not considered further here). As both program and properties are expressed in the same logic, the invariant P is proven by proving the implication $I \wedge \Box[\mathcal{N}]_v \longrightarrow \Box P$, i.e. P holds initially, and holds for all steps $\mathcal{N}$ can make. The key to proving this is the following INV rule of TLA [14]:

$$\frac{I \longrightarrow P \qquad P \wedge \mathcal{N} \longrightarrow P' \qquad P \wedge v' = v \longrightarrow P'}{I \wedge \Box[\mathcal{N}]_v \longrightarrow \Box P} \tag{INV}$$

TLA is mechanised in Isabelle/HOL using possible world semantics [6]. This embedding is shallow, which enables direct use of existing Isabelle/HOL tools and theorems. Moreover, the Hume embedding is also shallow, which simplifies the expression layer integration.

Hume boxes are executed in a two-step lock step algorithm [7]: in the first execute phase all runnable boxes are executed sequentially; this is followed by a super-step, which copies box outputs to wires. This is embedded by two (enumeration) meta-variables: a scheduler s and a program counter pc.

The scheduling is formalised by an action S, which updates the scheduling variable s. The scheduler depends on whether pc' equals the (defined) "last box" in the enumeration type.

Definition 3. *By giving the value of this "last box" predicate as argument, the scheduler is defined as follows:*

$$S \ last\_box \equiv s' = (\mathit{if}\ s = Execute \wedge last\_box\ \mathit{then}\ Super\ \mathit{else}\ Execute)$$

Each Hume wire is represented by a variable, and to achieve the lock-step scheduling, each box has one result buffer variable for each output. This is illustrated in Fig. 1, which shows the example discussed in Sect. 5. In addition, each box has a state/mode variable (e.g. copy_st) of the enumeration type consisting of *Runnable*, *Blocked*, and *Matchfail*: a *Runnable* box can be executed; *Matchfail* denotes that the box has failed in matching the inputs and cannot be executed; a *Blocked* box has failed asserting the output buffer with the output wires, and cannot be executed. All the result buffers and wires are of type Val. In addition each program has one heap $h \in$ Heap and a $p \in$ Resources which specifies resource properties. Every box has one action for each phase.

In the super-step, box outputs are checked, and if successful the result buffer is copied to the wires. For heap structures, this is a shallow copy of the references on the stack, thus the heap is left unchanged. In the execute phase, only the current box (identified by pc) is executed in a given step. Moreover, it is only executed when it is not *Blocked*. In a box execution, there is first a check that there is a match that will succeed (a box may not be total). If this check succeeds, $E, h \vdash e \Downarrow (v, h', p)$ is used to represent the execution of the expression layer e, under the environment E, with a correct variable (Var) to value (Val) mapping and the current heap h.

To enable usage of the inductively defined judgement $E, h \vdash e \Downarrow (v, h', p)$ within the TLA-embedded expression layer, it must be seen as a function, accepting the old heap h, environment E and expression e as input, and returning the new heap h', the return value v and resources used p.

Definition 4. *We define the* exe *function as follows:*

$$((v, h', p) = exe\ E\ h\ e) \equiv (E,\ h\ \vdash\ e\ \Downarrow\ (v, h', p))$$

The *exe* function is then used to update the result buffer, heap h and resource variable p in the TLA representation. The proof of TLA invariants of the coordination layer relies on pre- and post-conditions of the *exe* function. To achieve this, the *exe* function must be linked with the VDM logic for proofs of properties of the form $E, h \vdash e \Downarrow (v, h', p)$. This is achieved by the following theorem, which is the key for the integration between the TLA and VDM logic:

Theorem 2 (vdmexe[2]). $[\![((v, h', p) = exe\ E\ h\ e); \emptyset \rhd e : A]\!] \Longrightarrow A\ E\ h\ h'\ v\ p$

Proof. The assumption applied to the *soundness* theorem gives $\emptyset \vDash e : A$. By the definition of *validity in context*, this gives $\vDash \emptyset \longrightarrow (\vDash e : A)$ which gives (G1) $\vDash e : A$. Moreover, the definition of *exe* and the assumption of *vdmexe*, implies $E, h \vdash e \Downarrow (v, h', p)$. The goal then follows from unfolding (G1), by using the definition of *validity*, followed by an application of it. □

This integration works directly due to the shallow TLA embedding and the shallow assertion language for a VDM property. VDM properties are then explored within TLA, since the *vdmexe* theorem turns the VDM property into a HOL predicate, enabling the VDM proof to be independent of TLA. We will now illustrate how the VDM and TLA logics are combined in the proof of a Hume invariant $\Box P$. This approach will be known as the "*standard Hume/TLA invariant proof structure.*"

Definition 5 (the standard Hume/TLA invariant proof structure). *As a first step the* INV *rule above is applied. The base (initial state)* $I \Rightarrow P$ *and "unchanged"* $P \wedge v' = v \Rightarrow P'$ *cases are trivial and not discussed further.*

---

[2] This is theorem vdmexe in `Integrated.thy`.

In the main $P \wedge \mathcal{N} \Rightarrow P'$ case, $\mathcal{N}$ is a conjunction of the scheduler S and all the box actions. It starts by case-analysis on s, creating two cases. The first case, $s = $ Super is achieved purely within the TLA logic. The second case, $s = $ Execute is followed by a case analysis on pc. *If P' depends on the result of execution* pc, *then it is followed by a case-split on* pc_st $= $ Blocked *(the box state/mode variable). Let e be the expression layer of this box. If the check for a match succeeds, then the proof of P' depends on a sufficiently strong A such that $\emptyset \triangleright e : A$ can be proved by the VDM-logic. The* vdmexe *theorem is then applied to enable the use of A in the main TLA proof of P'.*

5   Example — a Verified List-Copy Configuration

To illustrate the integrated reasoning infrastructure, we will verify a resource property over the heap, for our running example shown in Fig. 1[3]. The *copy* box performs a list-copy over its input list, producing two identical lists; the *fuse* box takes these two lists and combines them into one list, using only the smaller of the two elements from the input lists. We first define these two functions in let-normal-form:

$copy\ [x]\ \equiv$ case x of
    $($CONS $[h,t]) \rightarrow$ let $y\ =\ copy\ [t]$ in CONS $[h,y]$ otherwise   NIL $[]$
$fuse\ [x_0, x_1] \equiv$ case x_0 of $($CONS $[h_0, t_0]) \rightarrow$ case x_1 of $($CONS $[h_1, t_1]) \rightarrow$
    let $y\ =\ fuse\ [t_0, t_1]$ in let $b\ =\ (h_0 < h_1)$ in
        if b then CONS $[h_0, y]$ else CONS $[h_1, y]$
    otherwise   NIL $[]$ otherwise   NIL $[]$

Here, the *fuse* box accepts two inputs (x, y), binding them in the environment, and the *copy* box returns two values. This is captured by the following interface: $(fuse\_res', h', r') = exe\ \emptyset(x := w1, y := w2)\ h\ (fuse\ [x, y])$. For *copy* we model the fact that the input from $w3$ is forwarded directly to its first output as follows: $(copy\_res1', (copy\_res2', h', r')) = (w3, exe\ \emptyset(x := w3)\ h\ (copy\ [x]))$. The super-step is similar to the one already described, although the copy box checks and updates two wires.

In this example the box network is open, with input wire $w3$ and output wire $w4$. Therefore we have to extend $\mathcal{N}$ with an additional conjunct *env*, which models the environment. Both $w3$ and $w4$ are assumed to be updated by other boxes (or streams). In the coordination-layer proof below, we model a single, non-overlapping evaluation where wire $w3$ initially contains a list structure $(mList)$ and is never updated, while wire $w4$ consumes the result.

We specify the layout of a list structure by the following inductive definition *mList*. Informally, $(n, a, U, h) \in mList$ means that at address a in heap h we find a list structure with n CONS and 1 NIL cells, covering the addresses in U.

---

[3] This example is theory `ListCopy.thy` of the Isabelle/HOL embedding.

$$\frac{h\ a = \text{Some (NIL, [])}}{(0, a, \{a\}, h) \in mList}\ \text{MLISTNIL} \qquad \frac{\begin{array}{c} h\ a = \text{Some (CONS}, [r, r']) \\ a \notin U \qquad (n, r', U, h) \in mList \end{array}}{(n+1, a, U \cup \{a\}, h) \in mList}\ \text{MLISTCONS}$$

The following definition is useful to express that address a contains a list of length n: $list\ h\ a\ n \equiv \exists\ U.\ (n, a, U, h) \in mList$

We are interested in the heap consumption, specified as a relation between the pre-heap h and the post-heap h'. We define these resource properties as entries in the *function specification table* $\mathcal{F}$. The specification for *copy* states, that provided the argument x points to a list structure of length n in the pre-heap h, the size of the post-heap h' is at most the size of the pre-heap plus $n+1$. Thus, the heap consumption of the *copy* function is $n + 1$. Furthermore, the result of the function (in v) is a list of length n at location r' in the post-heap h'. The remaining clauses assure that the input data structure is not modified. The clause $h \sim_{(\text{dom } h')-U'} h'$ states that the heaps h and h' contain the same values at addresses (dom h') $- U'$, i.e. only the values in U' are modified. The clause $U' \cap (\text{dom } h) = \emptyset$ states that the copy of the list does not overlap with the input list, and the $(n, r, U, h') \in mList$ clause states that the structure of the input list is indeed unchanged. Analogously, the specification for *fuse* states, that provided the arguments x_0 and x_1 point to list structures, of the same length n_0 and n_1, at locations r_0 and r_1 in the pre-heap h, the size of the post-heap h' is at most the size of the pre-heap plus $n_0 + 1$. The result of the function is a list of length n_0 at location r' in the post-heap.

$\mathcal{F}\ copy\ [x] \equiv \lambda E\ h\ h'\ v\ p.\ \forall n\ r\ U.$
$\quad E\ x\ =\ r\ \wedge\ (n, r, U, h) \in mList\ \longrightarrow$
$\quad\quad |\ \text{dom } h'\ | \leq |\ \text{dom } h\ | +n + 1\ \wedge\ (\exists r'\ U'.\ v = r'\ \wedge\ (n, r', U', h) \in mList\ \wedge$
$\quad\quad h \sim_{(\text{dom } h')-U'} h'\ \wedge\ U' \cap (\text{dom } h) = \emptyset\ \wedge\ (n, r, U, h') \in mList)$
$\mathcal{F}\ fuse\ [x_0, x_1] \equiv \lambda E\ h\ h'\ v\ p.\ \forall n_0\ n_1.$
$\quad (\exists r_0\ U_0.\ E\ x_0\ =\ r_0\ \wedge\ (n_0, r_0, U_0, h) \in mList)\ \wedge$
$\quad (\exists\ r_1\ U_1.\ E\ x_1\ =\ r_1\ \wedge\ (n_1, r_1, U_1, h) \in mList\ \wedge\ n_0 = n_1)\ \longrightarrow$
$\quad\quad |\ \text{dom } h'\ | \leq |\ \text{dom } h\ | +n_0 + 1\ \wedge$
$\quad\quad (\exists n'\ r'\ U'.\ v = r'\ \wedge\ (n', r', U', h') \in mList\ \wedge\ n' = n_0)$

In order to prove these two assertions, we first construct for each function a context, with specifications for all function calls in its body. We then prove the good context predicate, for these contexts. In both functions we find one direct recursive call, and therefore construct a one-element context for each function.

Lemma 1. $goodContext\ \mathcal{F}\ \{(copy\ \vec{xs},\ \mathcal{F}\ copy\ \vec{xs})\}\ \wedge$
$\qquad\qquad goodContext\ \mathcal{F}\ \{(fuse\ \vec{xs}, \mathcal{F}\ fuse\ \vec{xs})\}$

Proof structure. The same structure as in the proof for Theorem 3, but using VDMAX when encountering the recursive call. ☐

Now the resource consumption can be proven in an empty context:

Theorem 3. $\emptyset\ \triangleright\ copy\ \vec{xs}\ :\ \mathcal{F}\ copy\ \vec{xs}\ \wedge\ \emptyset\ \triangleright\ fuse\ \vec{xs}\ :\ \mathcal{F}\ fuse\ \vec{xs}$

Proof structure. In both clauses, by first applying the syntax-directed rules, and by applying CTXTWEAK, VDMADAPT and Lemma 1 when encountering the recursive call. The proof of the remaining subgoal proceeds by case distinction over the structure of the input, and over the cases in the conditional[4].   □

On coordination layer the main theorem below states that at each point in the execution any wire and any expression-layer result is either empty ($\bot$), or contains a reference to a list structure with N elements ($list\ldots$).

Theorem 4. □ $\left(\begin{array}{l} (w1 = \bot \vee \; list\ h\ w1\ N)\ \wedge\ (w2 = \bot \vee \; list\ h\ w2\ N) \\ \wedge\ (w3 = \bot \vee \; list\ h\ w3\ N)\ \wedge\ (w4 = \bot \vee \; list\ h\ w4\ N) \\ \wedge\ (copy\_res1 = \bot \vee \; list\ h\ copy\_res1\ N) \\ \wedge\ (copy\_res2 = \bot \vee \; list\ h\ copy\_res2\ N) \\ \wedge\ (fuse\_res = \bot \vee \; list\ h\ fuse\_res\ N) \end{array} \right)$

Proof structure. Standard TLA reasoning reduces the proof of each conjunct as a separate invariant, which is outlined below[5].   □

We will focus on the proof of one conjunct, shown as Lemma 5. The other conjuncts are verified similarly. We start with the proof for an auxiliary theorem, relating the expression-layer result to the coordination-layer structure.

Lemma 2. $list\ H\ V\ M\ \wedge\ (W, H', S) = exe\ \emptyset(x := V)\ H\ (copy\ [x]) \longrightarrow list\ H'\ V\ M$

Proof structure. This is proven from the expression-layer specification of *copy* using the Integration Theorem (vdmexe). □

Note that this property asserts that after box-execution the input V is still a *list*. Capital letters represent free variables. The invariant in Lemma 3 ensures that no other boxes (incl. the environment) can execute when $copy\_res1 \neq \bot$.

Lemma 3. □$(copy\_res1 \neq \bot \longrightarrow w1 = \bot \wedge\ w2 = \bot \wedge w3 = \bot \wedge\ fuse\_res = \bot)$

Proof. The proof follows the 'standard Hume/TLA invariant proof structure' and follows from □$(w3 \neq \bot \longrightarrow w1 = \bot \wedge\ w2 = \bot \wedge copy\_res1 = \bot \wedge copy\_res2 = \bot \wedge\ fuse\_res = \bot)$, which can be proven directly using the same structure.   □

The following invariant asserts that wires and expression-layer results are well-formed, and that box executions do not interfere.

Lemma 4. □$(w3 = \bot \vee \; list\ h\ w3\ N)$

Proof structure. This is proved using the 'standard Hume/TLA invariant proof structure' with the same strengthening as in the proof of Lemma 3.   □

Lemma 5. □$(copy\_res1 = \bot \vee \; list\ h\ copy\_res1\ N)$

Proof. The proof follows the 'standard Hume/TLA invariant structure', strengthened by Lemmas 3 and 4, instantiating the free variables of Lemma 2.   □

---

[4] These are theorems `copy_resources_ok` and `fuse_resources_ok` in `ListCopy.thy`.
[5] This is the main theorem in the theory file `ST.thy`.

The proofs of the other conjuncts of Theorem 4 have the same structure, using lemmas over the expression-layer result of *copy* and *fuse* similar to Lemma 2. Since the entire expression-layer heap is discarded after execution, the size of the live heap at coordination-layer is the sum of all data structures reachable from the wires and results. From the 7 *list* predicates in Theorem 4 we can immediately conclude that $7N + 7$ is such a bound. Moreover, Lemma 3 and similar lemmas for the other expression-layer results restrict the possible combinations of non-$\perp$ values in the wires and results: after executing *copy* only $w1, w2$, *copy_res1* and *copy_res2* are non-$\perp$; after executing *fuse* only $w4$ and *fuse_res* are non-$\perp$. Therefore, we can refine the upper bound on the size of the live heap to $4N + 4$.

The (unoptimised) proof of *copy* takes 329 steps, with several instantiations of heap structures, address sets and list predicates. In particular, establishing the validity of the separation clause is the most complex part of the proof. To tackle this issue it would be possible to enhance the expression-level logic with concepts from separation logic [20], which enables reasoning about heap structures, without having to explicitly encode that the rest of the heap is unmodified.

6   Related Work

Our VDM-style, resource-aware program logic builds on our logic in [1], especially in handling mutual recursion and parameter adaptation, where the source language was an abstraction of JVM bytecode, but without algebraic data-types or higher-order functions as in Hume. In our formalisation we use techniques studied in Nipkow's Hoare-style logic for a simple while language in [18] and the Hoare-style logic for Java-light by von Oheimb [22], both formalised in Isabelle/HOL. Our choice of a VDM-style logic was partially driven by the study of variants of Hoare-style and VDM-style logics explored in Kleymann's thesis [13]. Isabelle/HOL formalisations of a program logic for a call-by-value, functional language are studied in [15]. Other related reasoning infrastructures, mostly for object-oriented languages, are: the Jive system [17], building on a Hoare-style logic for a Java subset [19]; the LOOP project's encoding of a Hoare-style logic, with extensions for reasoning about abrupt termination and side-effects, in PVS/Isabelle [11]; the *Why* system [4], with *Krakatoa* [16] as front-end, using Coq for formalisation and interactive proofs of JML-annotated Java programs.

Our choice of TLA for the coordination layer comes from the stateful nature of both systems, whereas approaches such as process algebras are stateless. We have previously used TLA to reason about scheduling algorithms [7]. In a shallow embedding of the expression layer directly in Isabelle/HOL, we have managed to automate the verification of 'standard Hume/TLA invariant proof structure' by developing a set of special purpose tactics. However, this does not enable the type of resource reasoning achieved here, and we have no soundness guarantees of the embedding. Details can be found in the second author's PhD thesis [6]

Our integration of the two formalisations follows the "state-behaviour integration" approach, exemplified by csp2b [3], CSP||B [21] and CSP-OZ [5]. However, in this integration computation is state based (B or Z), and the communication uses a stateless *process algebra* [2]. In Hume on the other hand, computation is in a (stateless) purely functional language, and communication is in a (stateful) finite state machine language. All these tools are motivated by using suitable tools for the different aspects of a system. csp2b [3] works by translating the CSP (process algebra) [10] into a B machine, while CSP||B [21] and CSP-OZ [5] give a CSP semantics to the computational aspect (B and Object-Z). In our case, both the TLA and VDM representations are built on top of Isabelle/HOL, and integration is naturally achieved by "unlifting" into the Isabelle/HOL level, and no (resource preserving) translation is required.

7   Conclusion and Future Work

We have presented an integrated Isabelle/HOL formalisation of the two language layers of Hume. Our formalisation combines a high level of abstraction through the VDM-style program logic for the expression layer, ensured through the meta-theoretic soundness result, with a direct, shallow embedding of a TLA logic for the coordination layer. By formalising the most suitable style of logics for these two layers in a theorem prover, we obtain a powerful reasoning infrastructure. The expression layer soundness result has been formalised in the theorem prover. We have applied this infrastructure to one Hume program, verifying a basic resource property of the code, refining the latter through proofs of the availability of wire-values. This example shows that while the proofs can become lengthy, the proof strategies that can be applied follow naturally from the respective logics.

Notably, the TLA proofs follow a common structure, and we have explored their automation, through proof tactics, in the stand-alone coordination layer embedding [6]. In our integrated system, the proofs are (manually) driven by this structure at the coordination layer. Where needed, we make use of the VDM logic to prove the required properties for expressions. For resource properties only simple inequalities, e.g. over heap sizes, have to be proven. As discussed at the end of Sect. 5, the main structure of the proof follows naturally from the rules of the logics and the integration theorem. One complication, however, is to assert disjointness of data structures, requiring explicit reasoning over sets of addresses. Here techniques from separation logic could help [20] to raise the level of abstraction further. Finally, note that the Isabelle/HOL mechanisation currently only works for Isabelle 2007, and we are in the process of porting it to the latest version of Isabelle (Isabelle 2013), which we plan to publish in the Archive of Formal Proofs (http://afp.sourceforge.net). The theories for this paper are available at: http://www.macs.hw.ac.uk/~dsg/projects/hume-reasoning.html#FOPARA13.

References

1. Aspinall, D., Beringer, L., Hofmann, M., Loidl, H.-W., Momigliano, A.: A program logic for resources. Theoret. Comput. Sci. **389**(3), 411–445 (2007)
2. Baeten, J.C.M.: A brief history of process algebra. Theoret. Comput. Sci. **335**(2–3), 131–146 (2005)
3. Butler, M.J.: csp2B: a practical approach to combining CSP and B. Form. Asp. Comput. **12**(3), 182–198 (2000)
4. Filliâtre, J.-C.: Why: a multi-language multi-prover verification tool. Research report 1366, LRI, Université Paris Sud, March 2003
5. Fischer, C.: CSP-OZ: a combination of object-Z and CSP. In: Formal Methods for Open Object-Based Distributed Systems (FMOODS '97), pp. 423–438 (1997)
6. Grov, G.: Reasoning about correctness properties of a coordination programming language. Ph.D. thesis, Heriot-Watt University (2009)
7. Grov, G., Michaelson, G., Ireland, A.: Formal verification of concurrent scheduling strategies using TLA. In: International Conference on Parallel and Distributed Systems (ICPADS'07), pp. 1–6. IEEE, Hsinchu, December 2007
8. Grov, G., Merz, S.: A Definitional Encoding of TLA* in Isabelle/Hol. Archive of Formal Proofs, Formal proof development, November 2011. http://afp.sf.net/entries/TLA
9. Hammond, K., Michaelson, G.J.: Hume: a domain-specific language for real-time embedded systems. In: Pfenning, F., Macko, M. (eds.) GPCE 2003. LNCS, vol. 2830, pp. 37–56. Springer, Heidelberg (2003)
10. Hoare, C.A.R.: Communicating Sequential Processes. Prentice-Hall, Englewood Cliffs (1985)
11. Huisman, M., Jacobs, B.: Java program verification via a Hoare logic with abrupt termination. In: Maibaum, T. (ed.) FASE 2000. LNCS, vol. 1783, p. 284. Springer, Heidelberg (2000)
12. Jones, C.: Systematic Software Development Using VDM. Prentice Hall, Englewood Cliffs (1990)
13. Kleymann, T.: Hoare logic and VDM: machine-checked soundness and completeness proofs. Ph.D. thesis, LFCS, University of Edinburgh (1999)
14. Lamport, L.: The temporal logic of actions. ACM Trans. Program. Lang. Syst. **16**(3), 872–923 (1994)
15. Longley, J., Pollack, R.: Reasoning about CBV functional programs in Isabelle/HOL. In: Slind, K., Bunker, A., Gopalakrishnan, G.C. (eds.) TPHOLs 2004. LNCS, vol. 3223, pp. 201–216. Springer, Heidelberg (2004)
16. Marché, C., Paulin-Mohring, C., Urbain, X.: The krakatoa tool for certification of Java/JavaCard programs annotated in JML. J. Logic Algebraic Program. **58**(1–2), 89–106 (2004)
17. Müller, P., Meyer, J., Poetzsch-Heffter, A.: Programming and interface specification language of JIVE. Fernuniversität Hagen, Technical report (2000)
18. Nipkow, T.: Hoare logics for recursive procedures and unbounded nondeterminism. In: Bradfield, J.C. (ed.) CSL 2002 and EACSL 2002. LNCS, vol. 2471, p. 103. Springer, Heidelberg (2002)
19. Poetzsch-Heffter, A., Müller, P.O.: A programming logic for sequential Java. In: Swierstra, S.D. (ed.) ESOP 1999. LNCS, vol. 1576, p. 162. Springer, Heidelberg (1999)
20. Reynolds, J.: Separation logic: a logic for shared mutable data structures. In: Symposium on Logic in Computer Science (LICS'02), pp. 55–74. IEEE Computer Society, Copenhagen, July 2002

21. Schneider, S., Treharne, H.: CSP theorems for communicating B machines. Form. Asp. Comput. Appl. Form. Methods **17**(4), 390–422 (2005)
22. von Oheimb, D.: Hoare logic for Java in Isabelle/HOL. Concurr. Comput. Pract. Exp. **13**(13), 1173–1214 (2001)

On Paths-Based Criteria for Polynomial Time Complexity in Proof-Nets

Matthieu Perrinel[(⊠)]

ENS de Lyon, CNRS, Inria, UCBL, Université de Lyon. Laboratoire LIP,
Lyon, France
matthieu.perrinel@ens-lyon.fr

Abstract. Several variants of linear logic have been proposed to characterize complexity classes in the proofs-as-programs correspondence. Light linear logic (LLL) ensures a polynomial bound on reduction time, and characterizes in this way the class $Ptime$. In this paper we study the complexity of linear logic proof-nets and propose two sufficient criteria, one for elementary time soundness and the other one for $Ptime$ soundness, based on the study of paths inside the proof-net. These criteria offer several benefits: they provide a bound for any reduction sequence and they can be used to prove the complexity soundness of several variants of linear logic. As an example we show with our criteria a strong polytime bound for the system L^4 (light linear logic by levels).

1 Introduction

Implicit computational complexity is a research field aiming to characterize complexity classes by syntactically restricting models of computation. The main application is to achieve automated certification of a program's complexity. Due to its focus on resources management, linear logic (LL) [9] is a promising setting for this field. One of the interests of the linear logic approach is that it admits higher order types: functions are basic objects (e.g. functions can take functions as arguments and return functions).

In the linear logic approach, programs are proofs and program execution is done by the elimination of the cut rule in the proof. Proofs are either presented as sequent calculus derivations or as *proof-nets*, a graph based syntax for proofs. Programming in proof-nets is unnatural for most people. Fortunately, the proofs-as-programs correspondence states that a logical system corresponds to a type system for the λ-calculus [3]. λ-calculus is not used directly as a programming language but functional programming languages (e.g. Haskell) are based on it.

Most of the works controlling complexity in linear logic define a subsystem of LL enjoying some bounds on the length of cut-elimination sequences. Typically, the subsystem is defined in such a way that the programs are decomposed in *strata* and communication between strata is constrained. So syntax defines strata which in turn controls interaction. However a bunch of distinct subsystems have been defined in this way, corresponding to different notions of strata. How are these systems related and are there general principles underlying them?

© Springer International Publishing Switzerland 2014
U. Dal Lago and R. Peña (Eds.): FOPARA 2013, LNCS 8552, pp. 127–142, 2014.
DOI: 10.1007/978-3-319-12466-7_8

To investigate these questions we propose here a kind of reverse approach: instead of defining strata by syntax we will define them by interaction. We believe this will contribute to establish these strata-based systems on solid ground. In a second step this could help in designing more general systems, and possibly also in analyzing the intrinsic limitations of strata-based systems.

Concretely we will consider a general language, LL, and define criteria on proofs based on interaction, expressed here by relations between subterms. These criteria entail bounds on the length of cut-elimination sequences. They can then be used either directly, to prove bounds on the complexity of a LL proof, or indirectly to prove that a LL subsystem entails complexity bounds. Concretely, the relations between subterms that we consider are defined by studying some paths in the proof, by means of context semantics [4].

Note that it is harder to control complexity in a higher order than in a first-order language. Thus, variants of LL for $Ptime$ have to enforce strict control. Therefore, many polynomial time λ-terms can not be typed in those variants. For example, the λ-calculus type-system $DLAL$ [3] (obtained from the LL subsystem LLL [10]) is $Ptime$ *extensionally complete*. It means that for any function f computable in polynomial time, there exists a λ-term computing f typable in $DLAL$. This is proved by showing that it is possible to simulate any Turing machine for a polynomial number of steps with a $DLAL$ typed term. However, $DLAL$ is not *intensionally complete*: there are λ-terms which compute in polynomial time but are not typable in $DLAL$.

Contributions. In this paper, for any proof-net G, we define two relations $\twoheadrightarrow$ and $\succcurlyeq_2$ between some special elements of G called "boxes". A proof-net is said stratified if $\twoheadrightarrow$ is acyclic, and controls dependence if $\succcurlyeq_2$ is acyclic. A stratified proof-net normalizes in a number of steps bounded by an elementary function of its size. A proof-net satisfying both criteria normalizes in a number of steps bounded by a polynomial on its size. The elementary function and the polynomial only depend on the depth of the proof-net in terms of boxes and the depth of the $\twoheadrightarrow$ and $\succcurlyeq_2$ relations. Our approach has a number of benefits:

(i)   strong vs weak complexity bounds;
(ii) use of the criteria to prove complexity bounds for variants of linear logic;
(iii) better understanding of existing linear logic systems for complexity.

Concerning (i), a programming language comes with a reduction strategy which determines the reduction order. For example: do we reduce the arguments before passing them to functions (call by value) or not (call by name)? Complexity bounds are sometimes proved for farfetched strategies, which are unlikely to be implemented in a real programming language. The bounds proved in this paper do not depend on the strategy (*strong complexity bounds*).

As to (ii), we show how to use our approach to study variants of linear logic: we can establish the complexity soundness of a system by showing that all its proofs satisfy our criteria. Here, we will apply this technique to L^4, for which only a weak $Ptime$ bound was previously known. Note that it is relatively easy to prove that all proof-nets of a given system are stratified and control dependence. The more difficult work is done in the proof that those properties entail complexity bounds, and this is independent of the system. Factorizing proofs of complexity bounds may ease the search and the understanding of such proofs. Actually, an important progress had already been made in this direction by Dal Lago with context semantics [4]: he provided a common method to prove complexity bounds for several systems like ELL, LLL and SLL [11]. Here we go a step further by designing higher level criteria, based on context semantics.

Concerning point (iii), we believe the present work can shed a new light on variants of linear logic for complexity. Indeed, the elaboration of such a system can be divided in two steps: first finding an abstract property implying a complexity bound and then finding a way to entail this property by syntactic means. Several extensions of LLL have been studied, like L^4 [1] and MS [13]. As those systems verify our criteria, we think those criteria illustrate a common property underlying these logics. Moreover we have found some λ-terms satisfying our criteria without being in any system of the above list. Thus, it seems we could define more expressive systems by being closer to our criteria.

Related works. In the search for an expressive system for complexity properties, Dal Lago and Gaboardi have defined the type system $dlPCF$ [5] which characterizes exactly the execution time of PCF programs. Type-checking in $dlPCF$ is undecidable, but one can imagine restricting $dlPCF$ to a decidable fragment. Their framework can be seen as a top-down approach. Here we follow a bottom-up approach: we take inspiration from previous decidable type systems characterizing $Ptime$ and relax conditions losing neither soundness nor decidability.

Our main tool will be context semantics, a tool related to geometry of interaction [7]. Baillot and Pedicini used geometry of interaction to characterize elementary time [2]. Dal Lago adapted context semantics to study quantitative properties of cut-elimination [4]. From this point of view, an advantage of context semantics compared to the syntactic study of reduction is its genericity: some common results can be proved for different variants of linear logic, which allows to factor out proofs of complexity results for these various systems. We use the context semantics of Dal Lago, adapted to classical linear logic.

Here, we only give the statement of theorems, proofs can be found in [12].

2   Linear Logic

Linear logic [9] can be thought of as a refinement of System F [8] which focuses on the duplication of arguments. In LL, $A \Rightarrow B$ is decomposed into $!A \multimap B$. $!A$ means "infinitely many proofs of A" and $A \multimap B$ means "using one proof of A, I can prove B". In fact, $A \multimap B$ is a notation of $A^{\perp} \invamp B$. We can view $(\_)^{\perp}$ as a negation and $\invamp$ as a disjunction. The conjunction is written $\otimes$. Finally $\forall$ and $\exists$ allow us to quantify over the set of formulae. Compared to full linear logic, we use neither additives, nor constants and we add a modality: $\S$, introduced by Girard for the expressive power of LLL. Precisely, formulae of LL are defined inductively as follows (X ranges over a countable set of variables).

$$\mathcal{F} = X \mid X^{\perp} \mid \mathcal{F} \otimes \mathcal{F} \mid \mathcal{F} \mathcal{R} \mathcal{F} \mid \forall X \mathcal{F} \mid \exists X \mathcal{F} \mid !\mathcal{F} \mid ?\mathcal{F} \mid \S \mathcal{F}$$

As examples, let us notice that $\forall X.X \multimap X$ is provable (for any formula X, using one proof of X, we get a proof of X). On the contrary, $\forall X.X \multimap (X \otimes X)$ is not provable because, in the general case, we need two proofs of X to prove $X \otimes X$.

We define inductively $(\_)^{\perp}$ on $\mathcal{F}$, which can be viewed as a negation: $(X)^{\perp} = X^{\perp}$, $(X^{\perp})^{\perp} = X$, $(A \otimes B)^{\perp} = A^{\perp} \mathcal{R} B^{\perp}$, $(A \mathcal{R} B)^{\perp} = A^{\perp} \otimes B^{\perp}$, $(\forall X.A)^{\perp} = \exists X.A^{\perp}$, $(\exists X.A)^{\perp} = \forall X.A^{\perp}$, $(!A)^{\perp} = ?(A^{\perp})$, $(?A)^{\perp} = !(A^{\perp})$ and $(\S A)^{\perp} = \S(A^{\perp})$.

Definition 1. *A* proof-net *is a graph-like structure defined inductively by the graphs of Fig. 1 (G and H being proof-nets). Edges are labelled by formulae.*

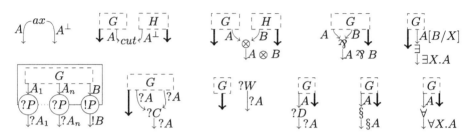

Fig. 1. Construction of proof-nets. For the $\forall$ rule, we require X not to be free in the formulae labelling the other conclusions of G.

Readers familiar with linear logic may notice the absence of the digging principle ($!A \multimap !!A$). We removed it from this article to simplify the definitions. The way we deal with digging is described in [12].

The set of edges is written E_G. The rectangle in the left-most proof-net on the second row of Fig. 1 is called a *box*. Formally a box is a subset of the nodes of the proof-net. We say that an edge (l, m) belongs to box B if l is in B. The number of boxes containing an edge e is its *depth* written $\partial(e)$. ∂_G is the maximum depth of an edge of G. The set of boxes of G is B_G. Let us call B the box in Fig. 1. The node labelled $!P$ is the *principal door* of B, its outgoing edge is written $\sigma(B)$. The $?P$ nodes are the *auxiliary doors* of box B. $D_G(B)$ is the set of doors of B. The doors of box B do not belong to box B.

Lists are written in the form $[a_1; ...; a_n]$, $l_1 @ l_2$ represents the concatenation of l_1 and l_2, and $.$ represents "push" ($[a_1; ...; a_n].b = [a_1; ...; a_n; b]$). If X is a set, $|X|$ is the cardinal of X. If $b, h, n \in \mathbb{N}$, we define b_h^n by $b_0^n = n$ and $b_{h+1}^n = b^{b_h^n}$.

The λ-terms correspond, through the proofs-as-programs paradigm, to proof-nets. Intuitively, proof-nets are λ-terms where applications and abstractions are respectively replaced by $\otimes$ and $\mathcal{R}$ and with additional information on duplication. Cut-elimination is a relation, described in Fig. 2, on proof-nets which corresponds to β-reduction. Proof-nets are stable under cut-elimination.

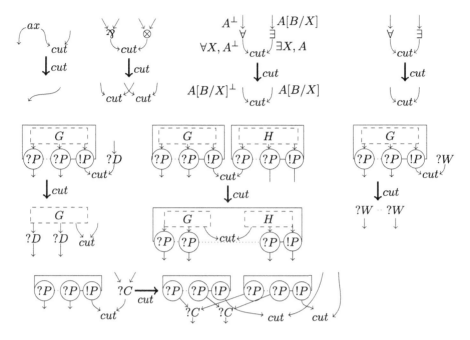

Fig. 2. Rules of cut-elimination. In the $\forall/\exists$ rule, the substitution of the variable X by B takes place on the whole net.

3   Context Semantics

Let us first give an informal explanation. The usual way to prove strong bounds on a rewriting system is to assign a weight T_G to each term G such that, if G reduces to H, $T_G > T_H$. In LL, the $!P/?C$ step makes the design of such a weight hard: a whole box is duplicated, increasing the number of edges, cuts,... Let us suppose that G reduces to H, an element (box, edge or node) x' of H is said to be a *residue* of an element x of G if x' "comes" from x. In Fig. 3, e, e_1, e_2, e_3 and e_4 are residues of e. A duplicate of $x \in G$ is a residue of x which has at most 1 residue (it can not be copied). In Fig. 3, the duplicates of e are e_1, e_3 and e_4. Then, $\sum_{e \in E_G} |\{\text{duplicates of } e\}|$ does not increase, even during $!P/?C$ steps. We will define a weight based on this sum.

Context semantics determines, among the paths in a proof-net G, which paths are preserved by cut-elimination (such paths are called *persistent* in the literature [7]). Computing those paths is somehow like reducing the proof-net, and the persistent paths starting at the principal door of a box correspond to the duplicates of this box. In context semantics, persistent paths are captured by tokens (*contexts*) travelling across the proof-net according to some rules. The following definitions introduce the components of the tokens.

A *signature* is a list of $\mathbf{1}$ and $\mathbf{r}$. A signature corresponds to a list of choices of premises of $?C$ nodes, to designate a particular duplicate of a box. The signature

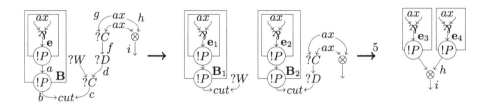

Fig. 3. Cut-elimination of a proof-net

$t.r$ means: "I choose the right premise, and in the next $?C$ nodes I will use t to make my choices". The set of signatures is written S.

A *potential* is a list of signatures: a signature corresponds to the duplication of one box, but an element is copied whenever any of the boxes containing it is cut with a $?C$ node. The set of potentials is written P. A potential is meant to represent duplicates. The duplicates of e in Fig. 3, e_1, e_3 and e_4, will be respectively represented by potentials $[[\mathtt{l}]; []]$, $[[\mathtt{r}]; [\mathtt{r}]]$ and $[[\mathtt{r}]; [\mathtt{l}]]$. The *canonical potentials*, will characterize exactly the potentials corresponding to a duplicate.

A *trace element* is one of the following characters: $\mathfrak{N}_l, \mathfrak{N}_r, \otimes_l, \otimes_r, \forall, \exists, \S, !_t, ?_t$ with t a signature. A trace element means "I have crossed a node with this label, from that premise to its conclusion". A *trace* is a non-empty list of trace elements. The set of traces is T. A trace is a memory of the path followed, up to cut-eliminations. We define duals of trace elements: $\mathfrak{N}_l^{\perp} = \otimes_l$, $!_t^{\perp} = ?_t$,... and extend the notion to traces by $([a_1; \cdots ; a_k])^{\perp} = [a_1^{\perp}; \cdots ; a_k^{\perp}]$.

A *polarity* is either $+$ or $-$. It will tell us in which way we are crossing the arrows. We define $+^{\perp} = -$ and $-^{\perp} = +$.

A *context* is a tuple (e, P, T, p) with $e \in E_G$, $P \in \mathsf{P}$, $T \in \mathsf{T}$ and p a polarity. It can be seen as a state of a token that will travel around the net. It is located on edge e (more precisely its duplicate corresponding to P) with orientation p and carries information T about its past travel.

The nodes define two relations $\rightsquigarrow$ and $\hookrightarrow$ on contexts. The rules are presented in Fig. 4. Observe that these rules are deterministic. For any rule $(e, P, T, p) \rightsquigarrow (g, Q, U, q)$ presented in Fig. 4, we also define the dual rule $(g, Q, U^{\perp}, q^{\perp}) \rightsquigarrow (e, P, T^{\perp}, p^{\perp})$. We define $\mapsto$ as the union of $\rightsquigarrow$ and $\hookrightarrow$. In other words, $\mapsto$ is the smallest relation on contexts including every instance of $\rightsquigarrow$ rules in Fig. 4 together with every instance of their duals and every instance of the $\hookrightarrow$ rule.

For every sequence $(e_1, P_1, T_1, p_1) \rightsquigarrow (e_2, P_2, T_2, p_2) \rightsquigarrow \cdots \rightsquigarrow (e_n, P_n, T_n, p_n)$, the sequence of directed edges $(e_1, p_1), \cdots , (e_n, p_n)$ is a path (i.e. the head of e_i is the same node as the tail of e_{i+1}). The $\hookrightarrow$ relation breaks this property as it is non-local, in the sense that it deals with two non-adjacent edges. It is the main relation that distinguishes Dal Lago's context semantics from geometry of interaction. The trace keeps track of the history of previously crossed nodes to enforce path persistence: the $\mapsto$ paths are preserved by cut-elimination. The study of *paths*, sequences of the shape $C_1 \mapsto C_2 \mapsto ...$, will give us information on complexity.

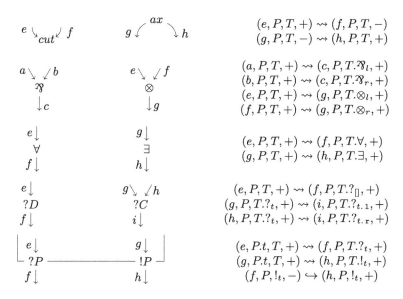

Fig. 4. Exponential rules of the context semantics

As an example, the path in the first proof-net of Fig. 3 $(e, [[\mathbf{r}]; [\mathbf{1}]], [\mathcal{R}_r], +) \mapsto$
$(a, [[\mathbf{r}]], [\mathcal{R}_r; !_{[\mathbf{1}]}], +) \quad \mapsto \quad (b, [], [\mathcal{R}_r; !_{[\mathbf{1}]}; !_{[\mathbf{r}]}], +) \quad \mapsto \quad (c, [], [\mathcal{R}_r; !_{[\mathbf{1}]}; !_{[\mathbf{r}]}], -) \mapsto$
$(d, [], [\mathcal{R}_r; !_{[\mathbf{1}]}; !_{[]}], -) \mapsto (f, [], [\mathcal{R}_r; !_{[\mathbf{1}]}], -) \mapsto (g, [], [\mathcal{R}_r; !_{[]}], -) \mapsto (h, [], [\mathcal{R}_r; !_{[]}], +) \mapsto$
$(i, [], [\mathcal{R}_r; !_{[]}; \otimes_r], +)$ becomes the path $(e_4, [[]], [\mathcal{R}_r], +) \quad \mapsto \quad (h, [], [\mathcal{R}_r; !_{[]}], +) \quad \mapsto$
$(i, [], [\mathcal{R}_r; !_{[]}; \otimes_r], +)$ in the third proof-net of Fig. 3.

We want to capture the potentials which correspond to duplicates of a box. The definition can be difficult to understand. To give the reader a grasp of it, we will introduce the notion of $\mapsto$-copy progressively, proceeding by successive refinements. For the sake of simplicity, we will start with the case of depth 0.

- First, we could say that t corresponds to a duplicate of box B iff t corresponds to a sequence of choices of residues along a cut-elimination sequence, and the box residue we chose either will not be part of a cut, or the cut will open it. The $\mapsto$-paths are exactly the paths preserved by cut-elimination. So, we could make the first attempt: "t corresponds to a duplicate of B iff $(\sigma(B), [], [!_t], +) \mapsto^*$ $(e, P, T, p) \not\mapsto$". However, this definition would allow potentials which refuse choices, corresponding to residues which have several residues themselves (e.g. $[]$ for B in Fig. 3). Indeed $(\sigma(B), [], [!_{[]}], +) \mapsto^* (c, [], [!_{[]}], -) \not\mapsto$. The duplicates of B in this figure are B_1 and B_2, which correspond to $[\mathbf{1}]$ and $[\mathbf{r}]$. $[]$ corresponds to B, which can be copied.
- Thus, our second try would be "(B, t) corresponds to a duplicate iff $\exists n \in$ $\mathbb{N}, \forall u \in \mathsf{S}, (\sigma(B), [], [!_{u.t}], +) \mapsto^n \not\mapsto$". However, this definition would allow potentials which make too many choices. For example $(B, [\mathbf{1}; \mathbf{r}])$ in Fig. 3 satisfies this definition. Indeed $(\sigma(B), [], [!_{[\mathbf{1};\mathbf{r}]}], +) \mapsto^* (d, [], [!_{[\mathbf{1}]}], -) \not\mapsto$. So we

add the condition that the left-most trace element in the last context must be $!_{[]}$, the signature must be used entirely.

Such a signature will be called a *copy* of $(B, [])$. If $B_k \subset \cdots \subset B_1$, duplicates of B_k will be represented by $[t_1; \cdots ; t_k]$ with $[t_1; \cdots ; t_{k-1}]$ corresponding to a duplicate of B_{k-1} and t_k a copy of $(B_k, [t_1; \cdots ; t_{k-1}])$.

Definition 2. *Let $\to$ be a relation on contexts, a $\to$-copy of (B, P) (with $B \in B_G$ and $P \in \mathsf{P})$ is a signature t such that there exists $n \in \mathbb{N}$ such that*

$$\forall u \in \mathsf{S}, (\sigma(B), P, [!_{u.t}], +) \to^n (e, Q, [!_u], -) \not\to$$

The set of $\to$-copies of (B, P) is denoted $C_\to(B, P)$. Intuitively, $C_\to(B, P)$ represents the duplicates of B, given the duplicates of the outer boxes.

Definition 3. *Let $\to$ be a binary relation on contexts and $e \in E_G$ such that $e \in B_{\partial(e)} \subset ... \subset B_1$. The set $L_\to(e)$ of canonical potentials for e is the set of potentials $[s_1; ...; s_{\partial(e)}]$ such that $\forall i \leq \partial(e), s_i \in C_\to(B_i, [s_1; \cdots ; s_{i-1}])$.*

So, a $\to$-canonical potential for e is the choice, for all box B_i containing e, of a $\to$-copy of B_i. In particular, in the case of $\to = \mapsto$, $L_\mapsto(e)$ corresponds to all duplicates of e. For example, in Fig. 3 $L_\mapsto(e) = \{[[\mathtt{l}]; []]; [[\mathtt{r}]; [\mathtt{l}]]; [[\mathtt{r}]; [\mathtt{r}]]\}$. We define $L_\to(B) = L_\to(\sigma(B))$.

The next theorem is due to Dal Lago [4]. The intuition behind it is that each cut-elimination step either erases a node or copies a box. Thus, if we know the number of duplicates of each edge, we can bound the number of cut-elimination steps. This result allows to prove strong complexity bounds for several systems.

Theorem 1 (Dal Lago's weight theorem). *For every proof-net G, the length of any cut-elimination sequence beginning by G is bounded by:*

$$T_G = \sum_{e \in E_G} |L_\mapsto(e)| + 2 \cdot \sum_{B \in B_G} \left(|D_G(B)| \sum_{P \in L_\mapsto(B)} \sum_{t \in C_\mapsto(B,P)} |t| \right)$$

Moreover, G is acyclic: *there exists no path of the form $(e, P, [!_s], b) \mapsto^+ (e, P, [!_t], b)$.*

4   Stratification

4.1   Motivations

Stratification designates a restriction of a framework, which forbids the identification of two objects belonging to two morally different "strata". Russell's paradox in naive set theory relies on the identification of two formulae which belong morally to different strata. The non-terminating λ-term $\Omega = (\lambda x.(x)x)\lambda y.(y)y$ depends on the identification of a function and its argument. In recursion theory, to create from the elementary sequences $\theta_m(n) = 2^n_m$ (tower of exponential of height m in n), the non elementary sequence $n \mapsto 2^n_n$, we also need to identify n

and m which seem to belong to different strata. Stratification restrictions have been applied to those frameworks (naive set theory, linear logic, lambda calculus and recursion theory) to entail coherence or complexity properties [1].

ELL [10] can be seen as linear logic deprived of the dereliction ($!X \multimap X$) and digging ($!X \multimap !!X$) principles. This is a stratification restriction on linear logic. The stratum of an edge is the depth of the edge in terms of box inclusion. One can observe in the rules of cut-elimination that without the $?D$ dereliction node (here, we did not present the node of digging), the depth of an edge never changes during cut-elimination, so during cut-elimination, a residue of e can be cut with a residue of f only if e and f have same depth. Any proof-net of ELL reduces to its normal form in a number of steps bounded by an elementary function of its size [6]. In [1], Baillot and Mazza present an analysis of the concept of stratification and L^3, a generalization of ELL. Their stratification condition is enforced by a labelling of edges and also entails elementary time.

Here, we present an even more general stratification condition. This generalization is not given by a LL subsystem but by a criterion on proof-nets. Then, to prove that a system is elementary time sound, we only have to prove that all the proof-nets of the system satisfy the criterion. ELL and L^3 satisfy the criterion.

4.2 Preliminary Intuition: Stratification on λ-Calculus

Our definition of stratification is based on context semantics paths and may be difficult to grasp at first read. To motivate the criterion, we first state a criterion on λ-calculus, the formal system whose terms are generated by $\Lambda = x \mid \lambda x.\Lambda \mid (\Lambda)\Lambda$.

We define *hole-terms* as λ-terms with a variable $\circ$ appearing free exactly once. If $t \in \Lambda$, $h[t]$ denotes $h[t/\circ]$ and, if t is not a variable, t is said a *subterm* of $h[t]$. For $t \in \Lambda$, $|t|$ is the size of t.

If $g[u] \to_\beta v$, the *residues* of u are the copies by β-reduction of u where free variables may have been substituted. Let us consider $t = (\lambda x.\lambda y.(x)(x)y)\lambda z.z \to_\beta \lambda y.(\lambda z.z)(\lambda z.z)y = t'$, then the residues of $\lambda z.z$ are the two occurrences of $\lambda z.z$ in t'. The residue of $(x)y$ is $(\lambda z.z)y$. Finally t and $\lambda x.\lambda y.(x)(x)y$ have no residue.

Let u, v be subterms of t, we capture "u belongs to a higher stratum than v" by the following relation $u \twoheadrightarrow v$.

Definition 4. *Let $t \in \Lambda$ and u, v be subterms of t, $u \twoheadrightarrow v$ if $t \to_\beta^* t'$ and there exists a subterm of t' of shape $(v')h[u']$ with u', v' residues of u, v.*

A λ-term is *stratified* if $\twoheadrightarrow$ is acyclic. Thus, Ω is not stratified because $\Omega \to_\beta (\lambda y.(y)y)\lambda y.(y)y$ so $\lambda y.(y)y \twoheadrightarrow \lambda y.(y)y$. For any stratified term t, we define S_t as the depth of $\twoheadrightarrow$ (i.e. the maximum n such that $\exists (t_i), t_0 \twoheadrightarrow \cdots \twoheadrightarrow t_n$).

Theorem 2. *If $t \in \Lambda$ is stratified, then there is a normalization sequence for t of length $\leq |t|_{3.S_t}^{|t|}$.*

Proof (sketch). Let t be a stratified λ-term. The strategy is to reduce first the set R_0 of subterms of t at stratum 0. By definition, these subterms have no residue inside the right part of an application. So there are never copied, they only have one duplicate. Thus we can reduce all the elements of R_0 in at most $|R_0|$ steps, obtaining a term t' in which elements of R_0 have no residue. We have $|t'| \leq |t|^{2^{|R_0|}} \leq |t|^{2^{|t|}}$.

If u' and v' are subterms of t' such that $u' \twoheadrightarrow v'$ and u', v' are residues of u, v, then $u \twoheadrightarrow v$. Thus, $S_{t'} < S_t$. In at most S_t such rounds of reduction, we reach a normal form.

4.3   Stratification on Proof-Nets

We define a relation $\twoheadrightarrow$ between boxes of proof nets. It loosely correspond to the relation on Λ. In terms of context semantics paths, $B \twoheadrightarrow C$ means that there is a path beginning by the principal door of B which enters C by its principal door.

$$B \twoheadrightarrow C \Leftrightarrow \exists P, Q \in \mathsf{P}, t \in \mathsf{S}, T \in \mathsf{T}, (\sigma(B), P, [!_t], +) \rightsquigarrow^* (\sigma(C), Q, T, -)$$

To illustrate the correspondence with the criterion on Λ, we can observe that in the proof-net of Fig. 5, $(\sigma(B_u), [], [!_\mathsf{e}], +) \mapsto^5 (\sigma(B_v), [], [!_\mathsf{e}; \otimes_l; ?_\mathsf{e}], -)$ so $B_u \twoheadrightarrow B_v$. Let u, v be the λ-terms corresponding to B_u and B_v, then the whole proof-net corresponds to $(\lambda x.h[(x)u])v$ which reduces to $h[(v)u]$ so $u \twoheadrightarrow v$.

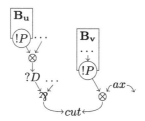

Fig. 5. This proof-net corresponds to $(\lambda x.h[(x)u])v$ for some h.

Definition 5. *A proof-net G is stratified if $\twoheadrightarrow$ is acyclic.*

For example, in Fig. 6, $(\sigma(B), [], [!_{[1]}], +) \rightsquigarrow^* (\sigma(C), [], [!_{[]}; \otimes_l; !_{[\mathtt{r}]}], -)$ so $B \twoheadrightarrow C$. This is the only relation in $\twoheadrightarrow$ so the proof-net is stratified.

The weak bounds for ELL and L^3 were proved using a stratum by stratum strategy, for a specific notion of stratum. They prove that reducing the cuts at strata $\leq i$ does not increase too much the size of the proof-net at stratum $i + 1$. Similarly, we will bound the number of copies of a box when we only reduce cuts in the strata $\leq i + 1$ by the maximum number of copies of a box when reducing only cuts in strata $\leq i$. Thus, we need a notion of copy corresponding to reduction of cuts only in strata $\leq i$. This means we need a relation $\mapsto_i$ on contexts which simulates cut-elimination restricted to strata $\leq i$.

First, we define the *stratum* of a box B, written $S(B)$ as the depth of B in terms of $\twoheadrightarrow$, i.e. $\max\{s | \exists (B_i)_{i \leq s}, B_0 \twoheadrightarrow B_1... \twoheadrightarrow B_s\}$. Then, the stratum of a

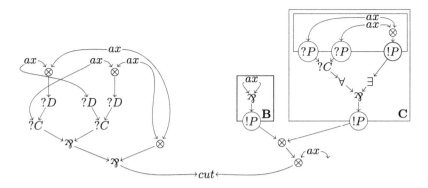

Fig. 6. This proof-net corresponds to $(\lambda\langle f, g\rangle.\langle(f)g, (g)f\rangle)\langle\lambda x.x, \lambda y.\langle y, y\rangle\rangle$.

context C is the stratum of the box from which the context comes from: more formally, if there exists $B \in B_G$, $P \in \mathsf{P}$ and $t \in \mathsf{S}$ such that $(\sigma(B), P, [!_t], +) \rightsquigarrow^*$ C, $S(C)$ is defined as $S(B)$. There are contexts such that $S(C)$ is undefined (if the left-most trace element is not a $!_u$, for example). $S(C)$ is not ambiguous because $\rightsquigarrow$ is injective and $(\sigma(B), P, [!_t], +)$ has no antecedent by $\rightsquigarrow$ (because the trace of a context is non-empty).

Let $s \in \mathbb{N}$, we define $C \mapsto_s D$ by: $C \mapsto_s D$ iff $C \mapsto D$ and $S(D) \leq s$. Thus, if B is a box of stratum $> s$, then for every P, t, $(\sigma(B), P, [!_t], +) \not\mapsto$ so $C_{\mapsto_s}(B, P) = \{[]\}$. This is the expected behaviour: we forbid the reduction steps involving a box of stratum $> s$, so B will never be duplicated. For matters of readability, we will often write $L_s(x)$ for $L_{\mapsto_s}(x)$ and $C_s(x, P)$ for $C_{\mapsto_s}(x, P)$. For any $s \in \mathbb{N}$, $\mapsto_s \subseteq \mapsto$ so $\mapsto_s$-copies of a box B are suffixes of $\mapsto$-copies of B.

Lemma 1. *For any $s \in \mathbb{N}$, any copy $t \in C_\mapsto(B, P)$ there is a unique $t^{/s} \in C_s(B, P)$ such that $t^{/s}$ is a suffix of t. For any $s \in \mathbb{N}$ and for any $P = [t_1; ...; t_{\partial(B)}] \in L_\mapsto(B)$, there is a unique $P^{/s} = [t'_1; ...; t'_{\partial(B)}] \in L_s(B)$ such that for all $1 \leq i \leq \partial(B)$, t'_i is a suffix of t_i.*

By Theorem 1, proof-nets are acyclic. So no $\mapsto$ path may go through two contexts of the shape $(e, Q, [!_u], p)$ and $(e, Q, [!_v], p)$. In fact, we can prove the following refinement. Let us assume $e \in B_{\partial(e)} \subset \cdots \subset B_1$, then no $\mapsto$ path beginning by $(\sigma(B), P, [!_t], +)$ may go through two contexts of the shape $(e, [q_1; \cdots; q_{\partial(e)}], [!_u], p)$ and $(e, [r_1; \cdots; r_{\partial(e)}], [!_v], p)$ where $q_i = r_i$ whenever $B \twoheadrightarrow B_i$. This gives us the following "strong acyclicity" lemma.

Lemma 2 (strong acyclicity). *Let us suppose that G is stratified and $e \in E_G$. If $(e, P, [!_t], p) \mapsto_s^+ (e, Q, [!_u], p)$ then $P^{/s-1} \neq Q^{/s-1}$.*

Theorem 3. *If a proof-net G is stratified, then the length of its longest reduction sequence is bounded by $2_{3.S_G+1}^{3.n}$ with $n = |E_G|$.*

Proof (sketch). Let us consider a $\mapsto_s$ path beginning by $(\sigma(B), P, [!_t], +)$. Lemma 2 bounds the number of times we can go through the same $?C$ node with a $[!_u]$ trace by $\max_{(C,Q)} |C_{s-1}(C,Q)|^{\partial_G}$. So the length of any $\mapsto_s$-copy of (B,P) will be inferior to $|E_G| \cdot \max_{(C,Q)} |C_{s-1}(C,Q)|^{\partial_G}$. We get $|C_s(B,P)| \leq 2^{|E_G| \cdot \max_{(C,Q)} |C_{s-1}(C,Q)|^{\partial_G}}$. This gives an elementary bound on $|C_s(B,P)|$, by induction on s. Then, the result folows by Theorem 1.

5   Dependence Control

5.1   Motivations

Though stratification gives us a bound on the length of the reduction, elementary time is not considered as a reasonable bound. Figure 7 illustrates how the complexity arises, despite stratification. On this proof-net, the box A duplicates the box B and each copy of B duplicates C. If we extended this chain to n boxes, it will normalize in time 2^n. In [13], this situation is called a chain of *spindles*. We call "dependence control condition" any restriction on linear logic which aims to limit chains of spindles. The solution chosen by Girard [10] was to limit the number of $?P$-doors of each !-boxes to 1. To keep some expressivity, he introduced a new modality § with §-boxes which can have an arbitrary number of $?P$-doors.

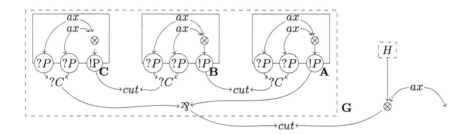

Fig. 7. If H is in normal form, this proof-net reduces in 32 cut-elimination steps.

However, this solution forbids many proof-nets whose complexity is polynomial. The complexity explodes in Fig. 7 because two copies of a box B merge with the same box A. A box with several auxiliary doors is harmful only if two of its auxiliary edges are contracted. Besides, we study the complexity of functions, not stand-alone proof-nets. We say that a proof-net G is in *polynomial time* if there is a polynomial P_G such that whenever G is cut with a proof-net H in normal form, the resulting proof-net normalizes in time $P_G(|E_H|)$. G is fixed and P_G depends on G. Thus, the sub-proof-net G of Fig. 7 normalizes in constant time.

In fact, what really leads to an exponential blowup is when the length of such a chain of spindles depends on the input, as in Fig. 8. If we replace the sub proof-net H (which represents 3) by a proof-net H' representing n, the resulting proof-net normalizes in time 2^n.

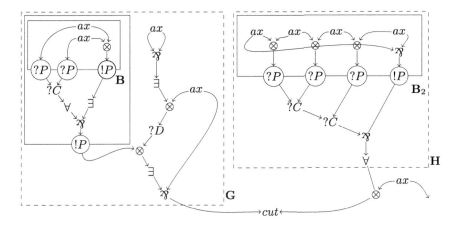

Fig. 8. The sub proof-net G is not polynomial time.

5.2   A Dependence Control Criterion

We will define a relation $B \succcurlyeq_2 C$ on boxes meaning that at least 2 residues of B have their principal doors cut with an auxiliary door of C (spindle from B to C). We say that a proof-net *controls dependence* if $\succcurlyeq_2$ is acyclic. Then, if a proof-net G is stratified and controls dependence, the length of a chain of spindles in reducts of G is bounded by the number of boxes of G.

Definition 6

$$B \succcurlyeq_2 C \Leftrightarrow \exists t \neq u \in \mathcal{S}, \begin{cases} (\sigma(B), P, [!_t], +) \mapsto^+ (\sigma(C), Q, [!_e], -) \\ (\sigma(B), P, [!_u], +) \mapsto^+ (\sigma(C), Q, [!_e], -) \end{cases}$$

If G controls dependence and $B \in B_G$, we define the *nest of B* (written $N(B)$) as the depth of B in terms of the $\succcurlyeq_2$ relation. N_G refers to $\max_{B \in B_G} N(B)$.

Theorem 4. *If G is stratified and controls dependence, let $n = |E_G|$, $N = N_G + 1$, $S = S_G + 1$ and $\partial = \partial_G + 1$, the maximal reduction length of G is bounded by*

$$n^{3 + 16 N \cdot \partial^{2 \cdot N \cdot S}}$$

We can represent binary words in linear logic by the proof-nets of conclusion $\mathbf{B} = \forall X.!(X \multimap X) \multimap !(X \multimap X) \multimap !(X \multimap X)$. Let us notice that the number of boxes in a cut-free binary words (or any other inductive data-type in Church encoding) is fixed. Let us suppose that G is a proof-net of type $\mathbf{B} \multimap A$ (A being a formula) and for any cut-free binary word l, G cut with l is stratified and controls dependence. Then, there exists a polynomial P such that for all normal proof-net l representing a binary word of length n, the application of G to l normalizes in at most $P(n)$ cut-elimination steps.

We can notice that the degree of the polynomial rises very fast. During the proof we used rough bounds. Otherwise, the statement of the bound would have been too complex. The bound is so high because, given S_G and N_G, we must consider the worst possible case (for example that there are boxes of nest N_G in each stratum). Given the exact $\twoheadrightarrow$ and $\succcurlyeq_2$ relations on a stratified proof-net G controlling dependence, one can statically infer tighter bounds (if we are not in the worst possible case) by following the proofs of Lemmas 24 and 25 in [12].

6   Applications

L^4 (Light Linear Logic by Levels) is a system introduced by Baillot and Mazza [1] which generalizes LLL. L^4 is defined as the set of proof-nets for which we can label each edge e with an integer $l(e)$ verifying the rules of Fig. 9, and whose boxes have at most one auxiliary door. We define l_G as $\max\{l(e)|e \in E_G\}$. Baillot and Mazza proved a weak polynomial bound for L^4 proof-nets for a particular strategy [1], but no strong bound[1]. Obtaining a strong polynomial bound is important to define a type system for λ-calculus based on L^4, because it is unclear whether the particular strategy on proof-nets of [1] could be converted into a β-reduction strategy.

Fig. 9. Relations between levels of neighbour edges in L^4

In L^4, the level of a box is stable by cut-elimination. This property has an equivalent in the context semantics presentation: the sum of the depth of the edge and the number of exponential trace elements is stable. Let $T \in \mathsf{T}$, the number of !, ? and § trace elements in T is denoted $\|T\|$. Notice that the following Lemma only holds for the $\leadsto$ relation, not for the $\mapsto$ relation. This makes the reasonings on L^4 more complex and partly explains why it was difficult to prove a strong bound for L^4.

Lemma 3. *If G is a L^4 proof-net and $(e, P, T, p) \leadsto_G^* (f, Q, U, q)$, then*

$$l(e) + \|T\| = l(f) + \|U\|$$

Lemma 4. *If G is a L^4 proof-net and $B \twoheadrightarrow B'$ then $l(\sigma(B)) > l(\sigma(B'))$.*

Thanks to Lemma 4, we can prove that L^4 proof-nets are stratified with strata of boxes being bounded by the maximum level of edges. It gives us an elementary bound on *cut* elimination. To prove a polynomial bound, one can prove that L^4 proof-nets control dependence. In fact, in L^4, the $\succcurlyeq_2$ relation is empty so acyclic.

---

[1] In fact, a proof of a strong bound is claimed in [13], but it contains flaws which do not seem to be easily patchable. See Appendix B of [12] for more details.

Theorem 5. *Let G be a L^4 proof-net, with $n = |E_G|$, of maximal level l, then the length of the longest reduction path is inferior to*

$$n^{3+16\partial_G^{2l_G+2}}$$

In L^4, binary words are represented using the Church encoding with the type: $\mathbf{B}_4 = \forall X.!(X \multimap X) \multimap !(X \multimap X) \multimap \S(X \multimap X)$. In Theorem 5, the polynomial only depends on the level and depth of the proof-net. Let G be a L^4 proof-net representing a function on binary words, i.e. the only conclusion of G has type $\mathbf{B}_4 \multimap A$ for some A. Then, there exists a polynomial P such that for all normal proof-net H representing a binary word of length n, the application of G to H normalizes in at most $P(n)$ cut-elimination steps.

Other systems. The framework MS [13] is a set of subsystems of ELL where ! connectives are indexed by integers. ELL is stratified so all proof-nets of MS are stratified. In [13], Vercelli characterizes the "most general" *Ptime* sound subsystems of MS. Those systems allow !-boxes with several auxiliary doors. In those systems, if $B \succcurlyeq_2 B'$, $\sigma(B)$ and $\sigma(B')$ are labelled by formulae of respective shape $!_n A$ and $=!_{n'} A'$, then $n < n'$. The dependence control follows immediately. The strong polynomial bound, however, was already proved in [13].

We also prove a strong bound for L_0^4, a refinement of L^4 [1]. L_0^4 does not enjoy stratification but we can derive a strong bound for L_0^4 from the strong bound for L^4. No polynomial bound was previously proved for this system.

Comparison with L^3. Our criteria allowed to show strong polynomial bounds for systems for which only weak bounds were known. In addition, it shows that the stratification constraints of L^3 could be relaxed. Indeed, we found stratified proof-nets controlling dependence corresponding to the λ-term $((\underline{2})\lambda n.((n)S)\underline{1})\underline{0}$ (with $\underline{n}$ being the representation of $n \in \mathbb{N}$ in Church numerals) and the λ-term with pair[2] $(\lambda\langle f, g\rangle.\langle(f)g, (g)f\rangle)\langle\lambda x.x, \lambda y.\langle y, y\rangle\rangle$ (Fig. 6). It seems that there are no L^3 proof-net corresponding to those terms. However, those examples are contrived, and it is still not clear how much expressive power can be gained in practice by relaxing the stratification conditions of L^3.

Comparison with MS. For any *Ptime* sound MS system S, the length of chains of spindles is bounded by an integer k_S. Let us fix S, we can extend the chain of spindles of G in Fig. 7 to k_S+1 spindles, so that G is still constant time but not in S. Our criteria are more general. First, we do not fix *a priori* a limit on the length of chains of spindles, but only forbid cycles. So G, even with an extended chain of spindles, satisfies our criteria. Let $t = \underline{k}(\lambda\langle x, y, z\rangle.\langle x, ((+)x)y, y\rangle)$ and $u = \lambda\langle x, y, z\rangle.\langle z, z, z\rangle$, then $(t)(u)(t)\cdots(u)t$ is stratified and controls dependence, whatever the length of the chain of applications, whereas in MS the maximum length of such a chain is bounded. Moreover, our bound is still valid in presence of dereliction $(?D)$ and digging (dealing with the latter is more complex and is only presented in the long version [12]).

---

[2] The pairs are here represented by using the connective $\otimes$.

7   Conclusion

We defined two criteria on proof-nets which imply bounds on the complexity of cut-elimination. These are then used to prove strong bounds for systems for which only weak bounds were known. A major advantage of our approach is that, once our general lemmas are established, proving bounds for various systems is quite simple. There are *Ptime* proof-nets which do not verify our criteria, however the expressive power of those criteria is still unclear. In future work, we plan to define more expressive systems based on these.

Let us comment on decidability issues. One can compute all the $\mapsto$ paths in a proof-net, for example by reducing the proof-net. So, stratification and dependence control of a proof-net are decidable. However, as we are interested by the complexity of functions, the interesting problem of certifying complexity of a proof-net G is "Is there any cut-free proof-net H such that G cut with H is not stratified or does not control dependence?". This problem seems undecidable. As a future work, we want to design a decidable type system, inspired by our criteria, capturing *Ptime*.

References

1. Baillot, P., Mazza, D.: Linear logic by levels and bounded time complexity. Theor. Comput. Sci. **411**(2), 470–503 (2010)
2. Baillot, P., Pedicini, M.: Elementary complexity and geometry of interaction. Fundamenta Informaticae **45**(1–2), 1–31 (2001)
3. Baillot, P., Terui, K.: Light types for polynomial time computation in lambda calculus. Inf. Comput. **207**(1), 41–62 (2009)
4. Dal Lago, U.: Context semantics, linear logic, and computational complexity. ACM Trans. Comput. Logic **10**(4), 1–32 (2009)
5. Dal Lago, U., Gaboardi, M.: Linear dependent types and relative completeness. In: Logic in Computer Science. IEEE (2011)
6. Danos, V., Joinet, J.B.: Linear logic and elementary time. Inf. Comput. **183**(1), 123–137 (2003)
7. Danos, V., Regnier, L.: Proof-nets and the Hilbert space. London Mathematical Society Lecture Note Series. Cambridge University Press, Cambridge (1995)
8. Girard, J.Y.: Une extension de l'interpretation de gödel a l'analyse, et son application a l'elimination des coupures dans l'analyse et la theorie des types. In: Fenstad, J.E. (ed.) Studies in Logic and the Foundations of Mathematics, vol. 63, pp. 63–92. North Holland, Amsterdam (1971)
9. Girard, J.Y.: Linear logic. Theor. Comput. Sci. **50**(1), 1–102 (1987)
10. Girard, J.Y.: Light linear logic. Inf. Comput. **143**(2), 175–204 (1998)
11. Lafont, Y.: Soft linear logic and polynomial time. Theor. Comput. Sci. **318**(1–2), 163–180 (2004)
12. Perrinel, M.: On paths-based criteria for polynomial time complexity in proof-nets (long version) (2013). http://arxiv.org/abs/1201.2956
13. Vercelli, L.: On the Complexity of Stratified Logics. Ph.D. thesis, Scuola di Dottorato in Scienze e Alta Tecnologia, Università degli Studi di Torino - Italy (2010)

Collected Size Semantics for Strict Functional Programs over General Polymorphic Lists

Olha Shkaravska[1]([✉]), Marko van Eekelen[2,3], and Alejandro Tamalet[4]

[1] Max Planck Institute for Psycholinguistics, Nijmegen, The Netherlands
olhsha@mpi.nl
[2] Institute for Computing and Information Sciences (iCIS),
Radboud University Nijmegen, Nijmegen, The Netherlands
M.vanEekelen@cs.ru.nl
[3] Faculty of Management, Science and Technology,
Open University of the Netherlands, Heerlen, The Netherlands
[4] Globant, Rosario, Argentina

Abstract. Size analysis can be an important part of heap consumption analysis. This paper is a part of ongoing work about typing support for checking output-on-input size dependencies for function definitions in a strict functional language. A significant restriction for our earlier results is that *inner* data structures (e.g. in a list of lists) all must have the same size. Here, we make a big step forwards by overcoming this limitation via the introduction of higher-order size annotations such that variate sizes of inner data structures can be expressed. In this way the analysis becomes applicable for *general*, polymorphic nested lists.

1 Introduction

Bounds on the resource consumption of programs can be used, and are often needed, to ensure correctness and security properties, in particular in devices with scarce resources as mobile phones and smart cards. Both the memory and the time consumption of a program often depend on the sizes of input and intermediate data. In many cases, analysis of size behavior is an important part of resource analysis, e.g. using lower and upper bounds of size dependencies to check and infer non-linear bounds on heap consumption [17,20]. Here, we consider size analysis of *strict* first-order functional programs over polymorphic non-cyclic *lists*. Function signatures are predefined in a program. A size dependency of a program is a *size function* that maps the size of inputs onto the sizes of the corresponding output. By size of a list we mean the number of the elements in it. For instance, the typical size dependency for a program append, that appends two lists of length n and m, is the function $append(n, m) = n + m$.

This work is part of the AHA project [20] which is sponsored by the Netherlands Organisation for Scientific Research (NWO) under grant nr. 612.063.511. and by the CHARTER project, EU Artrmis nr. 100039.

© Springer International Publishing Switzerland 2014
U. Dal Lago and R. Peña (Eds.): FOPARA 2013, LNCS 8552, pp. 143–159, 2014.
DOI: 10.1007/978-3-319-12466-7_9

In the article [16] size functions were defined by conditional multiple-choice rewriting rules. However, the type system from that article did not cover general lists. It only covered programs over 'matrix-like' structures, e.g. $L_n(L_m(\alpha))$ leaving no way to express variate sizes of internal lists. This substantially restricts application of the approach, since the case of programs over lists of lists with variate lengths is the most frequent one.

This paper is devoted to collecting size dependencies using *multivalued* size functions. We use multivalued size functions to annotate types making it possible to express that there can be more than one possible output size (like e.g. in the case of inserting an element to a list if it is not there already: the result will either have the same size or it will be one element larger).

In this paper, we remove the restriction of [16] and generalise the approach to obtain a general solution that generates conditional rewriting rules for size dependencies of first-order polymorphic programs over lists, for which the size(s) of an output depends only on the sizes of inputs.

We use an ML-like strict first-order language which is defined in Sect. 2. In Sect. 3 we define the type system which allows *size variables of higher-order kinds*, such that, e.g., a size variable M in the type $L_n(L_M(\alpha))$ represents the size $M(pos)$ of an internal list depending on its position *pos* in the outer list, where $0 \le pos \le n - 1$. Moreover, we extend (checking and inferring of) multivalued size functions defined by higher-order rewriting rules. We define soundness and sketch its proof. Section 4 relates our work to other resource analysis work.

It is not surprising that the presented research is inspired by sized-types and dependent-ML frameworks [5, 13, 23]. There sized types were used to prove termination and to assure other correctness properties of a program. Lists annotated by n denoted lists of length *at most n*. This is a limitation for size analysis since it makes upper bounds for decreasing size dependencies rather imprecise. For instance, with such interpretation of sized lists we would have to replace the dependency $n - m$, where n and m are annotations of input lists, just with n. For a better size analysis we initially wanted to have double-index annotations of the form $L_{n_1 \le length \le n_2}(\alpha)$, that allows to express lower and upper bounds on the length of the lists. Later we discovered that inferring such lower and upper bounds, especially for nested lists, can be done if we infer lower and upper bounds of multivalued functions that represent all possible lengths of lists. The ratio behind this approach is explained in more detail and by examples in the technical report [15].

However higher-order rewriting systems may be considered not only as a tool for deriving lower and upper bounds for list lengths. The may be considered as standalone recurrence relations to be solved by known methods. By solving of a recurrence relation one means finding a closed form for the function it defines. Solving non-linear recurrence relations is a difficult problem that does not enjoy any universal approach. Solutions are provided for some classes of them. Two of the coauthors of the presented paper recently published a result about nonlinear polynomial recurrences [14]. The discussion about solving *size-analysis-related* higher-order recurrences, e.g. by possible reduction them to first-order ones, is behind the scope of the presented paper.

Yet another argument for using higher-order rewriting rules for size dependencies is the prospect of an extension of the presented analysis to higher-order programs in the spirit of [9].

2 Language

The type system is designed for a strict first-order functional language over integers, booleans and (polymorphic) lists. Language expressions are defined by the grammar below where c ranges over integer and boolean constants False and True, x and y denote program variables of integer and boolean types, l ranges over lists, z denotes a program variable of a zero-order type, g ranges over higher-order program variables, unop is a unary operation, either $-$ or $\neg$, binop is one of the integer or boolean binary operations, and f denotes a function name.

$$Basic\ b ::= c \mid \text{unop } x \mid x \text{ binop } y \mid \text{Nil} \mid \text{Cons}(z, l) \mid f(g_1, \ldots, g_l, z_1, \ldots, z_k)$$
$$Expr\ e ::= b \mid \text{if } x \text{ then } e_1 \text{ else } e_2 \mid \text{let } z = b \text{ in } e_1$$
$$\mid \text{match } l \text{ with } \mid \text{Nil} \Rightarrow e_1$$
$$\mid \text{Cons}(z_{hd}, l_{tl}) \Rightarrow e_2$$
$$\mid \text{letfun } f(g_1, \ldots, g_l, z_1, \ldots, z_k) = e_1 \text{ in } e_2$$

The syntax distinguishes between let-binding of variables and letfun-binding of functions (function definitions). We prohibit head-nested let-expressions and restrict subexpressions in function calls to variables to make type checking straightforward. Program expressions of a general form may be equivalently transformed into expressions of this form. We consider this language as an intermediate language where a general language like ML may be compiled into.

3 Type System

We consider a type system constituted from zero-order and higher-order types and typing rules for each program construct. Size annotations represent lengths of finite lists. Syntactically, size annotations are (higher-order) arithmetic expressions over constants, size variables and multivalued-function symbols. Let $\mathcal{R}$ be a numerical ring used to express and solve the size equations. Constants and size variables are *layered*:

- *The layer zero* is empty. It corresponds to the unsized types Int, Bool and α, where α is a type variable. Elements of these types have no size annotations.
- The *first layer* is the type $\mathcal{R}^{(1)} = \mathcal{R}$ of numerical zero-order constants (i.e. integers) and size variables, denoted by a and n, respectively (possibly decorated with subscripts). They represent lengths of outermost lists. Examples are $\mathsf{L}_5(\alpha)$ with $a = 5$, or $\mathsf{L}_n(\mathsf{L}_5(\alpha))$ where n is a first-layer expression.

- The *second layer* consists of constants and variables of type $\mathcal{R}^{(2)} = \mathcal{R} \to \mathcal{R}$, denoted by B and M, respectively. They represent lengths of nested lists in a list. For instance, in the typing $\mathsf{I} : \mathsf{L}_n(\mathsf{L}_M(\alpha))$ the function $\lambda\, pos.M(pos)$ represents the length of the *pos*-th list in the master list I. Indexes start at 0, so $M(0)$ is the length of the head of the master list, and $M(n-1)$ is the length of its last element. Constants of the type $\mathcal{R} \to \mathcal{R}$ may be defined by an arithmetic expression or by a table. For instance, in $[[1,2],[3,4,5],[\,]]$ the length of the master list is $a = 3$ and B is given by the table $B(0) = 2$, $B(1) = 3$, $B(2) = 0$. For $pos \geq 2$, $B(pos)$ may be any number.
- In general, the s-th *layer* consists of numerical $(s-1)$-th-order constants and variables of type $\mathcal{R}^{(s)} = \mathcal{R} \to \mathcal{R}^{(s-1)}$, denoted by a^s and n^s. They represent lengths of lists of "nestedness" s. For instance in $\mathsf{I} : \mathsf{L}_{n^1}(\ldots \mathsf{L}_{n^s}(\alpha)\ldots)$ the function $\lambda\, i_1 \ldots i_{s-1}.\, n^s(i_1)\ldots(i_{s-1})$ represents the length of the i_{s-1}-th list in the i_{s-2}-th list in ... in the i_1-th list of the master list I.

Let $\mathcal{R}^*$ denote the union $\bigcup_{s=1}^{\infty} \mathcal{R}^{(s)}$ and let n^* range over size variables of $\mathcal{R}^*$. Let $\overline{n}^*$ denote a vector of variables $(n_1^*, \ldots, n_k^*)$ for some $k \geq 0$.

Layering is extended to multivalued size functions, according to their return types (but not their parameter types):

- Let $(\mathcal{R}^*)^k$ denote a k-fold product of $\mathcal{R}$. A function of the layer 1 is a function $f : (\mathcal{R}^*)^k \to 2^{\mathcal{R}}$ for some $k \geq 0$ that represents all possible sizes (depending on parameters from $(\mathcal{R}^*)^k$) of outer lists. For instance, if $f(n) = \{n, n+1\}$ in $\mathsf{I} : \mathsf{L}_{f(n)}(\alpha)$, then the length of I is either n or $n+1$.

  Another example is the output type of the function over a list of lists concatenating the elements of an input list: $\mathsf{concat} : \mathsf{L}_n(\mathsf{L}_M(\alpha)) \to \mathsf{L}_{concat(n,M)}(\alpha)$, where *concat*: $\mathcal{R}^{(1)} \times \mathcal{R}^{(2)} \to 2^{\mathcal{R}}$. In this case it is easy to spot the closed form $concat(n, M) = \sum_{i=0}^{n-1} M(i)$.
- A function of the layer s is a function of the type $(\mathcal{R}^*)^k \to (\mathcal{R} \to \ldots \to \mathcal{R} \to 2^{\mathcal{R}})$ that maps parameters from $(\mathcal{R}^*)^k$ to $s-1$-order multivalued functions of the type $\mathcal{R} \to \ldots \to \mathcal{R} \to 2^{\mathcal{R}}$. Its value $f(\overline{n}^*)(pos_1)\ldots(pos_{s-1})$ defines all possible sizes of the pos_{s-1} list in the pos_{s-2}-th list ... in the pos_1-the list of the master list.

If a function is single-valued, we will omit the curly brackets in its value. As yet another example consider a function definition

$$\mathsf{tails} : \mathsf{L}_n(\alpha) \to \mathsf{L}_{tails_1(n)}(\mathsf{L}_{tails_2(n)}(\alpha))$$

that creates the list of all non-empty tails of the input list:

$$\mathsf{tails(l)} = \mathsf{match}\ \mathsf{l}\ \mathsf{with}\ |\ \mathsf{Nil} \Rightarrow \mathsf{Nil}$$
$$|\ \mathsf{Cons(hd, tl)} \Rightarrow \mathsf{let}\ \mathsf{l'} = \mathsf{tails(tl)}\ \mathsf{in}\ \mathsf{Cons(l, l')}$$

For instance, on $[1, 2, 3]$ it outputs $[[1, 2, 3], [2, 3], [3]]$. Later we will prove that *tails$_1$* $: \mathcal{R} \to 2^{\mathcal{R}}$ is the identity *tails$_1$*$(n) = n$ and *tails$_2$* $: \mathcal{R} \to (\mathcal{R} \to 2^{\mathcal{R}})$ for $n \geq 1$ is defined by *tails$_2$*$(n)(pos) = n - pos$, if $0 \leq pos \leq n - 1$.

A *size expression* p is constructed from size constants, variables, multivalued-function symbols and operations of all layers. We will denote functions of the first and second layers via f and g, respectively. Admissible operations are arithmetic operations $+$, $-$, $*$, λ-abstraction and application. Layering is defined for size expressions as it has been defined for multivalued size functions. *A size expression is of layer s if it returns a value of order $s - 1$ of type $\mathcal{R} \rightarrow \ldots \rightarrow \mathcal{R} \rightarrow 2^{\mathcal{R}}$.* When necessary, we denote a size expression of the layer s via p^s. For instance:

$$p^1 ::= a, \; n, \; pos \mid f(p_1, \ldots, p_k) \mid p^1 \{+, -, *\} p^1 \mid p^2(p^1)$$
$$p^2 ::= B, \; M \mid g(p_1, \ldots, p_k) \mid \lambda \, pos. \, p^1 \mid p^3(p^1)$$

where pos is a special variable of type $\mathcal{R}$ used to denote the position of an element in a list, and p_{+1} abbreviates $\lambda \; pos. \, p(pos)$. We also assume that constants (e.g. a) and size variables (e.g. n) represent singleton sets.

Zero-order annotated types are defined as follows:

$$
\begin{aligned}
\tau^0 \quad &::= \mathsf{Int} \mid \mathsf{Bool} \mid \alpha \\
\tau^{s', s} \quad &::= \mathsf{L}_{p^{s'}}(\mathsf{L}_{p^{s'+1}}(\ldots \mathsf{L}_{p^s}(\tau^0) \ldots)) \quad \text{for } 1 \leq s' \leq s, \\
\tau^s \quad &::= \tau^{1, s}
\end{aligned}
$$

where α is a type variable. It is easy to see that $\tau^{s', s} = \mathsf{L}_{p^{s'}}(\tau^{s'+1, s})$. The types τ^0 and τ^s are types of program expressions, whereas $\tau^{s', s}$ are only used in definitions and proofs but not in function types.

Let τ ranges over zero-order types. The sets $TV(\tau)$ and $SV(\tau)$ of type and size variables of a type τ are defined inductively in the obvious way. All empty lists of the same underlying type represent the same data structure. So, $SV(\mathsf{L}_0(\tau)) = \emptyset$ forall τ and $\mathsf{L}_0(\mathsf{L}_m(\mathsf{Int}))$ represents the same structure as $\mathsf{L}_0(\mathsf{L}_0(\mathsf{Int}))$.

Zero-order types without type variables or size variables are *ground types*:

$$Ground\,Types \quad \tau^\bullet \quad ::= \quad \tau \text{ such that } SV(\tau) = \emptyset \wedge TV(\tau) = \emptyset$$

The semantics of ground types is defined in Sect. 3.1. Here we give some examples: $\mathsf{L}_2(\mathsf{Bool})$, $\mathsf{L}_2(\mathsf{L}_B(\mathsf{Bool}))$, and $\mathsf{L}_{concat(2, B)}(\mathsf{Bool})$, where $B(pos) = pos$ on $0 \leq pos \leq 1$. It is easy to see that $concat(2, B) = 0 + 1 = 1$. Examples of their inhabitants are $[\mathsf{True}, \; \mathsf{True}]$, $[[], [\mathsf{True}]]$ and $[\mathsf{True}]$, respectively. Examples of non-ground types are α, $\mathsf{L}_n(\mathsf{Int})$, $\mathsf{L}_n(\mathsf{L}_M(\mathsf{Bool}))$ and $\mathsf{L}_{concat(n, M)}(\mathsf{Bool})$ with unspecified n and M.

Let τ° denote a zero-order type where size expressions are all size variables or constants, like, e.g., $\mathsf{L}_n(\alpha)$ and $\mathsf{L}_n(\mathsf{L}_M(\alpha))$. Function types are then defined inductively:

$$Function\,Types \quad \tau^f \quad ::= \quad \tau_1^f \times \ldots \times \tau_{k'}^f \times \tau_1^\circ \times \ldots \times \tau_k^\circ \rightarrow \tau_0$$

where k' may be zero (i.e. the list $\tau_1^f, \ldots, \tau_{k'}^f$ is empty) and $SV(\tau_0)$ contains only size variables of $\tau_1^\circ, \ldots, \tau_k^\circ$.

Multivalued size functions f in the output types of function signatures are defined by conditional rewriting rules. It is desirable to find closed forms for functions defined by such rewriting rules. This is a topic of ongoing work.

A context Γ is a mapping from zero-order program variables to zero-order types. A signature Σ is a mapping from function names to function types. The definition of $SV(-)$ is straightforwardly extended to contexts: $SV(\Gamma) = \bigcup_{x \in dom(\Gamma)} SV(\Gamma(x))$.

3.1 Heap Semantics

In our semantic model, the purpose of the heap is to store lists.[1] Therefore, a heap is a finite collection of locations ℓ that can store list elements. A location is the address of a cons-cell consisting of a head field hd, which stores a list element, and a tail field tl, which contains the location of the next cons-cell of the list or the NULL address. Formally, a program value is either an integer or boolean constant, a location or the null-address, and a heap is a finite partial mapping from locations and fields into program values:

$$
\begin{aligned}
Address &\quad \mathbf{adr} ::= \ell \mid \text{NULL} &\quad \ell \in Loc \\
Val &\quad v \quad ::= c \mid \mathbf{adr} &\quad c \in \mathsf{Int} \cup \mathsf{Bool} \\
Heap &\quad h \quad : \quad Loc \rightharpoonup \{\mathsf{hd}, \mathsf{tl}\} \rightharpoonup Val
\end{aligned}
$$

We will write $h.\ell.\mathsf{hd}$ and $h.\ell.\mathsf{tl}$ for the results of applications $h\,\ell\,\mathsf{hd}$ and $h\,\ell\,\mathsf{tl}$, which denote the values stored in the heap h at the location ℓ at its fields hd and tl, respectively. Let $h.\ell.[\mathsf{hd} := v_h, \ \mathsf{tl} := v_t]$ denote the heap equal to h everywhere but in ℓ, which at the hd-field of ℓ gets the value v_h and at the tl-field of ℓ gets the value v_t.

The semantics w of a program value v with respect to a specific heap h and a *ground type* $\tau^\bullet$ is a set-theoretic interpretation given via the four-place relation $v \models_{\tau^\bullet}^h w$. Integer and boolean constants interpret themselves, and locations are interpreted as *non-cyclic lists*. Let $p^1(\overline{n}_0^*)$ denote the set of values of some expression p^1 applied to some values $\overline{n}_0^*$. Then

$$
c \models_{\mathsf{Int} \cup \mathsf{Bool}}^h c, \qquad \text{NULL} \models_{\mathsf{L}_{p^1(\overline{n}_0^*)}(\tau^\bullet)}^h \text{[]} \quad \text{iff} \ \ 0 \in p^1(\overline{n}_0^*),
$$

$$
\ell \models_{\mathsf{L}_{p^1(\overline{n}_0^*)}(\tau^\bullet)}^h w_{\mathsf{hd}} :: w_{\mathsf{tl}} \ \text{iff} \ h.\ell.\mathsf{hd} \models_{\tau^\bullet(0)}^{h|_{dom(h)\setminus\{\ell\}}} w_{\mathsf{hd}} \ \text{and} \ h.\ell.\mathsf{tl} \models_{\mathsf{L}_{p^1(\overline{n}_0^*)-1}(\tau_{+1}^\bullet)}^{h|_{dom(h)\setminus\{\ell\}}} w_{\mathsf{tl}}
$$

where $h|_{dom(h)\setminus\{\ell\}}$ denotes the heap equal to h everywhere except in ℓ, where it is undefined. Subtracting ℓ in the heaps of the recursive definition assures absence of cyclic lists since we exclude the reference to the same ℓ from the

---

[1] We introduce heap semantics to instrument the proof of the soundness of the typing system. As an anonymous reviewer pointed out, for the presented first-order setting without sharing it would be sufficient to use set-theoretical denotations in the operational-semantics rules to prove the soundness. However we plan to continue research in this direction for more general settings, where heap semantics may be an adequate model.

substructures. Next, $(p^s)_{+1}$ and τ_{+1} are abbreviations for $\lambda\,pos.\ p^s(pos+1)$ and $\lambda\,pos.\ \tau(pos+1)$, respectively and the application of a type to a first-layer size expression $\tau(p^1)$ is defined as follows:

$$\tau^0(p^1) = \tau^0, \qquad\qquad \tau^{1,\,s}(p^1) = \tau^{1,\,s},$$

$$(\mathsf{L}_{p^{s'}}(\tau^{s'+1\,s}))(p^1) := \mathsf{L}_{p^{s'}(p^1)}(\tau^{s'+1\,s}(p^1)),\ \text{for } s' \geq 2$$

3.2 Operational Semantics of Program Expressions

The first-order operational semantics is standard. We introduce a *frame store* as a mapping from program variables to program values. This mapping is maintained when a function body is evaluated. Before evaluation of the function body starts, the store contains only the actual parameters of the function. During evaluation, the store is extended with the variables introduced by pattern matching or let-constructs. These variables are eventually bound to the actual parameters. Thus there is no access beyond the current frame. Formally, a frame store s is a finite partial map from variables to values, $Store\ s\colon ProgramVars \rightharpoonup Val$.

Using a heap, a frame store and mapping $\mathcal{C}$ (*closures*) from function names to function bodies, the operational semantics of program expressions is defined inductively in a standard way. Here we give some of the rules as examples. The full operational semantics is given in the technical report [15].

$$\frac{c \in \mathsf{Int} \cup \mathsf{Bool}}{s;\ h;\ \mathcal{C} \vdash c \rightsquigarrow c;\ h}\ \mathrm{OSCons} \qquad \frac{}{s;\ h;\ \mathcal{C} \vdash \mathsf{z} \rightsquigarrow s(\mathsf{z});\ h}\ \mathrm{OSVar}$$

$$\frac{\begin{array}{cc} h.s(\mathsf{l}).\mathsf{hd} = v_{\mathsf{hd}} & h.s(\mathsf{l}).\mathsf{tl} = v_{\mathsf{tl}} \\ s[\mathsf{hd} := v_{\mathsf{hd}}, \mathsf{tl} := v_{\mathsf{tl}}];\ h;\ \mathcal{C} \vdash e_2 \rightsquigarrow v;\ h' \end{array}}{s;\ h;\ \mathcal{C} \vdash \begin{array}{l} \mathsf{match}\ \mathsf{l}\ \mathsf{with} \mid \mathsf{Nil} \Rightarrow e_1 \qquad\qquad \rightsquigarrow v;\ h' \\ \qquad\qquad\qquad\quad \mid \mathsf{Cons}(\mathsf{hd},\ \mathsf{tl}) \Rightarrow e_2 \end{array}}\ \mathrm{OSMatch\text{-}Cons}$$

$$\frac{s;\ h;\ \mathcal{C}[f := ((\mathsf{g}_1,\ldots,\mathsf{g}_{k'},\ \mathsf{z}_1,\ldots,\mathsf{z}_k) \times e_1)] \vdash e_2 \rightsquigarrow v;\ h'}{s;\ h;\ \mathcal{C} \vdash \mathsf{letfun}\ f(\mathsf{g}_1,\ldots,\mathsf{g}_{k'},\ \mathsf{z}_1,\ldots,\mathsf{z}_k) = e_1\ \mathsf{in}\ e_2 \rightsquigarrow v;\ h'}\ \mathrm{OSLetFun}$$

$$\frac{\begin{array}{c} s(\mathsf{z}'_1) = v_1 \quad \ldots \quad s(\mathsf{z}'_k) = v_k \\ \mathcal{C}(\mathsf{f}) = (\mathsf{g}_1,\ldots,\mathsf{g}_{k'},\ \mathsf{z}_1,\ldots,\mathsf{z}_k) \times e_f \\ [\mathsf{z}_1 := v_1,\ldots,\mathsf{z}_k := v_k];\ h;\ \mathcal{C} \vdash e_f[\mathsf{g}_1 := \mathsf{f}_1,\ldots,\mathsf{g}_{k'} := \mathsf{f}_{k'}] \rightsquigarrow v;\ h' \end{array}}{s;\ h;\ \mathcal{C} \vdash \mathsf{f}(\mathsf{f}_1,\ldots,\mathsf{f}_{k'},\ \mathsf{z}'_1,\ldots,\mathsf{z}'_k) \rightsquigarrow v;\ h'}\ \mathrm{OSFunApp}$$

Note that in the function-application rule above, the function variables from the function definition do not become variables in $\mathcal{C}$, since $\mathcal{C}$ does not contain higher-order (function) variables because we deal with first-order programs. $\mathcal{C}$ contains only higher-order constants (functions). In the presented work function arguments in LetFun rule play a role of placeholders and is a syntactic sugar. To make it a classic first-order language one has to replace a "higher-order" function definition of f with the collection of function definitions without higher-order placeholders, just enumerating all function instantiations that are possible (at the current call of f). To make it fully higher order, extension of the language in the spirit of [9] should be studied.

3.3   Typing Rules

A typing judgement is a relation of the form $D, \Gamma \vdash_\Sigma e : \tau$, i.e. given a set of constraints D, a zero-order context Γ and a higher-order signature Σ, an expression e has a type τ. The set D of disequations and memberships is relevant only when a rule for pattern-matching and constructors are applied. When the nil-branch is entered on a list $\mathsf{L}_{p^1(\overline{n}^*)}(\alpha)$, then D is extended with $0 \in p^1(\overline{n}^*)$. When the cons-branch is entered, then D is extended with $m \geq 1$, $m \in p(\overline{n}^*)$, where m is a fresh size variable in D. When a constructor is applied, D is extended with position-delimiting disequations.

Given types $\tau = \mathsf{L}_{p^1(\overline{n}^*)}(\ldots \mathsf{L}_{p^s(\overline{n}^*)}(\alpha) \ldots)$ and $\tau' = \mathsf{L}_{p'^1(\overline{n}^*)}(\ldots \mathsf{L}_{p'^s(\overline{n}^*)}(\alpha) \ldots)$, let the entailment $D \vdash \tau \to \tau'$ abbreviate the collection of rules that (conditionally) rewrite $p^1(\overline{n}^*) \to p'^1(\overline{n}^*)$ etc.:

$$
\begin{array}{l}
D \\
D, m_1 \in p'^1(\overline{n}^*),\ 0 \leq pos \leq m_1 - 1 \\
\quad m_1,\ pos \text{ are fresh for } D \\
\cdots
\end{array}
\qquad
\begin{array}{l}
\vdash p^1(\overline{n}^*) \to p'^1(\overline{n}^*) \\
\vdash p^2(\overline{n}^*)(pos) \to p'^2(\overline{n}^*)(pos)
\end{array}
$$

$$
D, \left\{
\begin{array}{l}
m_1 \in p'^1(\overline{n}^*),\ 0 \leq pos_1 \leq m_1 - 1, \ldots, \\
m_s \in p'^s(\overline{n}^*)(pos_1) \ldots (pos_{s-1}), \\
0 \leq pos_s \leq m_s - 1
\end{array}
\right\}
\vdash
\left\{
\begin{array}{l}
p^s(\overline{n}^*)(pos_1) \ldots (pos_s) \to \\
p'^s(\overline{n}^*)(pos_1) \ldots (pos_s)
\end{array}
\right.
$$
$$
m_1, pos_1, \ldots, m_s, pos_s \text{ are fresh for } D
$$

A notation $p \to p'$ means that $p = p'$ in the axiomatics of $\mathcal{R}$. An arrow is introduced because the type system is used to infer rewriting rules defining size functions. The inference process amounts to backward application of the typing rules, so that at the end of the process a size function appears on the left-hand side of the rewriting rules. Examples are given further.

The typing judgment relation is defined by the following rules:

$$
\frac{}{D, \Gamma \vdash_\Sigma \imath : \mathsf{Int}} \ \text{IConst}
\qquad
\frac{}{D, \Gamma \vdash_\Sigma \mathbf{b} : \mathsf{Bool}} \ \text{BConst}
$$

$$
\frac{D \vdash \tau' \to \tau}{D, \Gamma,\ \mathbf{z} : \tau \vdash_\Sigma \mathbf{z} : \tau'} \ \text{Var}
\qquad
\frac{D \vdash \tau' \to \mathsf{L}_0(\tau)}{D, \Gamma \vdash_\Sigma \mathsf{Nil} : \tau'} \ \text{Nil}
$$

$$
\frac{
\begin{array}{l}
D \\
D \\
1 \leq m \in p^1(\overline{n}^*),\ 1 \leq pos \leq m;\ D \vdash \tau'_2(pos) \to \tau_2(pos - 1)
\end{array}
\quad
\begin{array}{l}
\vdash \tau' \to \mathsf{L}_{p^1(\overline{n}^*)+1}(\tau'_2) \\
\vdash \tau'_2(0) \to \tau_1
\end{array}
}{D, \Gamma,\ \mathsf{hd} : \tau_1,\ \mathsf{tl} : \mathsf{L}_{p^1(\overline{n}^*)}(\tau_2) \vdash_\Sigma \mathsf{Cons}(\mathsf{hd}, \mathsf{tl}) : \tau'} \ \text{Cons}
$$

where m is fresh in $D, \Gamma, \tau_1, \tau_2$.

Backward application of the CONS-rule to

$$n \geq 1; \; \mathsf{l}: \mathsf{L}_n(\alpha), \; \mathsf{l}': \mathsf{L}_{tails_1(n-1)}(\mathsf{L}_{tails_2(n-1)}(\alpha)) \vdash_\Sigma \mathsf{Cons}(\mathsf{l}, \mathsf{l}'): \mathsf{L}_{tails_1(n)}(\mathsf{L}_{tails_2(n)}(\alpha))$$

allows to infer the rewriting rules for the sizes of the inner lists of the output for tails: $n \geq 1 \vdash tails_2(n)(0) \rightarrow n$ and $n \geq 1, \; 1 \leq pos \leq n-1 \vdash tails_2(n)(pos) \rightarrow tails_2(n-1)(pos-1)$.

The IF-rule "collects" the size dependencies of both branches:

$$\frac{\begin{array}{c} D \vdash \tau \rightarrow \tau_1 \mid \tau_2 \\ \Gamma(\mathsf{x}) = \mathsf{Bool} \quad D, \Gamma \vdash_\Sigma e_t: \tau_1 \quad D, \Gamma \vdash_\Sigma e_f: \tau_2 \end{array}}{D, \Gamma \vdash_\Sigma \text{ if } \mathsf{x} \text{ then } e_t \text{ else } e_f: \tau} \; \text{IF}$$

$$\frac{\mathsf{z} \notin dom(\Gamma) \quad D, \Gamma \vdash_\Sigma e_1: \tau_z \quad D, \Gamma, \mathsf{z}: \tau_z \vdash_\Sigma e_2: \tau}{D, \Gamma \vdash_\Sigma \text{ let } \mathsf{z} = e_1 \text{ in } e_2: \tau} \; \text{LET}$$

$$\frac{\begin{array}{c} D, 0 \in p^1(\overline{n}^*), \; \Gamma, \; \mathsf{l}: \mathsf{L}_{p^1(\overline{n}^*)}(\tau) \vdash_\Sigma e_{\mathsf{Nil}}: \tau' \quad \mathsf{hd}, \mathsf{tl} \notin dom(\Gamma) \\ D, m \geq 1, \; m \in p^1(\overline{n}^*), \; \Gamma, \mathsf{hd}: \tau(0), \; \mathsf{l}: \mathsf{L}_{p^1(\overline{n}^*)}(\tau), \; \mathsf{tl}: \mathsf{L}_{m-1}(\tau_{+1}) \vdash_\Sigma e_{\mathsf{Cons}}: \tau' \end{array}}{D; \; \mathsf{l}: \mathsf{L}_{p^1(\overline{n}^*)}(\tau) \vdash_\Sigma \begin{array}{l} \text{match } \mathsf{l} \text{ with } \mid \mathsf{Nil} \Rightarrow e_{\mathsf{Nil}} \\ \qquad\qquad\qquad\quad \mid \mathsf{Cons(hd, tl)} \Rightarrow e_{\mathsf{Cons}} \end{array}: \tau'} \; \text{MATCH}$$

where $m \notin SV(D)$. Note that if in the MATCH-rule p^1 is single-valued, the statements in the nil and cons branches are $p^1(\overline{n}^*) = 0$ and $p^1(\overline{n}^*) \geq 1$, respectively.

$$\frac{\begin{array}{c} \Sigma(f) = \tau_1^f \times \ldots \times \tau_{k'}^f \times \tau_1^\circ \times \cdots \times \tau_k^\circ \rightarrow \tau_0 \\ \Sigma(\mathsf{g}_1) = \tau_1^f, \ldots, \Sigma(\mathsf{g}_{k'}) = \tau_{k'}^f \\ \mathsf{z}_1: \tau_1^\circ, \ldots, \mathsf{z}_k: \tau_k^\circ \vdash_\Sigma e_1: \tau_0 \quad \Gamma \vdash_\Sigma e_2: \tau' \end{array}}{\Gamma \vdash_\Sigma \text{ letfun } f(\mathsf{g}_1, \ldots, \mathsf{g}_{k'}, \mathsf{z}_1, \ldots, \mathsf{z}_k) = e_1 \text{ in } e_2: \tau'} \; \text{LETFUN}$$

$$\frac{\begin{array}{c} \Sigma(f) = \tau_1^f \times \ldots \times \tau_{k'}^f \times \tau_1^\circ \times \ldots \times \tau_k^\circ \rightarrow \tau_0 \\ \text{the type of } \mathsf{g}_\imath \text{ is an instance of the type } \tau_i^f; \\ D \vdash \tau \rightarrow \sigma(\tau_0) \quad D \vdash C \end{array}}{D, \Gamma, \mathsf{z}_1: \tau_1, \ldots, \mathsf{z}_k: \tau_k \vdash_\Sigma f(\mathsf{g}_1, \ldots, \mathsf{g}_{k'}, \mathsf{z}_1, \ldots, \mathsf{z}_k): \tau} \; \text{FUNAPP}$$

where σ is an instantiation of the formal size variables with the actual size expressions, and C consists of equations between size expressions that are constructed in the following way. If $\tau_i^\circ = \mathsf{L}(\ldots \mathsf{L}_{n^s}(\tau^{\circ\prime}) \ldots)$ and $\tau_\imath = \mathsf{L}(\ldots \mathsf{L}_{p_i^s(\overline{n}^*)}(\tau') \ldots)$, then $\sigma(n^s) := p_i^s(\overline{n}^*)$. If $\tau_i^\circ = \tau_{i'}^\circ$, then the corresponding size expressions are equal, that is C contains $p_i^s = p_{i'}^s$. Further, if $\tau_i^\circ = \mathsf{L}(\ldots \mathsf{L}_{a^s}(\tau^{\circ\prime}) \ldots)$, then C contains $p_i^s(\overline{n}^*) = a^s$. Eventually $\sigma(\tau_0)$ for $\tau^0 = \mathsf{L}(\ldots \mathsf{L}_{f(\ldots, n^s, \ldots)}(\ldots \mathsf{L}(\alpha) \ldots) \ldots)$ is defined as $\mathsf{L}(\ldots \mathsf{L}_{f(\ldots, p^s(\overline{n}^*), \ldots)}(\ldots \mathsf{L}(\alpha) \ldots) \ldots)$.

As an example of a case when C is needed, consider a call of a function scalarprod : $\mathsf{L}_m(\mathsf{Int}) \times \mathsf{L}_m(\mathsf{Int}) \rightarrow \mathsf{Int}$ on actual size arguments $\mathsf{l}_1: \mathsf{L}_{n+1}(\mathsf{Int})$ and $\mathsf{l}_2: \mathsf{L}_{m-1}(\mathsf{Int})$. Then C contains $n+1 = m-1$. It will hold if D contains $n = m-2$.

Example 1: Inferring Rewriting Rules for concat. Consider the function concat, which given a list of lists appends all the inner lists:

$$\text{concat(l)} = \text{match l with } | \text{ Nil} \Rightarrow \text{Nil} \\ | \text{ Cons(hd, tl)} \Rightarrow \text{append(hd, concat(tl))}$$

The rewriting rules defining the type for concat : $\mathsf{L}_n(\mathsf{L}_M(\alpha)) \to \mathsf{L}_{concat(n,M)}(\alpha)$ are

$$\vdash concat(0, M) \to 0 \\ n \geq 1 \vdash concat(n, M) \to M(0) + concat(n-1, \lambda\, pos.\, M(pos+1))$$

Now we show how the typing rules are used to infer this rewriting system. We apply the rules as in a subgoal-directed backward-style proof.

1. The LETFUN rule defines the main goal: $\mathsf{l}\colon \mathsf{L}_n(\mathsf{L}_M(\alpha)) \vdash_\Sigma e_\text{concat}\colon \mathsf{L}_{concat(n,M)}(\alpha)$, where e_concat denotes the body of concat.
2. Apply the MATCH-rule. In the nil-branch we obtain the subgoal $n = 0$;
   $tv|\mathsf{L}_n(\mathsf{L}_M(\alpha)) \vdash_\Sigma \mathsf{Nil}\colon \mathsf{L}_{concat(n,M)}(\alpha)$.
3. Continue with the nil-branch. Apply the NIL rule and obtain $n = 0 \vdash \mathsf{L}_{concat(n,M)}(\alpha) \to \mathsf{L}_0(\tau^?)$.
4. Instantiate $\tau^? = \alpha$. Unfold the definition of type rewriting:
   $n = 0 \vdash concat(n, M) \to 0$.
5. Now, consider the cons-branch. The subgoal there is
   $n \geq 1$; hd : $\mathsf{L}_M(\alpha)(0)$, tl : $\mathsf{L}_{n-1}(\mathsf{L}_M(\alpha)_{+1}) \vdash_\Sigma$ append(hd, concat(tl)) : $\mathsf{L}_{concat(n,M)}(\alpha)$.
6. Unfold the definition of $(-)_{+1}$:
   $n \geq 1$; hd : $\mathsf{L}_{M(0)}(\alpha)$, tl : $\mathsf{L}_{n-1}(\mathsf{L}_{M_{+1}}(\alpha)) \vdash_\Sigma$ append(hd, concat(tl)) : $\mathsf{L}_{concat(n,M)}(\alpha)$.
7. The expression in the judgment above is a sugared let-construct. So, we apply the LET-rule. In the binding we get the goal: $n \geq 1$; tl : $\mathsf{L}_{n-1}(\mathsf{L}_{M_{+1}}(\alpha)) \vdash_\Sigma$ concat(tl) : $\tau^?$.
8. Using FUNAPP-rule we instantiate the type $\tau^? := \mathsf{L}_{concat(n-1,M_{+1})}(\alpha)$.
9. Therefore, the subgoal for the let-body is
   $n \geq 1$; hd : $\mathsf{L}_{M(0)}(\alpha)$, l' : $\mathsf{L}_{concat(n-1,M_{+1})}(\alpha) \vdash_\Sigma$ append(hd, l') : $\mathsf{L}_{concat(n,M)}(\alpha)$.
10. Apply the FUNNAPP-rule. In this rule use the type append : $\mathsf{L}_{n_1}(\alpha') \times \mathsf{L}_{n_2}(\alpha') \to \mathsf{L}_{n_1+n_2}(\alpha')$ and $\sigma(n_1) := M(0)$, $\sigma(n_2) := concat(n-1, M_{+1})$. We obtain the predicate
    $n \geq 1 \vdash \mathsf{L}_{concat(n,M)}(\alpha) \to \mathsf{L}_{M(0)+concat(n-1,M_{+1})}(\alpha)$.
11. Unfold the definition of type rewriting and the definition of the operation $(-)_{+1}$: $n \geq 1 \vdash concat(n, M) \to M(0) + concat(n-1, \lambda\, pos.\, M(pos+1))$.

Example 2: Inferring Rewriting Rules for tails. Now, we will infer the rewriting rules for the size annotations in the type

$$\text{tails} : L_n(\alpha) \rightarrow L_{\mathit{tails}_1(n)}(L_{\mathit{tails}_2(n)}(\alpha))$$

of the function tails as defined on page 3.

1. The LETFUN rule defines the main goal: $| : L_n(\alpha) \vdash_\Sigma e_{\text{tails}} : L_{\mathit{tails}_1(n)}(L_{\mathit{tails}_2(n)}(\alpha))$, where e_{tails} denotes the body of tails.
2. Apply the MATCH-rule. In the nil-branch we obtain the subgoal $n = 0$;
   $tv|L_n(\alpha) \vdash_\Sigma \text{Nil}: L_{\mathit{tails}_1(n)}(L_{\mathit{tails}_2(n)}(\alpha))$.
3. Continue with the nil-branch. Apply the NIL rule and obtain
   $n = 0 \vdash L_{\mathit{tails}_1(n)}(L_{\mathit{tails}_2(n)}(\alpha)) \rightarrow L_0(\tau^?)$.
4. Trivially, instantiate $\tau^? := L_{\mathit{tails}_2(n)}(\alpha)$. Unfold the definition of the type rewriting:
   $n = 0 \vdash \mathit{tails}_1(n) \rightarrow 0$.
   Note, that the rewriting rules for $\mathit{tails}_2(n)$ in this branch are absent, since $n_1 \in \{n = 0\}$, $0 \le pos \le n_1 - 1$ is an empty set.
5. Now, consider the cons-branch. The subgoal there is
   $n \ge 1; \ |: L_n(\alpha), \ \text{tl}: L_{n-1}(\alpha_{+1}) \vdash_\Sigma \text{Cons}(\text{l}, \text{tails}(\text{tl})): L_{\mathit{tails}_1(n)}(L_{\mathit{tails}_2(n)}(\alpha))$.
6. In the type of tl unfold the definition of $(-)_{+1}$:
   $n \ge 1; \ |: L_n(\alpha), \ \text{tl}: L_{n-1}(\alpha) \vdash_\Sigma \text{Cons}(\text{l}, \text{tails}(\text{tl})): L_{\mathit{tails}_1(n)}(L_{\mathit{tails}_2(n)}(\alpha))$.
7. The expression in the judgment above is a sugared let-construct. So, we apply the LET-rule. In the binding we have the subgoal: $n \ge 1; \ \text{tl}: L_{n-1}(\alpha) \vdash_\Sigma \text{tails}(\text{tl}): \tau^?$.
8. Using FUNAPP-rule we instantiate the type $\tau^? := L_{\mathit{tails}_1(n-1)}(L_{\mathit{tails}_2(n-1)}(\alpha))$.
9. Therefore, the subgoal for the let-body is
   $n \ge 1; \ | : L_n(\alpha), \ l' : L_{\mathit{tails}_1(n-1)}(L_{\mathit{tails}_2(n-1)}(\alpha)) \vdash_\Sigma \text{Cons}(\text{hd}, l') : L_{\mathit{tails}_1(n)}(L_{\mathit{tails}_2(n)}(\alpha))$.
10. Applying the CONS-rule we obtain

$$
\begin{array}{ll}
n \ge 1 & \vdash L_{\mathit{tails}_1(n)}(L_{\mathit{tails}_2(n)}(\alpha)) \rightarrow L_{\mathit{tails}_1(n-1)+1}(L_{\mathit{tails}_2(n)}(\alpha)) \\
n \ge 1 & \vdash (L_{\mathit{tails}_2(n)}(\alpha))(0) \rightarrow L_n(\alpha) \\
n \ge 1, \ 1 \le pos \le n \vdash & L_{\mathit{tails}_2(n)}(\alpha)(pos) \rightarrow (L_{\mathit{tails}_2(n-1)}(\alpha))(pos - 1)
\end{array}
$$

11. Unfold the definition of type-typewriting. For tails_1 we obtain $n \ge 1 \vdash \mathit{tails}_1(n) = \mathit{tails}_1(n - 1) + 1$, and for tails_2 applied to 0 and to $pos \ge 1$ we obtain

$$
\begin{array}{ll}
n \ge 1 & \vdash \mathit{tails}_2(n)(0) \rightarrow n \\
n \ge 1, \ 1 \le pos \le n \vdash & \mathit{tails}_2(n)(pos) \rightarrow \mathit{tails}_2(n - 1)(pos - 1)
\end{array}
$$

respectively.

It is easy to see that $\mathit{tails}_1(n) = n$ is a closed form for the obtained rewriting system for f: $\mathit{tails}_1(0) = 0$ and $\mathit{tails}_1(n) \rightarrow \mathit{tails}_1(n - 1) + 1$ with $n \ge 1$. Further,

$tails_2(n)(pos) = n - pos$ for $0 \leq pos \leq n - 1$ solves the rewriting system for g. Indeed, by induction on $n \geq 2$, $tails_2(n)(pos) = tails_2(n - 1)(pos - 1) = (n - 1) - (pos - 1) = n - pos$ for $pos \geq 1$, with the base $tails_2(1)(0) = 1$, and having $tails_2(n)(pos) = n$ for $pos = 0$.

3.4 Semantics of Typing Judgments (Soundness)

The set-theoretic semantics of typing judgments is formalised later in this section as the soundness theorem, which is defined by means of the following two predicates. One indicates if a program value is *valid* with respect to a certain heap and a ground type. The other does the same for sets of values and types, taken from a frame store and a ground context $\Gamma^{\bullet}$:

$$
\begin{aligned}
Valid_{\mathsf{val}}(v, \tau^{\bullet}, h) &= \exists_w.\ v \models^{h}_{\tau^{\bullet}} w \\
Valid_{\mathsf{store}}(vars, \Gamma^{\bullet}, s, h) &= \forall_{x \in vars}.\ Valid_{\mathsf{val}}(s(x), \Gamma^{\bullet}(x), h)
\end{aligned}
$$

Let a valuation ϵ^s map size variables to constants of the layer s, and let an instantiation η map type variables to ground types:

$$
\begin{aligned}
Valuation \quad & \epsilon^s : SizeVariables^s \to (\mathcal{R} \to \ldots \to \mathcal{R} \to 2^{\mathcal{R}}) \\
Instantiation\ \eta^s : & \ TypeVariables^s \to \tau^{\bullet\,s}
\end{aligned}
$$

Let ϵ and η be the direct sums of some $\epsilon^1, \ldots, \epsilon^k$ and $\eta^1, \ldots, \eta^k$ respectively. We will usually write application of η and ϵ to types τ and size relations D as subscripts. For example, $\eta(\epsilon(\tau))$ becomes $\tau_{\eta\epsilon}$ and $\epsilon(D)$ becomes D_{ϵ}. Note that D contains no type variables and hence $D_{\eta} = D$. Valuations and instantiations distribute over size functions in the following way: $(\mathsf{L}_{p(\overline{n}^*)}(\tau))_{\eta\epsilon} = \mathsf{L}_{p(\overline{n}^*_\epsilon)}(\tau_{\eta\epsilon})$.

Informally, the soundness theorem states that, assuming that the zero-order context variables are *valid*, i.e., that they indeed point to lists of the sizes mentioned in the input types, then the result in the heap will be *valid*, i.e., it will have the size indicated in the output type.

Theorem 1 (Soundness). *For any store s, heaps h and h', closure $\mathcal{C}$, expression e, value v, context Γ, quantifier-free formula D, signature Σ, type τ, size valuation ϵ, and type instantiation η such that*

- *$dom(s) = dom(\Gamma)$, $\epsilon \colon SV(\Gamma) \cup SV(D) \to \mathcal{R}$ and $\eta \colon TV(\Gamma) \to \tau^{\bullet}$,*
- *the expression e when evaluated in h evaluates to v, and the new heap is h', i.e., $s; h;\ \mathcal{C} \vdash e \rightsquigarrow v; h'$,*
- *D_{ϵ} holds,*
- *$D, \Gamma \vdash_{\Sigma} e : \tau'$,*
- *$Valid_{\mathsf{store}}(dom(s), \Gamma_{\eta\epsilon}, s, h)$,*

then v is valid according to its return type τ' in h', i.e., $Valid_{\mathsf{val}}(v, \tau'_{\eta\epsilon}, h')$.

Proof. The proof is done by induction on the size of the derivation tree for the operational-semantic judgment. This is possible because we assume that the evaluation of e terminates (with a value v). We have to prove $Valid_{\mathsf{val}}(v, \tau'_{\eta\epsilon}, h')$, i.e., that there is a w such that $v \models^{h'}_{\tau'_{\eta\epsilon}} w$. In the proof we omit some technical lemmata and easier cases. They can be found in the technical report.

OSVar: In this case $e = \mathsf{z}$, $v = s(\mathsf{z})$ and $h' = h$. Since $dom(s) = dom(\Gamma)$, there is a τ such that $\Gamma(\mathsf{z}) = \tau$, and because $Valid_{store}(dom(s), \Gamma_{\eta\epsilon}, s, h)$, there is a w such that $s(\mathsf{z}) \models^h_{\tau_{\eta\epsilon}} w$. Now from the VAR typing rule, we have $D \vdash \tau' \to \tau$. Since D_ϵ holds, we obtain $v \models^{h'}_{\tau'_{\eta\epsilon}} w$.

OSCons: In this case $e = \mathsf{Cons(hd, tl)}$, $v = \ell$ for some location $\ell \notin dom(h)$ and $h' = h.\ell.[hd := s(\mathsf{hd}), tl := s(\mathsf{tl})]$. From the CONS typing rule we have that $\mathsf{hd}\colon \tau_1$ and $\mathsf{tl}\colon \mathsf{L}_{p^1(\overline{n}^*)}(\tau_2)$, and for some τ'_2 the judgments $D \vdash \tau' \to \mathsf{L}_{p^1(\overline{n}^*)+1}(\tau'_2)$, $D \vdash \tau'_2(0) \to \tau_1$ and $n \in p^1(\overline{n}^*), 1 \le pos \le n, D \vdash \tau'_2(pos) \to \tau_2(pos - 1)$ hold. Since $Valid_{store}(dom(s), \Gamma_{\eta\epsilon}, s, h)$, there exist w_{hd} and w_{tl} such that $s(\mathsf{hd}) \models^h_{\tau_{1\eta\epsilon}} w_{hd}$ and $s(\mathsf{tl}) \models^h_{\mathsf{L}_{p^1(\overline{n}^*_\epsilon)}(\tau_{2\eta\epsilon})} w_{tl}$. Therefore

$$h'.\ell.hd \models^h_{\tau_{1\eta\epsilon}} w_{hd}$$

and

$$h'.\ell.tl \models^h_{\mathsf{L}_{p^1(\overline{n}^*_\epsilon)}(\tau_{2\eta\epsilon})} w_{tl}.$$

By the definition of h' we have $h = h'|_{dom(h')\setminus\{\ell\}}$, thus, $h'.\ell.hd \models^{h'|_{dom(h')\setminus\{\ell\}}}_{\tau_{1\eta\epsilon}} s(\mathsf{hd})$ and $h'.\ell.tl \models^{h'|_{dom(h')\setminus\{\ell\}}}_{\mathsf{L}_{p^1(\overline{n}^*_\epsilon)}(\tau_{2\eta\epsilon})} s(\mathsf{tl})$. From the judgment $D \vdash \tau'_2(0) \to \tau_1$ we obtain $h'.\ell.hd \models^{h'|_{dom(h')\setminus\{\ell\}}}_{\tau'_{2\eta\epsilon}(0)} w_{hd}$. Now we want to show that

$$h'.\ell.tl \models^{h'|_{dom(h')\setminus\{\ell\}}}_{\mathsf{L}_{p^1(\overline{n}^*_\epsilon)}(\tau'_{2\eta\epsilon+1})} w_{tl},$$

and then by the definition of model relation we can obtain the desired result: $\ell \models^{h'}_{\tau'_{\eta\epsilon}} w_{hd} :: w_{tl}$. The judgment $n \in p^1(\overline{n}^*), 1 \le pos \le n, D \vdash \tau'_2(pos) \to \tau_2(pos - 1)$ is equivalent to $n \in p^1(\overline{n}^*), 0 \le pos \le n - 1, D \vdash \tau'_2(pos + 1) \to \tau_2(pos)$. Recall that τ_{+1} is defined as $\lambda\, pos.\, \tau(pos + 1)$, thus we have the judgment $n \in p^1(\overline{n}^*), 0 \le pos \le n - 1, D \vdash (\tau'_2)_{+1}(pos) \to \tau_2(pos)$. Now by definition of rewriting rules for types we have $D \vdash \mathsf{L}_{p^1(\overline{n}^*)}((\tau'_2)_{+1}) \to \mathsf{L}_{p^1(\overline{n}^*)}(\tau_2)$. Using $h'.\ell.tl \models^{h'|_{dom(h')\setminus\{\ell\}}}_{\mathsf{L}_{p^1(n^*_\epsilon)}(\tau_{2\eta\epsilon})} w_{tl}$, we get $h'.\ell.tl \models^{h'|_{dom(h')\setminus\{\ell\}}}_{\mathsf{L}_{p^1(n^*_\epsilon)}(\tau'_{2\eta\epsilon+1})} w_{tl}$.

OSLet: In this case e is $\mathsf{let}\ \mathsf{z} = e_1\ \mathsf{in}\ e_2$, where $s; h; \mathcal{C} \vdash e_1 \rightsquigarrow v_1; h_1$ and $s[\mathsf{z} := v_1]; h_1; \mathcal{C} \vdash e_2 \rightsquigarrow v; h'$. From the LET typing rule we have that $\mathsf{z} \notin dom(\Gamma)$, $D, \Gamma \vdash_\Sigma e_1 : \tau$ and $D, \Gamma, \mathsf{z}\colon \tau \vdash_\Sigma e_2 : \tau'$. Applying the induction hypothesis to the antecedents of the operational semantics, we get that $Valid_{val}(v_1, \tau_{\eta\epsilon}, h_1)$ and that if $Valid_{store}(dom(s[\mathsf{z} := v_1]), \Gamma_{\eta\epsilon} \cup \{\mathsf{z}\colon \tau_{\eta\epsilon}\}, s[\mathsf{z} := v_1], h_1)$ then $Valid_{val}(v, \tau'_{\eta\epsilon}, h')$.

Fix some $\mathsf{z}' \in dom(s[\mathsf{z} := v_1])$. If $\mathsf{z}' = \mathsf{z}$, then $Valid_{val}(v_1, \tau_{\eta\epsilon}, h_1)$ implies $Valid_{val}(s[\mathsf{z} := v_1](\mathsf{z}), \tau_{\eta\epsilon}, h_1)$. If $\mathsf{z}' \ne \mathsf{z}$, then $s[\mathsf{z} := v_1](\mathsf{z}') = s(\mathsf{z}')$. Sharing of data structures in the heap is benign (no destructive pattern matching and assignments), hence $s(\mathsf{z}') \models^h_{\Gamma_{\eta\epsilon}(\mathsf{z}')} w'_z$ implies $s(\mathsf{z}') \models^{h_1}_{\Gamma_{\eta\epsilon}(\mathsf{z}')} w'_z$ and then $s[\mathsf{z} := v_1](\mathsf{z}') \models^{h_1}_{\Gamma_{\eta\epsilon}(\mathsf{z}')} w_{z'}$. So, $Valid_{val}(s[\mathsf{z} := v_1](\mathsf{z}'), \Gamma_{\eta\epsilon}(\mathsf{z}'), h_1)$. Hence, $Valid_{store}(dom(s[\mathsf{z} := v_1]), \Gamma_{\eta\epsilon} \cup \{\mathsf{z}\colon \tau_{\eta\epsilon}\}, s[\mathsf{z} := v_1], h_1)$ and we can now apply the induction hypothesis.

OSMatch-Cons: In this case $e = \text{match I with} \mid \text{Nil} \Rightarrow e_1 \mid \text{Cons(hd, tl)} \Rightarrow e_2$. for some l, hd, tl, e_1 and e_2. The typing context has the form $\Gamma = \Gamma' \cup \{l : L_{p^1(\overline{n}^*)}(\tau)\}$ for some Γ', τ and f. From the operational semantics we know that $h.s(l).hd = v_{hd}$ and $h.s(l).tl = v_{tl}$, for some v_{hd} and v_{tl}, that is, $s(l) \neq \text{NULL}$. Due to the validity of $s(l)$ there exists $1 \le n_0 \in p^1(\overline{n}^*_\epsilon)$. From the validity $s(l) \models^h_{L_{p^1(\epsilon(\overline{n}^*))}(\tau_{\eta\epsilon})} w_{hd} :: w_{tl}$, the validities of v_{hd} and v_{tl} follow:

$$v_{hd} \models^h_{\tau_{\eta\epsilon}(0)} w_{hd} \text{ and } v_{tl} \models^h_{L_{\overline{n}^*_\epsilon} -1((\tau_{\eta\epsilon})+1)} w_{tl}.$$

From the MATCH typing rule we have that $D, n_0 \ge 1 \in p^1(\overline{n}^*)$; $\Gamma'' \vdash_\Sigma e_2 : \tau'_{\eta\epsilon}$, where $\Gamma'' = \Gamma \cup \{\text{hd}: \tau(0), \text{tl}: L_{p^1(\overline{n}^*)-1}(\tau+1)\}$.

From $Valid_{\text{store}}(dom(s), \Gamma_{\eta\epsilon}, s, h)$ and the results above, we obtain that $Valid_{\text{store}}(dom(s'), \Gamma''_{\eta\epsilon}, s', h)$, where $s' = s[\text{hd} := v_{hd}][\text{tl} := v_{tl}]$. With $\epsilon' = \epsilon[n_0 := length_h(s(l))]$, the induction hypothesis yields $Valid_{\text{val}}(v, \tau_{\eta\epsilon'}, h')$.

Now, since $n_0 \notin SV(\tau')$ (and thus, $\tau_{\eta\epsilon} = \tau_{\eta\epsilon'}$), we have $Valid_{\text{val}}(v, \tau_{\eta\epsilon}, h')$.

OSLetFun: Here $e = \text{letfun } f(f_1, \ldots, f_{k'}, z'_1, \ldots, z'_k) = e_1 \text{ in } e_2$, where

$$s; h; \mathcal{C}[f := ((g_1, \ldots, g_{k'}, z'_1, \ldots, z'_k) \times e_1)] \vdash e_2 \rightsquigarrow v; h'.$$

From the LETFUN typing rule we have that $\Gamma \vdash_\Sigma e_2 : \tau'$. Applying the induction hypothesis to these judgments with the same η and ϵ, we obtain $Valid_{\text{val}}(v, \tau'_{\eta\epsilon}, h')$ as desired.

OSFunApp: In this case $e = f(f_1, \ldots, f_{k'}, z'_1, \ldots, z'_k)$, with $\mathcal{C}(f) = (g_1, \ldots, g_{k'}, z'_1, \ldots, z'_k) \times e_1)$ and $[z_1 := v_1, \ldots, z_k := v_k]$; h; $\mathcal{C} \vdash e_f[g_1 := f_1, \ldots, g_{k'} := f_{k'}] \rightsquigarrow v$; h'. We want to apply the induction hypothesis to this judgment.

Since all functions called in e are defined via letfun, there must be a node in the derivation tree of the original typing judgment of the form $\text{True}, y_1 : \tau^\circ, \ldots, y_k : \tau^\circ_k \vdash_\Sigma e_f : \tau_0$. Let σ be the substitution over type variables and size variables that ensures this instance of the FUNAPP-rule. In particular, $D \vdash \tau \rightarrow \sigma(\tau_0)$. Take η' and ϵ' such that $\eta'(\alpha) = \eta(\sigma(\alpha))$, and $\epsilon'(n^*_{ij}) = \epsilon(\sigma(n^*_{ij}))$. From the induction hypothesis we have that if

$$Valid_{\text{store}}((y_1, \ldots y_k), (y_1 : \tau^\circ_{1\,\eta'\epsilon'}, \ldots, y_k : \tau^\circ_{k\,\eta'\epsilon'}), [y_1 := v_1, \ldots, y_n := v_n], h)$$

then $Valid_{\text{val}}(v, \tau_{0\eta'\epsilon'}, h')$. From $Valid_{\text{store}}(dom(s), \Gamma_{\eta\epsilon}, s, h)$ we get the validity of the values of the actual parameters: $v_i \models^h_{\Gamma_{\eta\epsilon}(l_i)} w_i$ for some w_i, with $1 \le i \le k$. Since $\Gamma_{\eta\epsilon}(l_i) = \tau^\circ_{i\,\eta'\epsilon'}$, the left-hand side of the implication holds, and one obtains $Valid_{\text{val}}(v, \tau_{0\,\eta'\epsilon'}, h')$. It is easy to see that

$$\tau'_{\eta\epsilon} = (\sigma(\tau_0))_{\eta\epsilon} =$$
$$\tau_0[\ldots \alpha := \eta(\sigma(\alpha)) \ldots][\ldots n^*_{ij} := \epsilon(\sigma(n^*_{ij})) \ldots] =$$
$$\tau_{0\,\eta'\epsilon'}$$

Therefore from obtain $Valid_{\text{val}}(v, \sigma(\tau_{0\,\eta'\epsilon'}), h')$ we obtain $Valid_{\text{val}}(v, \tau'_{\eta\epsilon}, h')$.

$\square$

4   Related Work

This research extends our work [17–19,21] about shapely function definitions that have a single-valued, exact input-output polynomial size functions. Our non-monotonic framework resembles [1] in which the authors describe *monotonic* resource consumption for Java bytecode by means of Cost Equation Systems (CESs), which are similar to, but more general than recurrence equations. CESs express the cost of a program in terms of the size of its input data. In a further step, a closed-form solution or upper bound can be found by using existing Computer Algebra Systems, or a by a specially designed by the authors recurrence solver. However, they consider non-monotonic size functions only if they are linear, e.g. $s(x, y) = x - y$.

Our approach is related to size analysis with polynomial quasi-interpretations [2,4]. There, a program is interpreted as a *monotonic* polynomial extended with the max operation.

Hofmann and Jost presented a heap space analysis [11] to infer linear space bound of functional programs with explicit memory deallocation. It uses type annotations and an amortisation analysis that assign a *potential*, i.e. hypothetical free space, to data structures. The type system ensures that the potential to the input is an upper bound on the total memory required to satisfy all allocations. They have extended their analysis to object-oriented programs [12], although without an inference procedure. Brian Campbell extended this approach to infer bounds on *stack* space usage in terms of the total size of the input [6], and recently as max-plus expressions on the depth of data structures [7]. Again, the main difference with our work is that we not require linear size functions. Recently, this analysis has been extended to include multivariate non-linear resource polynomials [10]. The difference with our work is that we also allow general polynomials including non-monotonic polynomials like $x^2 - y^2$ where [10] allows only non-negative linear combinations of base polynomials.

In his thesis, Pedro Vasconcelos [22] uses abstract interpretation to automatically infer linear approximations of the sizes of recursive data types and the stack and heap of recursive functions written in a subset of *Hume*.

Several papers have studied programming languages with *implicit computational complexity* properties [3,8]. This line of research is motivated both by the perspective of automated complexity analysis and providing natural characterisations of complexity classes like PTIME or PSPACE. Resource analysis may also be performed within a *Proof Carrying Code* framework.

5   Conclusions and Future Work

We have presented a system that combines lower/upper bounds and higher-order size annotations to express, type check and infer reasonable approximations for polynomial size dependencies for strict functional programs using general lists.

Future   work   will   include   research   on   generalising   size   analysis on   algebraic   data   types   and   implementation   work   incorporating   the results of this paper in our polynomial size analysis prototype (see `resourceanalysis.cs.ru.nl/#prototypes`).

References

1. Albert, E., Arenas, P., Genaim, S., Puebla, G., Zanardini, D.: Cost analysis of java bytecode. In: De Nicola, R. (ed.) ESOP 2007. LNCS, vol. 4421, pp. 157–172. Springer, Heidelberg (2007)
2. Amadio, R.M.: Synthesis of max-plus quasi-interpretations. Fundam. Informaticae **65**(1–2), 29–60 (2004)
3. Atassi, V., Baillot, P., Terui, K.: Verification of ptime reducibility for system F terms: type inference in dual light affine logic. Logical Meth. Comput. Sci. **3**(4), 1–32 (2007)
4. Bonfante, G., Marion, J.Y., Moyen, J.Y.: Quasi-interpretations a way to control resources. Theor. Comput. Sci. **412**(25), 2776–2796 (2011)
5. Reistadand, B., Gifford, D.K.: Static dependent costs for estimating execution time. In: Proceedings of the Conference on Lisp and Functional Programming FP'94, pp. 65–78. ACM Press, January 1994
6. Campbell, B.: Space cost analysis using sized types. Ph.D. thesis, School of Informatics, University of Edinburgh (2008)
7. Campbell, B.: Amortised memory analysis using the depth of data structures. In: Castagna, G. (ed.) ESOP 2009. LNCS, vol. 5502, pp. 190–204. Springer, Heidelberg (2009)
8. Gaboardi, M., Marion, J.-Y., Ronchi Della Rocca, S.: A logical account of PSPACE. In: Proceedings of the 35th ACM SIGPLAN-SIGACT Symposium on Principles of Programming Languages POPL 2008, San Francisco, January 10–12, 2008, pp. 121–131 (2008)
9. Góbi, A., Shkaravska, O., van Eekelen, M.: Higher-order size checking without subtyping. In: Loidl, H.-W., Peña, R. (eds.) TFP 2012. LNCS, vol. 7829, pp. 53–68. Springer, Heidelberg (2013)
10. Hoffmann, J., Aehlig, K., Hofmann, M.: Multivariate amortized resource analysis. ACM Trans. Program. Lang. Syst. **34**(3), 14:1–14:62 (2012)
11. Hofmann, M., Jost, S.: Static prediction of heap space usage for first-order functional programs. SIGPLAN Not. **38**(1), 185–197 (2003)
12. Hofmann, M., Jost, S.: Type-based amortised heap-space analysis. In: Sestoft, P. (ed.) ESOP 2006. LNCS, vol. 3924, pp. 22–37. Springer, Heidelberg (2006)
13. Hughes, L.P.J., Sabry, A.: Proving the correctness of reactive systems using sized types. In: Proceedings of the 23rd ACM SIGPLAN-SIGACT Symposium on Principles of Programming Languages, POPL '96, pp. 410–423. ACM (1996)
14. Shkaravska, O., van Eekelen, M.: Univariate polynomial solutions of algebraic difference equations. J. Symbolic Comput. **60**, 15–28 (2014)
15. Shkaravska, O., van Eekelen, M., Tamalet, A.: Collected size semantics for functional programs over polymorphic nested lists. Technical report ICIS-R09003, Radboud University Nijmegen, July 2009
16. Shkaravska, O., van Eekelen, M., Tamalet, A.: Collected size semantics for functional programs over lists. In: Scholz, S.-B., Chitil, O. (eds.) IFL 2008. LNCS, vol. 5836, pp. 118–137. Springer, Heidelberg (2011)
17. Shkaravska, O., van Eekelen, M.C.J.D., van Kesteren, R.: Polynomial size analysis of first-order shapely functions. Log. Meth. Comput. Sci. **5**(2), 1–35 (2009)

18. Shkaravska, O., van Kesteren, R., van Eekelen, M.: Polynomial size analysis of first-order functions. In: Della Rocca, S.R. (ed.) TLCA 2007. LNCS, vol. 4583, pp. 351–365. Springer, Heidelberg (2007)
19. Tamalet, A., Shkaravska, O., van Eekelen, M.: Size analysis of algebraic data types. In: Achten, P., Koopman, P., Morazán, M. (eds.) Trends in Functional Programming, TFP'08, vol. 9. Intellect Publishers (2009)
20. van Eekelen, M., Shkaravska, O., van Kesteren, R., Jacobs, B., Poll, E., Smetsers, S.: AHA: amortized heap space usage analysis. In: Morazán, M. (ed.) Selected Papers of the 8th International Symposium on Trends in Functional Programming (TFP'07), pp. 36–53. Intellect Publishers, New York (2007)
21. van Kesteren, R., Shkaravska, O., van Eekelen, M.: Inferring static non-monotonically sized types through testing. In: Proceedings of 16th International Workshop on Functional and (Constraint) Logic Programming (WFLP'07). ENTCS, Paris, France, vol. 216C, pp. 45–63 (2007)
22. Vasconcelos, P.B.: Space cost analysis using sized types. Ph.D. thesis, School of Computer Science, University of St. Andrews, August 2008
23. Xi, H., Pfenning, F.: Dependent types in practical programming. In: Proceedings of the 26th ACM SIGPLAN Symposium on Principles of Programming Languages, San Antonio, pp. 214–227, January 1999

Author Index

Amadio, Roberto M. 1
Asăvoae, Mihail 19
Ayache, Nicolas 1

Bobot, Francois 1
Boender, Jaap P. 1

Campbell, Brian 1
Canavese, Daniele 38
Cesena, Emanuele 38

Di Pierro, Alessandra 58

Eguchi, Naohi 77

Garnier, Ilias 1
Grov, Gudmund 110

Kersten, Rody 93

Loidl, Hans-Wolfgang 110

Madet, Antoine 1
Mariuca Asăvoae, Irina 19

McKinna, James 1
Mulligan, Dominic P. 1

Ouchary, Rachid 38

Parisen Toldin, Paolo 93
Pedicini, Marco 38
Perrinel, Matthieu 127
Piccolo, Mauro 1
Pollack, Randy 1

Régis-Gianas, Yann 1
Roversi, Luca 38

Sacerdoti Coen, Claudio 1
Shkaravska, Olha 143
Stark, Ian 1

Tamalet, Alejandro 143
Tranquilli, Paolo 1

van Eekelen, Marko 93, 143
van Gastel, Bernard 93

Wiklicky, Herbert 58

Printed in the United States
By Bookmasters